A FRENCHWOMAN'S
IMPERIAL STORY

A FRENCHWOMAN'S IMPERIAL STORY

Madame Luce in Nineteenth-Century Algeria

REBECCA ROGERS

Stanford University Press
Stanford, California

Stanford University Press
Stanford, California

Printed in the United States of America on acid-free, archival-quality paper

Library of Congress Cataloging-in-Publication Data

Rogers, Rebecca, 1959– author.
 A Frenchwoman's imperial story : Madame Luce in nineteenth-century Algeria / Rebecca Rogers.
 pages cm
 Includes bibliographical references and index.
 ISBN 978-0-8047-8431-3 (cloth : alk. paper)
 1. Luce, Madame, 1804–1882. 2. Women teachers—France—Biography. 3. Muslim girls—Education—Algeria—History—19th century. 4. Education and state—Algeria—History—19th century. 5. Women—Algeria—Social conditions—19th century. 6. France—Colonies—Africa—History—19th century. I. Title.
 LA2375.F72R63 2012
 370.92—dc23
 [B]
 2012031058

Cover illustration: Detail from a photochrom postcard of Henriette Benaben's "School of Arab embroidery" on the rue Marengo in the Palais Oriental in Algiers, ca. 1899. In 1900 this institution carried on the legacy of Madame Luce's initial school for Muslim girls, created in 1845. Benaben's institution attracted visitors who were curious to see indigenous girls at work, eager to purchase their embroideries and to admire the Spanish ceramic tiles from Valencia that decorated the building. From "Views of People and Sites in Algeria" Photochrom print collection, Detroit Photographic Company. Library of Congress Prints and Photographs Division, Washington, DC. LC-DIG-ppmsc-05554.

Typeset by Bruce Lundquist in 10/15 Minion

To my family
On both sides of the ocean

CONTENTS

FIGURES

ACKNOWLEDGMENTS

This book, more than my previous ones, is laden with memories, emotions, and experiences that extend far beyond the parameters of my professional life. The research for this book led me to Algeria and the discovery of a country and a people far removed from my own history. And yet in many ways this book weaves together the threads of an adult life spent traveling between France and the United States questioning how education makes a difference, especially for girls. It is such a pleasure to acknowledge here how my encounters during these travels have enriched me and, I hope, the book that follows.

Several institutions have allowed me to pursue this project from article to book. The Université Marc Bloch kicked the adventure off by granting me a sabbatical in the spring of 2004. I have not forgotten that sorely needed respite from university politics. The history department at the University of Michigan welcomed me and provided the sort of intellectual community that explains why the project developed as it did. The Université Paris Descartes granted me a two-year research leave (a "délégation CNRS") that gave me time to write a book. I am immensely grateful to the CERLIS (Centre de recherche sur les liens sociaux), my research laboratory, and to its director, François de Singly, for believing that a historian is a congenial addition to a group of sociologists. This project has matured in the collegial atmosphere of the education department at Paris Descartes and benefited from the insights of colleagues and students from a wide range of disciplines. We may spend too much time filling out tables for five-year plans, but we also talk about each other's work, reminding ourselves in the process why we went into higher education.

Archivists throughout France and in England and Algeria have taken the time to answer my questions, find documents, and help me navigate unfamiliar archives. Particular thanks to Anne-Cécile Tizon-Germe and her staff at the departmental archives of the Loir-et-Cher in Blois. Their welcome and expertise during a very cold and snowy January of 2009 warmed my heart. Christophe Leblan at the departmental archives of the Oise sent me precious documents, Frédéric Gilly at the Centre des Archives d'Outre-Mer in Aix-en-Provence has cheerfully responded to inquiries for years, Kate Perry at Girton College sent me documents from the Bodichon collection, Moya Carey at the Victoria and Albert Museum in London allowed me to handle embroideries from Madame Luce's workshop, and archivists in the Quai Branly welcomed me into their offices and allowed me to print out vibrant color images of their embroidery collection. François Debarre remains my favorite genealogist (and father-in-law), even if he only contributed a few birth certificates to this book, compared with the thousands he uncovered for my previous book.

My research took me to Algeria for my first experience of the Maghreb outside of books and archives. Like so many, I am in debt to Robert Parks and the Centre d'études maghrébines en Algérie for helping me get access to archives and for the ways the center promotes exchanges between North African, European, and American scholars. The community at the Glycines in Algiers offered the perfect living place for a single woman seeking to get a feel for the city and the archives. Bouzid Khelili helped me navigate the Bibliothèque nationale and its collections, Meriem Messaoud allowed me to roam the stacks of colonial newspapers at the Bibliothèque Frantz Fanon, and the archivists at the Wilaya archives of Algiers patiently pulled years and years of General Council reports off the shelves. Amel Soltani at the National Museum of Antiquities encouraged my interest in their collections, and the guardian in the Saint-Eugène cemetery has my eternal gratitude for showing me Henriette Benaben's tombstone. This first trip to Algiers will remain forever colored in my mind by these encounters, as well as by the experience of walking the streets with Louafi Abid searching for movie houses, of savoring a beer on the roof of the Glycines at sunset while talking about Algerian history with Deborah Harrold, and of admiring that breathtaking view over the city and the Mediterranean from the Bibliothèque Frantz Fanon, without forgetting the cats whose pictures I took at the entrance to the library.

My unexpected middle-aged encounter with things Algerian has unquestionably added a great deal to my life. In France, I will treasure the time Leïla Sebbar spent with me over tea at the Coupole. Her gracious curiosity and the intensity of her engagement with my project not only encouraged me, but also set off thoughts for future work. Eugénie Luce's descendants, the Crouzet family and especially Claude Crouzet, welcomed me into their homes; showed me furniture, lace, and jewelry that came from Algeria; lent me books and documents; and enthusiastically responded to my interest in their family. They regret, of course, that I am writing the book in English.

Colleagues throughout the world have, as always, made a huge difference, especially as this short project ended up taking years and years to complete. It is a bit embarrassing to admit the number of talks I have given about this subject (twenty-three, but who's counting?) since the first one in 2003 in Basel. I cannot help but think that Madame Luce would be amused to learn that people have heard me speak of her adventures from Strasbourg to Sydney, from Amsterdam to Algiers, from Paris to Purdue, from São Paulo to Saint-Denis. As a result, I have had the good fortune to get feedback, interesting questions, and inspiration from a great many people. While I cannot possibly name everyone, I thank in particular those who invited me to speak at seminars and conferences, as well as those who have shared their friendship, their knowledge, and their interest in women's history and education over food and wine: Claudia Opitz, who inaugurated my tour of four continents in Basel; my Strasbourg friends and colleagues: Nicolas Bourguinat, Arlette Bothorel, Céline Grasser, Irini Jacoberger, Nathalie Hillenweck, Roland Pfefferkorn, and André Rauch; my British community across the English Channel: Michèle Cohen, Joyce Goodman, Jane Martin, Gary McCulloch, and Ruth Watts; without forgetting the Irish contingent: Mary O'Dowd, Deirdre Raftery, and especially Phil Kilroy; my new Brazilian friends Angela Xavier de Brito, Paula Leonardi, and Maria Alzira Colombo; and Mineke van Essen, who shares my interest in teachers. My American friends and colleagues made more difference than they can imagine, welcoming me to their universities and into their homes or getting in touch with me when in Paris. Thank you to Jim Albisetti, Laird Boswell, Tom Broden, Linda Clark, Suzanne Desan, Sarah Farmer, Dena Goodman, Cathy Kudlick, Howard Lay, Karen Offen, Lou Roberts, and Bonnie Smith. Steven Kaplan responded enthusiastically to an early proposal about Madame Luce, and Whitney Walton was the first person to suggest that I might have the makings of a biography.

Like Madame Luce, I have spent most of my adult life in my adopted country, France. French scholars and friends have accompanied this project from the outset: the Cliotines, and especially Françoise Thébaud, Pascale Barthélémy, and Michelle Zancarini-Fournel; the broader community of gender scholars: Nicole Pellegrin, Béatrice Rollet, and another transplanted American, Laura Lee Downs; and of course my companions in the field of education, the members of the Service d'Histoire de l'éducation. It has been exciting over the past few years to interact with the community of scholars working on colonization or empire. My thanks to those who invited me to speak, asked useful questions, and steered me toward new sources or scholarship, particularly Emmanuel Blanchard, Omar Carlier, Claire Fredj, Alain Messaoudi, Monique de Saint Martin, Christelle Taraud, Sylvie Thénault, and Christiane Veauvy. A number of people have helped me from afar translating Arabic and sending me source material, especially Kamel Chachoua, Michel Levallois, and Michel Megnin. In England, Meritxell Simon-Martin shared material on Barbara Bodichon concerning Madame Luce. In the United States Osama Abi-Mershed has patiently answered questions over the years. I know that such lengthy lists of names are a form of self-indulgence, but they convey, I hope, my conviction that scholarship is about dialogue and exchange, even though we all are ultimately responsible for what we write.

Some people deserve more specific thanks for the ways they have accompanied my intellectual travels in the new century. Some are old traveling companions, such as Sarah Curtis, who got her book about empire out before I did and who read big chunks of the manuscript. Or Susan Whitney, who introduced me to Ottawa, asked me tons of questions, and then read the entire manuscript when it was finally finished. Her six pages of comments pushed me to sharpen arguments, rethink the introduction, and get rid of my Gallicisms. Jean-Luc Pinol offered his time and expertise for two of the maps when he had many other things to do. Just like in our college days, Pat Howard Hudson read the introduction and chipped in her two cents. Mira Velimirovic would have read the introduction but opted instead for a more medically oriented stay in Paris; cousin Lisa Redburn told me she did not like my working title and she was right. Anne Epstein read the introduction and conclusion at a moment of self-doubt and gave me a response that allowed me to move on. The no-longer-anonymous readers for Stanford University Press, Julia Clancy-Smith and Whitney Walton, wrote just the sort of reader's reports one longs for: praise and only a few suggestions for revision. A bottle of Madiran was downed the evening their reports came in. Odile Goerg, Sheryl Kroen, Isabelle Laboulais, and Daniel Payot have listened to me endlessly on the topic of Madame Luce, helped me work out arguments, and read bits and pieces of the project as it developed. Their questions, their interest, and most especially their friendship have buoyed me during the eight years it took me to write this book. I have followed much of the advice given and appreciated the ways it has forced me to defend the ultimate decisions I have made. Above all, the collective response I received has bolstered me during these final months, which have not been a lot of fun. I can hear my family echoing this latter statement. Neither Olivier, nor Alice, nor Thomas has clamored to read the book in progress, but the Luce family tree is thanks to Olivier, and I am sure they all secretly love Madame Luce. They have accepted patiently the way she has pushed her way into our family. She is at times a cumbersome presence, and I think we will all appreciate seeing her nicely contained within the covers of a book.

The staff at Stanford University Press deserves special thanks for responding so quickly to questions on all subjects and for moving the manuscript so expertly through the phases of production. I am immensely grateful to Norris Pope in particular for taking the risk of publishing the biography of an unknown woman.

If my "quick" book took so long, it is partly because life intervened when my parents died one after the other in 2005 and 2007. Saying goodbye and sorting through their legacy brought vividly home all they have given me: a curiosity about others; a love of France; a passion for books, reading, and writing; and a tendency to keep too many postcards. Their presence lies lightly on this entire project. My mother, Jacqueline Rogers, would have been puzzled by my interest in Algeria while approving of the biographical focus and urging me to reread Camus (which I have not). My father, Thomas Rogers, lived long enough to know I was working on a biography; I will never forget the delight he took in hearing me tell the story of Madame Luce's life. It is his voice I heard when I made writerly choices, relayed by my sister, Susan Fox Rogers, whose own authorial voice blossomed as life intervened for her as well. Writer, editor, kayaker, teacher, my sister read the entire manuscript as well as rewrites and made just the right comments. Family matters, I write when describing Madame Luce's life. Family matters. Indeed.

A NOTE ON TERMINOLOGY

Most of the material used in writing this book was written in French using the language of the period. I have hesitated about how to refer to the populations living in Algeria when the French arrived. The expression "Algerian" is anachronistic in the nineteenth century because that term referred increasingly to the European settlers. As a result, I often use the terms I find in the sources, which I quote a good deal: indigenous, Arab, Muslim, Moor, Moresque, Kabyle, Negro, Negress. Readers should be aware that these are nineteenth-century usages which allow us as historians to understand how the French (or British or Americans) perceived and named the different populations they encountered. The expressions were used loosely and with a great deal of variation, depending on the speaker. I have also used the spellings of Arabic words or names as I found them in the sources.

· · ·

Arab: used generically to refer to nonurban inhabitants of Algeria, assumed to be Muslim.

Berber: an ethnic group in North Africa; historically they spoke the Berber language.

El Djezaïr: the Arabic name for Algiers.

Kabyle: the Berber population that inhabited Kabylia.

Kabylia: a term coined by the French to designate a region in northeast Algeria.

madrasa: an institution of secondary or higher learning under religious governance.

Moor: a male urban dweller, presumably Muslim, but distinguished from an Arab.

Moresque (Mooresque/Mauresque): a female urban dweller.

Muslim (Mussulman): used frequently to designate Arabs (or Moors) in addition to indicating an individual adhering to Islam.

zawiya: a traditional Muslim school that focused on religious learning.

. . .

French words are italicized and translated as needed in the text.

collège: a secondary level school.

école ouvroir: a school workshop.

lycée: a secondary level school with more qualified teachers than in a *collège*.

ouvroir: a training workshop.

A FRENCHWOMAN'S
IMPERIAL STORY

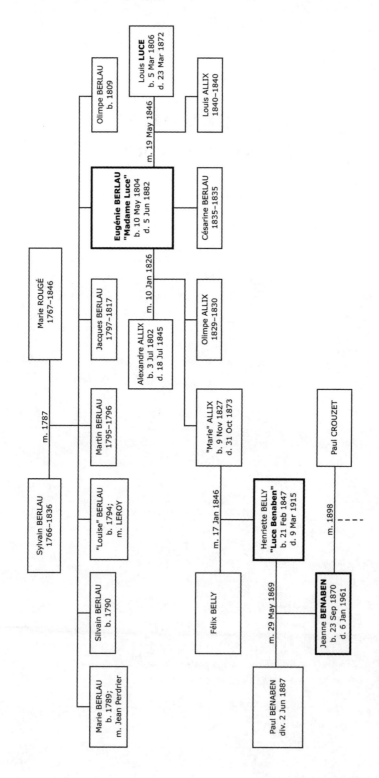

Madame Luce's family tree.

INTRODUCTION

This book explores the life and work of Eugénie Allix Luce, a provincial French schoolteacher. In 1832 she fled from her husband, leaving behind her five-year-old daughter, and migrated to the newly colonized soils of Algeria. There, she labored and loved for thirteen years before founding the first school for Muslim girls in 1845. Virtually single-handedly, she placed girls' education on the colonial agenda and forced the authorities to support what she described as her mission: "to change native morals, prejudices and habits, as quickly and as surely as possible, by introducing the greatest possible number of young Muslim girls to the benefits of a European education."[1] For fifteen years she taught French spelling and grammar, arithmetic, and sewing. When the tide of colonial politics turned against the "French" education of Arab girls, she trained them for another fifteen years in the arts of embroidery. At her death in France at the age of seventy-eight, her obituary noted: "Madame Luce devoted her youth, her intelligence, and her heart to the education of Arab girls. For forty years, without flagging a single day, she pursued her oeuvre: the regeneration of the Arab woman through work and instruction."[2] Who was this Madame Luce? And what difference does the story of her life make for our understanding of the French conquest of Algeria?

Some people's lives add only color and nuance to the past; others make us read the past differently. Madame Luce's life is one of the latter. Her story shows a woman's active participation in the colonization of Algeria. Her initial success and then her later disavowal reveal the place of gender in the evolution of colonial cultural politics. Madame Luce wrote Muslim women into the French "civilizing mission," and the attention she garnered in mid-century Algiers shows the ways that the French sought to advertise their gender egalitarianism for a time. The closure of her school spelled the end to that experiment but not to Luce's effect on attitudes toward women's roles within Muslim society. Her embroidery workshop taught women marketable skills and brought French and foreign visitors to her doorstep in the Casbah. Thanks to Madame Luce, Algerian embroideries circulated between Algiers, mainland France, and London, creating a legacy whose significance remains largely unexplored. Telling her story sheds light on the European and indigenous women who lived and often worked side by side, but it also shows that her life mattered, not just to her family and granddaughter, who carried on her work, but also to our way of thinking about the French colonization of Algeria.

ARCHIVAL STORIES AND THE PRACTICE OF HISTORY

My interest in Madame Luce began with an initial archival encounter. While pursuing the activities of French women teachers overseas and in the colonies in the French colonial archives in Aix-en-Provence, I stumbled upon the voluminous dossier about her school in Algiers. Mingled with letters and reports from the men who worked in the Government General of Algeria were those of an unusual French schoolmistress. Page after page were filled with grandiloquent statements about the role she sought to play in the French civilizing mission and the importance of including indigenous women in this mission. For instance, in 1850 she wrote to the prefect of Algiers: "I was intimately convinced that our efforts to effect the fusion of civilizations would come to naught, as long we were unable to have our morals, our habits and our beliefs penetrate within families. How else to achieve this goal but through the education of women, the touchstone of the family, women who were destined as daughters, wives, and mothers to either inspire love or hate of the French?"[3] Her voice captured my attention.

Eugénie Allix (the future Madame Luce) was forty-one years old in the summer of 1845 when she started her campaign to receive support for her school. On 14 July 1845, she wrote the queen of France, Marie Amélie de Bourbon-Sicile, pleading for help: "Without the means to create the sort of establishment which is necessary, I am seeking the generosity of your Royal Highness to aid in the foundation of an institution destined to improve the morality and to ensure the happiness of a people whose future is inextricably tied up with that of France."[4] In November her school was indeed up and running with a few students; it would take many more months and many more letters, however, for her to persuade the government to finance her efforts.

In March 1846 the articulate schoolteacher once more took up her pen to defend the school for Muslim girls that she had opened at her own cost in Algiers a few months earlier: "It is civilization itself, inoculated in Algeria through pacific means; it is the fusion of the races, a problem heretofore considered insoluble, which is resolved affirmatively through a new institution; it is, in addition, such an unexpected success and it so decisively counters indigenous prejudices, that once the first step is taken one can reasonably and without presumption hope for everything in the future."[5] Page after page pursues these arguments. The French conquest of Algeria required a woman's touch, Luce asserted. Women were the key to the pacification of relations; through girls' education the French would penetrate Muslim families and persuade them of the grandeur of the civilizing mission. In other words, the domestic was political and required attention. By January 1847 Madame Luce had managed to persuade the authorities to fund her school, but she had acquired a reputation for brashness and immodesty in the process.

Fifteen years later, in the summer of 1861, a commission of Arab notables and French administrators debated the wisdom of continuing to subsidize her school. As Commissioner Adolphe Michel noted: "The usefulness of the Arab-French school directed by Madame Luce has always been controversial." He went on to insist that it was "sheer illusion" to think that the reform of Algerian society would occur thanks to teaching urban Muslim girls to read, write, and calculate: "By raising them as Europeans, we have sullied them for Arab life; we are preparing concubines for Europeans rather than wives for native men."[6] Arab notables confirmed this negative vision of Madame Luce's school, feeling that it fostered a morally questionable fusion of the races. They argued heatedly against continued funding, stating that no respectable Muslim man would place his daughter in Luce's hands or choose to marry a graduate of her institution. On 19 September 1861 an official decree transformed Luce's Arab-French school for Muslim girls in Algiers into a vocational workshop. Although she sought to defend her school, ultimately she recognized that the tide had turned; authorities no longer supported the spread of book learning among Muslim girls. As a result, Madame Luce dropped from public visibility in Algiers and spent the next fifteen years teaching embroidery skills to girls. If one stops the story here, the colonial archives appear to chronicle the rise and fall of a female adventurer.

This book began as a project for an article about that rise and fall. The dossier in the colonial archives offered a tantalizing entry into colonial cultural politics and triggered my initial questions and investigation. From the outset, the colonial administration questioned Luce's motives and were troubled by the expression of her ambitions. There was something unseemly and unwomanly in her oft-repeated conviction that the authorities required the aid of both European and indigenous women in order to succeed in their civilizing mission. But as I toiled through the colonial archives, I increasingly questioned whether Adolphe Michel was right. Was Eugénie Luce really just an amoral adventurer, seeking financial advantage through the education of Muslim girls? Surely there would have been easier ways to earn money in colonial Algeria if that were indeed her main concern. Who was this woman who wielded such a trenchant pen and whose institution aroused such a passionate denunciation? Why would the provision of a modicum of book knowledge among indigenous girls provoke such indignant response? What explained the colonial volte-face with respect to a schoolteacher whose school had received tens of thousands of francs since the late 1840s? Increasingly, I wanted to learn more. A series of discoveries gradually persuaded me that there was enough material for a biography. The historian's craft involves far more than the critical reading of sources. It also requires imagination and at times serendipity, which I capture through a few snippets from my research diary.

7 March 2004, the University of Wisconsin Library (Madison)
God bless the Dewey decimal system! My audience at Madison asked me interesting questions about gender politics in the 1860s in Algeria. What do I know about gender politics then? Not much because there's so little work on the subject. Where might I find answers, I puzzled, as I roamed through the DT section concerning Algeria of the library. Travel narratives. Ah, that's a possibility—travelers might have interesting things to say. At eye level I spot Mrs. Rogers, *A Winter in Algeria, 1863–64*; I pull it off the shelf, along with a few other books with promising titles and disappointing content. My homonym Mrs. Rogers, however, represents one of those moments of epiphany in a historian's life. She has written a diary with subchapters on "The Status of Arab Women," on a visit to a Protestant orphanage, on the tale of five French nuns forced to leave Algiers and . . . on a visit to the Moorish school run by Madame Luce! And there, to my unbelieving eyes, I find six whole pages describing Madame Allix Luce, telling me about her early upbringing in France, shedding light on her unhappy marriage (a husband who really wanted to be a priest), and revealing she was known and written about by one of the most prominent British feminists of the time, Barbara Bodichon, who published an article on her in the *English Woman's Journal*. I can hardly believe Mrs. Rogers is giving me all of this, and that I have found it mostly because we share the same name and I was curious to read something that was not penned by a historian.

27 September 2004, Arsenal Library (Paris)
Went in search of the Saint-Simonian archives at the Arsenal today in the hopes I might find signs of my Madame Luce.[7] Napoleon III's advisor, Ismaÿl Urbain, a well-known Saint-Simonian who converted to Islam, clearly knew her, as he mentions her school

in his prose. I don't know the Arsenal well. The librarian directs me to an inventory where I find the last name Allix. A tremor of anticipation begins, although I know Allix is not a particularly unusual name. I order the register and wait a mere fifteen minutes. A large bound volume with letters stuck to the pages in alphabetical order arrives. I page my way to the appropriate folio, AL, and my breath stops—it's her! Her signature, clearly recognizable. She, like other women of her time, admired the Père Enfantin, as they called him.[8] I can hardly believe it. Four letters and a poem. I refrain from reading rapidly but rather start copying her prose, slowly and carefully, letting her words and her feelings envelop me. In 1840 she is living in Bône, she is in trouble, Enfantin appears to be a savior, an idea who keeps her mind and soul together. A third letter in 1845 is full of joy: her husband is dead, she has inherited money, her project for a school for Muslim girls is finally taking shape. And for the first time I read about the daughter she has not seen for thirteen years. Her husband's death has allowed her to reclaim this daughter. And then a final undated poem I don't really understand. Full of strong emotions, love, passion—requited or unrequited? I'm not really sure. But I spend the afternoon reading, copying, and smiling. What pleasure to glimpse a side of Eugénie I have never seen. Intimate correspondences evoke such different emotions compared with petitions and administrative reports. She's beginning to take shape. I don't yet know what I will do with her, but this gradual finding is a source of happiness.

14 October 2005, Center of Town (Strasbourg)

Took a break from student essays to bike into town today. Decided to explore my favorite used bookstore, the Somnambule. The little store is packed with books, piles on tables, but a rigor in the organizing principle that allows me to locate colonial history books with ease. First I stumble on Julien's weighty tome about the history of the colonization of Algeria, being sold for what seems like a pittance. Snatched that book up. I then turn to the big picture book for sale about Algeria. It's organized alphabetically; under "E" for "école" I find an interesting photo of a sewing school for girls in Kabylia, turn two more pages, and there she is! Madame Luce in person, taking up space at the back of her class. She's looking and gesturing with a ruler at a black woman in white who stands before a blackboard, a motley assembly of little girls at their feet. The caption: *L'école de jeunes filles mauresques dirigées par Madame Luce* [The school for young Moorish girls run by Madame Luce], the photographer is Félix Antoine Moulin [the image is shown in Chapter 4]. But what astonishes me more than the existence of the photo is Madame Luce's appearance in 1856. She is forty-two years old, her face is framed by ringlets. She's wearing a rather garish full-length gown that accentuates her corpulence, which is considerable. I had read she was fat, but that was not my vision of her. I had imagined her a bit like myself: slender, not massive. On the contrary she is vast and imposing; her physical presence commands respect. I leave the bookstore heavier with my new purchases and my head full of new images. This changes my relationship to Madame Luce, now that I can see her, and not just hear her.

4 April 2009, 14 rue de Verdun (Strasbourg)

I'm still rocking from my discovery of this afternoon, which has, as a result, prevented me from pursuing Luce's elusive girl students in my prose. Since the last time I checked, the European civil registers of Algeria have been digitized and are now available online. The miracles of modern technology. I was curious to see if Eugénie's daughter was pregnant before wedlock and so I started checking various birth certificates. Then I got curious about the Berlau family in Algeria, Eugénie's uncle. Back in 1835 a little Césarine Berlau dies. Let's see who that is . . . and, lo and behold, Eugénie is a mother again! She is listed as a "*lingère*" [laundress], her daughter "*de père inconnu*" [of unknown father], no mention of the forsaken husband Alexandre Allix. My, my, my, her early years in Algeria are far juicier than I expected. And so I decided to check the various records more carefully. Who, for instance, is this Louis Lucien Allix who is born and then quickly dies in Bône in 1840? Oh my goodness, yet another illegitimate child, although this time she claims the father is Alexandre Allix, schoolteacher in Vendôme, which is many thousands of miles from Bône. Louis Napoléon Luce, musician in the 26th regiment of the infantry, is one of the witnesses. One certainly suspects this must be the happy father and then the distraught father when little Louis dies 8 months later (or perhaps the relieved father—who knows?). The plot thickens. All this unsettles my vision of the *institutrice dévouée* [devoted schoolteacher].

19 October 2009, Algiers

Monday morning I awake feeling a bit anxious that there is still so much to accomplish: I need to talk with the head of the museum, I want to find Henriette Benaben's tombstone in the cemetery [Madame Luce's granddaughter], I want to see Madame Luce's dossier in the archives, I want to explore the library here at the Glycines, I need to check in with the Bibliothèque nationale to see if they have miraculously found material for me in their library, I need to change money and buy presents for my loved ones, and I haven't visited the Casbah. . . .

Getting to the Saint-Eugène cemetery is a bit of an expedition that involves speaking with quite a few of the Algerians who are waiting at the bus stop. After a substantial wait a bus arrives that is deemed appropriate and I am whisked off along the coast heading west. The men sitting around me are all intrigued by my expedition and one of them accompanies me off the bus when we arrive and walks me into the cemetery, assuring me along the way that things are very safe here and that he is himself a cop. The cemetery is beautiful and quiet, nestled under the Basilica Notre-Dame d'Afrique; it looks out onto the sea. Incredibly, the guardian of the cemetery has all of the archives and so he's able to find the date of burial and the plot in which Henriette Benaben,

Gravesite of Madame Luce's granddaughter, Henriette Benaben, née Belly, in the Saint-Eugène cemetery in Algiers. Although not cared for, the inscriptions on the stones are still legible in French and Arabic. The French reads: "Madame Luce Benaben, née Henriette Belly / She devoted her life to Muslim art / And to the welfare of the indigenous woman / 21 February 1847–9 March 1915." The Arabic reads: "Here lies Madame Luce Benaben, the head of the ex-bureau of Arab art. May God welcome her in his vast paradise." The form of the headstones demonstrates the affinity Henriette Benaben felt with Muslim culture.

née Belly, is buried, although he has less luck figuring out where Louis Luce and Marie Allix are buried, Eugénie's husband and daughter. After about fifteen minutes we're off into the cemetery, with a map in hand, to find Henriette. Hard to describe my emotions when we come upon the grave, very overgrown with vegetation but highly distinctive because Muslim-style amongst lots of Christian graves. "I thought it was that one," says the guardian, "because of the name." On one side of the tombstone there is an inscription in French and on the other side one in Arabic. From the hillside I gaze out onto the Mediterranean. Enough said.

6 March 2010, London

There are moments when one feels the British are truly civilized. Like at this moment, as I end my day of work at the Victoria and Albert Museum and am now settled in the café downstairs, richly inlaid with gold floral patterns, sipping a much appreciated tea. I have spent the previous two hours working in a frigid conservation room. Apparently textiles do not need heat, and so those who work on textiles do without. Very moving experience to see and handle objects, which most probably come from Madame Luce's

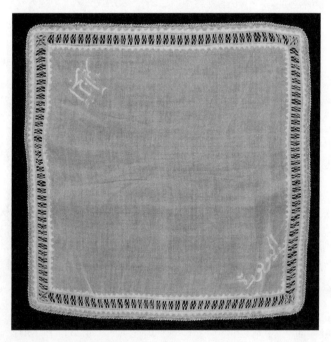

Embroidered handkerchief from the Luce workshop purchased by Mrs. L. F. M. Preston in the 1860s. Girls stitched and embroidered these handkerchiefs for sale, often personalizing them, as in this example, with the name Eleonora (the client's mother's name) and "El Djezaïr" (Algeria) in Arabic. Victoria and Albert Museum, T.211-1922.

workshop in 1868. A Mrs. Preston bought them—three inscribed handkerchiefs and a little sewing trousseau. Her daughter, Miss Preston, an invalid who divided her time between Rome, London, and the Isle of Wight, donated them to the V&A in 1922. I cannot claim I really know a great deal more about the objects than what I knew coming into the museum, but there is something about actually seeing and touching them that changes my appreciation. And then, thoroughly frozen, I go off to the print and drawing study room to see if I can view a watercolor by Barbara Bodichon, *A Landscape near Algiers*. Alas, I arrived too late, but the exceedingly helpful young woman at the desk sends me an e-mail image, and takes the time to print out two color images of the landscape that add delicate pastel touches to my vision of colonial Algiers.

Embroidered sewing trousseau from the Luce workshop purchased by Mrs. L. F. M. Preston in 1882. The piece of embroidered material folds into three to make a little trousseau, or wallet. Victoria and Albert Museum, T.209-1922.

These excerpts give a glimpse into the moments of excitement that punctuate the experience of historical research and explain my "taste for the archive" so powerfully described by Arlette Farge.[9] But perhaps I should have started with an excerpt from 1997 when I unexpectedly encountered Madame Luce in the guise of great-grandmother while researching a very different topic. One of the first French women secondary schoolteachers, Jeanne Crouzet-Benaben, published her memoirs, *Souvenirs d'une jeune fille bête* (Memories of a Silly Girl) in the 1950s. To my astonishment she described being raised by "Maman Luce," the woman who opened the first school for Muslim girls in 1845. I learned from these memoirs that Luce returned to France in her declining years and raised her great-granddaughter, Jeanne. Jeanne presents a fat, fun-loving old woman with a taste for bawdy humor and wine—quite a contrast to the determined proponent of the civilizing mission whose prose I had discovered several months earlier in the colonial archives. At the time, I was amused by the coincidence that my longstanding interest in French girls' education overlapped here with my new interest in education in the colonies. I had no idea that the memoirs would end up providing precious information about the Luce Benaben family.

BIOGRAPHY AND THE
POLITICS OF WOMEN'S HISTORY

The encounters described above transformed this project from an article into a historical biography. The more I learned about Eugénie Luce, the more I became interested in understanding what sort of woman would have the courage to give up all that was familiar to her for a life in the colonies. The more I read about colonial Algeria, the more I was struck by the absence of serious attention to the presence of European women or to the ways gender played a role in French colonization. And the more I pursued the different threads of Luce's life, the more I was intrigued by the things that remained today—in both historical and material terms—most notably the Algerian embroideries produced in her school and workshop. This book, then, presents a woman, her life work, and its legacy.

Madame Luce's story emerges from the sources as a series of snapshots: the colonial schoolteacher, the pioneering feminist, the Saint-Simonian fellow traveler, and the jovial great-grandmother. These perspectives come for the most part from those whose paths she crossed; the documents penned in her hand are limited to about fifteen years of her life, and they are all almost entirely located in the colonial archives. Like all biographers I have had to accept that there are holes in my story, years about which I know virtually nothing, feelings that were never recorded, dreams about which I can only speculate. Her life story must be reconstituted from these snapshots, whose angles, colors, and sharpness of definition vary widely, leaving a great deal in the shadows.

My desire to write about Madame Luce's adventures is clearly a sign of our times, and my method of writing openly acknowledges the interpretative nature of the biographical endeavor.[10] I cannot bring back to life the "real" Madame Luce, but I can show her influence on colonial cultural politics, her talent at drawing attention to herself, the interpretations others offered of her life and works, and the legacy she left. In other words, sources can illuminate the role she played in shaping the French civilizing mission. I bring to this book decades of experience writing about women's lives and the convert's enthusiasm to the biographical endeavor. I have long been interested in how individual girls and women respond to the messages that family, schools, books, and peers communicate, but this is my first venture into biography.[11] I have taken this step with the conviction that Madame Luce's story matters.

My tale of Eugénie Luce is not just another example of an approach at times described as "add women and stir." Her life brings to light an unusual story of a woman who dared, who fought, and who accomplished a good deal. She is not representative of the forgotten majority whose lives exemplify the female condition. Nor would I describe this project as being a form of Italian microhistory, although I share with this scholarship an interest in the local and the small scale. Rather, I argue throughout this book that knowledge of Eugénie Luce's life changes our vision of French colonization and brings to light the opportunities offered to determined women in early colonial Algeria. Luce left more traces than many, but there were others, such as Émilie de Vialar, who brought the first nuns to care for the ill in Algeria in 1835; Rosa Barroil, who ran a sewing workshop for poor girls in the 1860s; or Madame Parent, who ran the Arab-French school for girls in Constantine for several decades.[12] Knowledge of their lives offers a way to see how gender affected the civilizing mission.

Feminist biographies have long flourished in the English-speaking world and have received new life under the guise of the "new biography" and the influence of postmodern interpretations of the performative self.[13] In France, however, an early tradition of women writing about illustrious women did not, with a few exceptions, influence the first three decades of academic women's history.[14]

The tardy turn to biography in French women's history has historical roots. In general, French feminists were less committed than the British or the Americans to creating a pantheon of foremothers, for reasons that speak to differing national attitudes toward the individual and society.[15] This has influenced the writing of women's history in France. Only recently have French women historians, and myself, begun to explore biographical writing and advocate the study of individual women's lives as another way to challenge the gender politics of writing history.[16]

The difference in national traditions of biographical writing is particularly striking in the field of education. In Britain, Ireland, and the United States countless biographical studies and biographical dictionaries recount the efforts of women such as Sophie Barat, Catherine Beecher, Dorothea Beale, Frances Bus, Emily Davies, and Mary Lyon, if one limits the scope to the nineteenth century alone.[17] In France, infant school educators, notably Marie Pape Carpantier and Pauline Kergomard, have attracted academic interest, but the women teachers who founded schools and campaigned for access to more serious education remain very much in the shadows. In 2008 a scholar in education published a volume on famous women pedagogues, but the entries rarely acknowledge the scholarship on women's history, which would allow readers to understand the social and political effects of these women's educational ideals.[18] Notwithstanding the scholarship of Françoise Mayeur and myself, the French historical narrative continues to present women's access to knowledge as the product of church or state politics.[19] French students all recognize the name of Jules Ferry, who instituted free, obligatory, and secular primary education; but virtually none has heard of Madame Jules Favre, who trained the first generations of female secondary school professors. We still have much to learn about individual women's contributions to the politics of education and to the shaping of modern French society. The same goes without saying for all of the French colonies.

The commitment to uncovering women's experiences in the past remains a political project, even now, forty or so years after the emergence of the field in the academy.[20] Approaches to this project have changed over the years as knowledge has increased and historical fashions have challenged us to investigate new objects, explore new sources, reinterpret old ones, and position ourselves more centrally within a global world.[21] This book, then, is part of a collective effort in France to bring to light not only how the politics of gender have acted to erase the memory of countless women, but also how the history of individual women's lives reshapes our reading of the past.[22] I have sought throughout the book to situate Eugénie Luce and her family within their social context but also to highlight how knowledge of her actions changes our understanding of the French colonization of Algeria. Recovering her life also recovers a moment in Algeria when girls and women were part of a political project. This books seeks to render audible the silences of that history and set in perspective its material legacy—the celebration of women's manual skills and traditions.[23]

MADAME LUCE'S LIFE AND ADVENTURES

I begin this book by reconstructing the biographical details of Madame Luce's early life. The first two chapters explore the years before she became a public figure. Unfortunately, no private journal or familial correspondence allows us access to her private musings or her more intimate aspirations. Her origins and upbringing in the Loir-et-Cher have left little imprint on existing documentary sources. As a result, I have had to rely on stories she told friends and family about these years, stories that bear the imprint of the storyteller more than the historian.

Born in 1804, Eugénie Berlau shared with her Romantic contemporaries a taste for the quixotic and a keen awareness of the role of the individual in history. She cast her own life in this mold and later in life liked to compare herself to the novelist George Sand. She described herself acting out noble ambitions as she defended Arab womankind, although it remains unclear how she moved from being a provincial schoolteacher to being a proponent of France's civilizing mission in Algeria. She hints, however, that a faith in education underlay most of her life decisions. Certainly she came from a family that understood the value of schooling. The departmental archives offer insights into the familial culture that gave Eugénie Berlau the intellectual tools that would stand her in such good stead during the years to come. They also highlight inconsistencies and holes in the stories that she later told about herself.

Eugénie came of age in the 1820s; married a fellow schoolteacher, Alexandre Allix; and gave birth to two girls, one of whom died within the year. Influenced perhaps by the revolutionary effervescence that characterized the early years of the July Monarchy (1830–1848), she made the remarkable decision to abandon her husband and daughter, fleeing alone to Algeria in 1832. Chapter 2 puts this decision into historical perspective and describes the life that awaited a woman on her own in those early years of colonial conquest. Civil registers reveal that

Eugénie did more than just work and dream of founding a school for Muslim girls; she also encountered men and bore two illegitimate children, who both died as infants. In this respect Eugénie's experiences in Algeria mirror those of many European women at this time, who lived and loved more easily outside of the bonds of marriage. Unquestionably, Eugénie was an unusual woman, but she was far from alone in seeking a new life on colonial soils. Her flight to Algeria was not the product of pure happenstance, and it suggests that alongside the lure of the "Orient," a colonial "imaginary" existed during these years.[24] I argue that this imaginary was not just masculine; women also imagined that life might be better far from home.

Eugénie's encounter with the Saint-Simonian movement puts yet another spin on the motivations that led her to Algiers. Prosper Enfantin, the leader of this movement in the 1830s, inspired women to question their insubordinate status in French society. The radical equality between the sexes that he advocated offered some the means to challenge traditional gender roles and inspired women to fight for a more egalitarian society. In the 1830s and 1840s Algeria attracted many Saint-Simonian officers and civil administrators, but the presence of women who shared their worldview has never been mentioned. Eugénie's correspondence with Enfantin reveals a little-known aspect of early colonial Algeria: the fact that women also engaged in cultural politics.

The central section of this book, "Women in the Civilizing Mission," explores this facet of Eugénie's life. It writes women and gender back into the story of conquest and "pacification" while highlighting the role one woman played in these events. My analysis shows how women's and gender history modifies the early history of colonization, revealing the limits of a historiography that has not paid close attention to the presence of women as actors in the process.[25]

Focusing on the woman who became known as Madame Luce in the history of Algerian colonization shifts attention from the military and the masculine politics of settlement to the place women held within the nascent settler society. It brings to light the existence of women in the Saint-Simonian project with respect to Algeria. It shows how Muslim women figured into colonial politics, not just as veiled figures on the streets or languorous wives in harems, but as girls learning to recite French dialogues and to embroider following ancient patterns. The rise and fall of Madame Luce as a cultural power broker merits attention because this movement reveals the role gender played in colonial educational and social policies. I take seriously the moral condemnations that accompanied the decision to close her school. These attacks highlight the fragility of women's reputations when they stepped out of their prescribed roles and sought to influence politics. As a schoolteacher, however, Madame Luce achieved a brief moment of fame, and this tells us a great deal about French attitudes toward schooling and the place it held in the colonization of a land whose history remains today inextricably intertwined with that of France.

The book's final two chapters explore the historical and cultural legacies Madame Luce left behind. Chapter 6 highlights the cosmopolitan character of colonial Algiers and the role European (and particularly British) women played in the circulation of knowledge and material goods of Algeria. Although unrecognized in the histories of French feminism, Madame Luce became a heroine of sorts in the writings of early British feminists such as Barbara Bodichon and Bessie Rayner Parkes. My focus on Luce and her project lends itself to an exploration of transnational discussions and exchanges in colonial Algiers during the 1850s and 1860s, revealing the ways in which women and gender were very much a part of the cosmopolitanism known to characterize this city. The stories that emerge from these encounters carry the ochre hues of the Orientalist painters who sought to capture the Arab woman, and they come to life through the bustling activity and the artisanal productions of the Moorish girls and their teacher who so intrigued English travelers.

Chapter 7 explores in more detail what I have termed "The Remains of the Day." The inventory and will established at Madame Luce's death testify to the astute business acumen that guided her throughout much of her life. She died leaving a comfortable sum of money to the young girl whose memoirs do the most to bring her great-grandmother to life. But she also left a legacy in artisanal handicrafts that circulated widely across France, Great Britain, North America, and North Africa, thanks to universal and colonial exhibitions. Her granddaughter Henriette Benaben continued the workshop Luce established in Algiers and actively worked to assemble collections of "oriental embroideries" that now lie in the storerooms of museums in Algiers, Paris, and London. These collections constitute, no doubt, the most permanent and highly gendered legacy of Madame Luce's Arab-French school.

In 1931 the art historian Augustin Berque summed up Madame Luce's contribution to the early years of French colonization, praising the vocational training she offered Muslim girls and the fine examples of Turkish embroidery she managed to preserve through her actions with her granddaughter. He recognized that her name would be unfamiliar to most in this centennial celebration of the French conquest, and so he added: "France has always had such collaborators, whose lives have remained in the shadows while their agile fingers have woven the threads of the future."[26]

This statement rings remarkably true for the historian of women that I am. Indeed, yes, women more than men have remained in the shadows, and their contributions to the future are often overlooked and underestimated. I have spent my professional life emphasizing women's contribution to girls' education, but I never imagined writing about just one woman's efforts. Nor have I ever looked carefully at the material objects so frequently produced within girls' schools and pondered their significance. This book, then, is an effort not only to bring a rather remarkable woman out of the shadows, but also to shed light on what she and others created in terms of cultural and historical legacies. Above all, this book argues for the importance of peopling our histories with *both* men and women because both sexes have histories that are as inextricably intertwined as those of France and its former colonies.

A FINAL WORD ON VOICE

This project began with a voice in the archives. When I first encountered it almost fifteen years ago, I was struck by Eugénie Luce's claim to have made a difference. She wanted a place in history and actively sought to ensure that her story would be told and heard. Hers was a feminist story that offered an alternative to the violent and virile nature of the French conquest.[27] Exploring the nature of that story led me back in the end to that voice in the archives, back to the woman whose polite and elegant prose carried "a decisive ring which is quite extraordinary," as one British admirer wrote.[28] This, then, is a biography of a woman who sought public attention, who participated in the commemoration of her life, and who undoubtedly would have enjoyed knowing that an American academic teaching in France wanted to tell her tale to others.

I have struggled throughout this project with how to recount Madame Luce's adventures, in what language, addressing what audience, resorting to what claims to authority. English won the day, along with readability—I'm not a novelist's daughter for nothing. The footnotes and the conclusion deal directly with the historian's craft, offering insights on historiography and methods in Algerian, French, and women's history. In the body of the book, however, I have chosen to emphasize a life story. And although this book pursues questions about girls' schooling, access to knowledge, and work that have long interested me, it places at the center of the story the woman who defended Muslim girls' right to learn. Her trajectory, her ambitions, and the reactions she generated conjure up the social texture of Algiers during the early years of colonization. Above all, Madame Luce's life and its legacy bring both European women and Muslim girls squarely into the limelight. But it is my voice that frames the story.

PART I

Reconstructing a Woman's Life

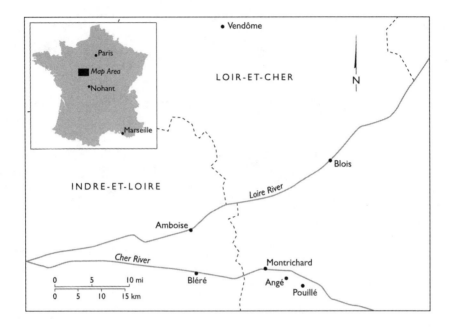

Previous page: Montrichard, where Eugénie Luce was born, and
surrounding towns in the Cher River valley.

1 GROWING UP IN PROVINCIAL FRANCE (1804–1832)

Véronique Eugénie Berlau[1] was born in Montrichard in the Loir-et-Cher on 20 Floréal Year XII (10 May 1804), eight short days before Napoleon Bonaparte's decision to crown himself emperor of France and a few weeks after the French civil code durably inscribed women's inferiority into law. The same year also saw the birth of the famous woman novelist George Sand. Like Sand, Eugénie defied many of the conventions defining appropriate womanly behavior. And like Sand, she acquired a measure of notoriety during the heady years of the July Monarchy (1830–1848). Unlike Sand, this notoriety is not visible in the pages of history because Eugénie left no written oeuvre and her battles for recognition took place in Algeria, not in metropolitan France. Although both women lie buried in villages not far distant in the rolling landscapes of central France, no tourists visit Montrichard in the Loir-et-Cher in search of Eugénie Luce, in contrast to Nohant-Vic in Indre, whose tourist industry thrives thanks to the reputation of George Sand.

The juxtaposition of the two women is not just a literary device. Madame Luce wrote to Sand in the 1860s and liked to associate her name with her illustrious contemporary. Perhaps she imagined parallels in their life stories; perhaps she had dreams of achieving similar notoriety. This we will never know. Luce left no written traces of her more introspective musings, nor did she devote her declining years to writing a memoir. As a result, very little remains to reconstitute her childhood and youth, her emotions upon marrying, her feelings about motherhood, or the heartbreak associated with losing infant children. Fortunately, she left some indications about her childhood and youth, but not all of them are accurate. What follows, then, confronts her own romantic rendering of her past with the available archival information. Neither version does justice to the complicated business of disentangling the role of individual decision from the web of social and economic constraints, but combined they do shed some light on the circumstances that would later lead this obscure provincial schoolteacher to flee France for Algeria, abandoning her husband and five-year-old daughter. We begin with the only available description of Madame Luce's youth and then turn to the archives, which reveal a somewhat different story.

A ROMANTIC FAMILY STORY

Sometime during the winter of 1857, the British feminist Bessie Rayner Parkes encountered Madame Luce through the intermediary of her close friend Barbara Bodichon. In letters to England to sister feminist Mary Merryweather, Parkes mentioned Madame Luce several times and offers the first relatively lengthy description of her new acquaintance:

Yesterday I spent part of the afternoon with Madame Luce who opened out and told me much of her private history. . . . She was one of a large family of 13 in Touraine, her maiden name was Eugénie Berlau. They were poor and at 16 she had a small school. At 21 she was married by her relations to a M. Allix, a man who had been educated in a seminary and had even sworn the Priesthood but threw it off before taking definitive vows and commenced as professor. This individual ill led her in various ways, beat and *pinched* her. She did not explain what his misdemeanors were except that that he took all her earnings from her school, which she still continued and she never had any of them for herself. Her father, M. Berlau, interfered several times, but there was no money to obtain a separation and she dreaded being in the newspapers. At length as a family in the neighborhood were going to Algiers, which was then hardly a conquered [territory] and certainly not a settled district [she left;] was not that a plucky thing to do? She left her little girl with her own family; coming to Algiers, she struggled on. . . . Her husband wrote over to the Algerine authorities to reclaim her, and they told her they must send her back. She declared that if they did she would try and throw herself off the deck of the vessel into the Mediterranean or if she could not do that would fly to Switzerland instantly on her arrival to seek the protection which French law would not afford. In which seeing it was a bad case and that she was getting her living honestly, she believes they wrote back to say there was no such person there. Was not that French?

This presentation is followed then by a description of Madame Luce's early intellectual influences:

Then she told me how much she had been influenced in her childhood and youth by a certain old woman who lived in Touraine and was a market gardener. How this old woman had a wonderful head, and how one of her sons was head of the Collège at Blois, but how she would never accept anything from him but preferred sending her vegetables to market on a donkey. How this old woman had somehow been educated at Chenonceau [under?] the eye of Madame Dupin, who was daughter to Louis the 15th and grandmother to George Sand. There is a complication for you. George Sands maiden name was Dupin, but Mad Luce declares that her grandmother was an illegitimate daughter of the Kings and lived at the royal chateau of Chenonceau where she was visited by Voltaire and Jean Jacques! See Madame Luce and my beloved George Sand both indirectly nourished by the same stream of thought, and the old connexions with the Capets, son of St Louis. The world is not very big and the people in it are very few. You cannot think how I delight in a bit of pedigree and a romantic family story.[2]

Whether Madame Luce really believed this fanciful retelling of George Sand's ancestry—Sand's grandmother Marie-Aurore Dupin was the illegitimate daughter of Maurice de Saxe, not the king of France—she clearly perceived that establishing a connection between her own modest origins and that of George Sand added an appropriate degree of "pedigree" and romance that would appeal to her British audience.

In this description of early poverty, an arranged marriage, and spousal mistreatment, the heroine resisted the forces of oppression, and Parkes was sensitive in her retelling to Madame Luce's early commitment to education and bold gestures. Parkes and her feminist friends defended women's right to work and achieve financial independence. Not only did Allix abuse his wife, he also deprived her of her earnings. Madame Luce provided a story, which deliberately played on feminist and romantic chords, particularly in her description of the old woman market gardener.

Four years later Parkes offered a far more detailed presentation of "Madame Luce, of Algiers" in three long articles of the feminist *English Woman's Journal*. Although Madame Luce's activities in Algiers formed the heart of this chronicle, her British friend was clearly intrigued by her upbringing, to which she devoted five pages. Writing for a British audience, Parkes wanted to give her readership a sense of the texture of Luce's family life as well as of the nature of women's lives in the French provinces in order that they "understand the influences which surrounded this remarkable woman in her younger years."[3] And while the articles unquestionably create a serious portrait of a woman worthy, the tone is leavened with touches of humor that must have come from the storyteller herself. Madame Luce collaborated actively in this project, providing a great deal of social realism that responded to Parkes's concern to translate French realities for a foreign audience.

Early Life and Labors

This is how Parkes begins the story: "A short account of the life and labors of Madame Luce, of Algiers, appeared four years ago in a Scotch journal. Having lately had access to the numerous private and official documents required by any writer seeking to do justice to one of the most remarkable of living French women, I offer to our readers a detailed account of her efforts in the cause of education and civilization, hoping thus to add one more portrait to the gallery of our contemporaries who have deserved the gratitude of their kind."[4] Parkes then (inaccurately) places Eugénie's birth on the sixth of June 1804 in the Hôtel de Ville of Montréchat, "a small town in Touraine containing a population of 2400 souls. Her father, an architect and engineer by profession, was at that time *Secrétaire de la mairie* at Montréchat." After noting the birth "on the Monday of the great Feast of Pentecost,"[5] the journalist moves back in time to describe the "mysterious" origins of the Berlau family. Eugénie's grandfather was an orphan, raised by a prior, who upon discovering a mathematical equation on the ground decided this was a sign from Providence to become a professor of mathematics. Eugénie was the twelfth child of her parents and grew up mainly in the countryside in an "old château in the environs of Montréchat." Despite this aristocratic setting, however, the Berlau family was not wealthy, since her father's salary as an architect and engineer was small and his domestic circle large: "neither his profession nor his land appear to have raised his income to 500 francs, or £200 a year." Parkes goes on to reflect, "How French households get on at all, and contrive to bring up their children, to settle their sons, and to marry their daughters, is a subject of constant astonishment to English people well acquainted with French interests."

Parkes describes Eugénie as a "dreamy, studious child," who acquired an education botanizing in the countryside around the castle, enjoying a freedom of action far different, Parkes explains, from that of her Parisian sisters: "mixing among the poorer neighbors, cognizant of their family histories, and involved in their experience." Raised in a "very natural way," Eugénie read indiscriminately in her father's library, mingled with country people, and sought to "inoculate the shepherds on the estate with a love for the beauties of literature; for which effort they probably expressed more gratitude than appreciation." Notwithstanding the absence of stern parental oversight, however, Parkes presents Eugénie as "extremely *sage*" (well-behaved) and pious; after her first communion at age eleven, she was so gifted at the catechism that the curé asked her to teach her fellow students.

This intellectually talented girl grew into a "very tall and strong" young woman, showing evidence of the "personal vigor and beauty" that her British friends appreciated more than half a century later, despite "manifold trials and labor." But Eugénie is more than just a do-gooder in the feminist retelling. Parkes emphasizes as well that she was a young lady with a mind and political opinions, thanks to the influence of her father, who had been a devoted royalist and had transmitted his hostility toward Napoleon Bonaparte to his daughter. On two occasions, she showed her commitment to the royalist cause by tearing up a Bonapartist banner discovered on the property of a married sister and then out-singing a young Bonapartist boy in a musical tournament in 1815: "Song after song proceeded for some time without any flagging, but the moment came when, alas! Master A—'s memory was completely exhausted, whereas Eugénie, to whom her papa brought sheets of royalist rhymes whenever he went to town, continued crowing triumphantly like a little cock, to master A—'s infinite disgust and mortification." When the guests tried to have them kiss and make up, the boy refused to honor "a young lady with such strong political principles and audacious lungs . . . and dealt her a hearty cuff, which it is whispered that Eugénie returned with interest."

Familial tragedy also marked Eugénie's early life when her older brother died at age twenty. Although only thirteen at the time, she sought to alleviate her parent's grief by persuading them to move back into town: "As a further means of creating a little more movement in the house, she opened a small school, of which the pupils were as old as herself, but at thirteen she was so tall and womanly that no one would have guessed her age." In these early years of the Bourbon Restoration (1815–1830), schools opened and closed without much control, but such an enterprise was nonetheless unusual. For several years Eugénie taught students, inspiring the local education inspector to encourage her, upon reaching eighteen, to pass a school teaching certificate.[6] These were created for women in 1819, so if she had listened to the inspector, she would have been among the first female rural schoolteachers to receive accreditation.

Love and Discord

Eugénie's youthful years were filled with more than just study, work, and concern over her parents, according to Parkes's retelling. She also fell in love with the son of a judge. This young man was not her parent's choice of a suitor, but they did not force her to marry the "young gentleman from Holland" they had chosen for her. Alas, her sweetheart died of consumption when she was still younger than twenty, and so "depressed and disheartened," she accepted the marriage arrangement her parents had made for her with M. Allix. She presented this decision as a response to her parents' "extreme anxiety to see her settled." She did not want to be a burden to them.

Eugénie's loquaciousness about her childhood faded into innuendo with respect to her married life: "Little is known, and nothing need be said, about this marriage, but that it was a very unhappy and unsuitable tie." Still, she did tell her British friends that her future husband had been raised for the priesthood but renounced his vows. No mention of the mistreatment she recounted to Parkes makes its way into the *English Woman's Journal*'s version of her history; instead, readers are told:

> Why he married, and why once married he did not make his young wife happy, is one of those sad mysteries which are best left in the shadowed privacy of domestic life. That Madame Allix three times returned to her father's house, and at last, with her father's consent fled to Algiers, then recently acquired by the French is enough to say; and so great was her distress, and so moving her representations, that on M. Allix sending to inquire for the fugitive, the Algerine authorities actually sent back word *that no such woman had been heard of in the colony!*

Parkes mentions the existence of a daughter, left in France with Eugénie's mother, but dwells lightly on domestic discord before plunging into the description of Madame Allix's early years in Algeria.

This presentation of Eugénie's early life highlights aspects of her character that clearly appealed: "a certain shrewd, practical simplicity of character"—so different from British representations of the frivolous French society woman—her strong will, her ability to rise above misfortune, and her determination to do something with her pedagogical talents. The story also contains a number of inaccuracies, such as her date of birth, the name of her native town, and the number of her siblings. The first two errors were probably inadvertent mistakes on the part of her British friends, but the issue of family size is more puzzling. Parkes carefully situates Eugénie's birth within the Christian calendar, born on the "great feast of Pentecost," celebrated as Whitsun in Great Britain, and then presents her as the twelfth child of her parents. This precision as to the number of children must have come from Eugénie herself, but why did she invent such a large family? Was this simply a penchant for exaggeration? Whatever the answers to such questions, the presentation bears all the marks of a good storyteller and does a nice job disrupting not just British representations of French womanhood, but also historical descriptions of women's lives in the early years of the nineteenth century. We have very few portraits of lower-middle-class girls acting independently, expressing political opinions, and teaching. The archival version confirms the socioeconomic context Parkes described but offers little opportunity to see the little girl teaching peasants to read, tearing Bonapartist banners in two, or vociferously singing royalist songs.

THE ARCHIVAL VERSION:
FAMILIAL AND LOCAL CULTURE

Eugénie was indeed born into the moderately educated lower middle classes in a small town in the Cher River valley, Montrichard—not Montréchat—in the Loir-et-Cher, 34 kilometers southwest from the department's prefecture, Blois. She grew up in pastoral surroundings marked by the presence of vineyards, woods, and the wide, drowsy river Cher. In the early nineteenth century, the town (with roughly two thousand inhabitants) held a market and served as an administrative hub, situated as it was at the crossroads of two major arteries within the department. Located in the diocese of Tours, Montrichard belonged to the Touraine in the early modern period, but in 1790 administrative redivisions placed it in the Blésois in the Loir-et-Cher.

Unlike neighboring Blois or Tours, Montrichard boasts no particularly famous local inhabitants. A history published in 1850 noted the existence of three "famous" men from Montrichard: Victor Palma-Cayet (1525–1610), who was a historian and subpreceptor to the future Henri IV and later taught Hebrew at the Collège de Navarre in Paris; G. Touchard-Lafosse (1780–1847), who was appointed a war commissioner under Napoleon and became a local historian; and the revolutionary politician Louis Frécine, who committed suicide upon Napoleon's return to power.[7] Like Madame Luce, none of these men is particularly well-known outside specialized historical circles. Today, Montrichard's tourist bureau vaunts the town's picturesque qualities, canoe rides on the Cher, and the proximity of the Loire Valley castles, not its illustrious former inhabitants.

According to stories Eugénie Luce later told Bessie Parkes, her family moved when she was four years old to a ramshackle castle that dominated the neighboring village of Angé along the river. Her grandfather Sylvain Berlau (1742–1809) was the mayor of this agricultural village of a little over six hundred inhabitants. He had received some education, as evidenced by his profession, listed variously in baptismal or civil registers as a geometer, a land surveyor, or a "grammarian geometer."[8] All of these professions required schooling in reading, writing, and arithmetic. From 1769 until 1788, he ran the boys' school in Montrichard, but his focus on teaching writing—a talent required for land surveying—led to his replacement by another teacher willing to spend more time teaching reading and grammar.[9]

Eugénie's grandfather was clearly not a wealthy man. He earned a living measuring land, teaching at times, and helping out both in the town hall and in the church of Montrichard and Angé. The prefect appointed mayors during the First Empire, but this does not necessarily tell us about his politics, particularly in such a small village. Probably his ability to read and write qualified him for this position in a community of wine growers. His death in 1809 brought a modest sum to his children: Eugénie's father, her uncle Léonard, and her aunt Marie-Catherine. The inheritance, valued at 7,667 francs, consisted of a house worth 5,000 francs and furniture worth the remaining sum.[10]

Eugénie's father, also named Sylvain Berlau, followed very much in his father's footsteps, working as a land surveyor, a geometer, and, toward the end of his life, a schoolteacher. Her mother, Marie Rougé, like most Frenchwomen of the time, emerges in the archives as a mother and a wife. Both of Eugénie's parents were natives of Montrichard, born within a year of each other—Sylvain in 1766 and Marie in 1767. In November 1787 when they married, all of the family members gathered for the occasion were capable of signing the marriage register, including the young bride herself. Her ability to sign her name positioned Marie Rougé among a relatively small percentage of "literate" women in the Loir-et-Cher. Educational surveys for the period between 1786 and 1790 reveal that only between 10 and 20 percent of women and 20 to 30 percent of men were capable of signing their marriage contracts.[11] As the daughter of a tradesman Marie Rougé may have acquired the rudiments of education from her father, or perhaps she attended her father-in-law's small school. In the revolutionary year IV (1796), Eugénie's father was listed in the census as a tradesman, and he and his wife were living at that time with three small children and one servant. All this defines a socioeconomic status above the working classes, but just barely.[12]

Eugénie's parents were not poor by contemporary standards, but they had to make do with Sylvain's modest income from land surveying and the proceeds from a little land; it seems that her uncle inherited the grandfather's property in Angé while Sylvain possessed a variety of plots in Montrichard that may have allowed him to produce and sell some wine. The need to establish the Berlau children, however, put a strain on the family's budget. Contrary to what Eugénie appears to have claimed, she was the sixth of seven children (rather than the twelve reported by Parkes), only five of whom lived into adulthood. Her oldest sister, Marie, was born shortly after their parents' marriage, followed in 1790 by the first son, named Sylvain (as familial tradition obliged). Marie Rougé was frequently pregnant or nursing a baby during the revolutionary decade, giving birth in 1794 to a daughter, Agnès Rose, known in the family as Louise; to a son, Martin Anselme, a year later, who lived only six months; and to another son, Jacques Étienne, in 1797. A final two girls were born in the first years of the new century: Eugénie in 1804 and Olimpe in 1809.

Eugénie's older siblings quickly left home although they stayed in the region. Her oldest brother, Sylvain, began his career in the family "business" working as a surveyor during the early years of the Napoleonic Empire. He was one of a crew of thousands who helped divide France's territory into departments. Her two older sisters married educated men like their father who were local landowners. Marie wed Jean Perdrier, who succeeded Eugénie's grandfather and then her uncle as mayor of the village of Angé from 1816 until 1840. Their imposing tombstone is still in good shape in Angé's cemetery more than 150 years after their deaths. Eugénie claimed that her brother Jacques Étienne went off to study at the *collège* in Poitiers, dying there in 1817.[13] His death certificate, however, states that he was a cooper and died in Angé at age twenty. He may indeed have spent some years studying, but by age twenty he had forsworn books for the wine-making business, like his uncle Léonard Berlau.

Eugénie's earliest memories were from her life in Angé growing up amidst the members of her extended family. Located 6 kilometers southeast of Montrichard, Angé was primarily a wine-growing village, with rolling hills to the south and the river Cher to the north. The castle where Eugénie grew up was in the center of the village, surrounded by pastures where she played with her younger sister, Olimpe, and a cousin her age. Although her family clearly valued schooling, she later described an education acquired informally, learning her catechism with the local priest and reading voraciously in her father's library. There is no archival evidence that Eugénie had any formal education, and there is no sign of a school in Angé. Girls' schools did exist in the larger towns of the area, including in Montrichard where a poor school run by nuns opened in 1810.[14] In Blois, the aspiring middle classes could send their daughters to the Ursulines or one of four lay boarding schools for *jeunes demoiselles*, but the limited resources of the Berlau family make it unlikely that her parents would have had the financial means to send her to board in any of the available schools, nor could the family afford a tutor.[15] By 1820, when Eugénie was sixteen, Montrichard boasted five girls' schools, including a boarding school run by Mademoiselle Rafarin, who may have given Eugénie lessons in the accomplishments.[16] Like most girls from Eugénie's social class at the time, she undoubtedly learned most of "her letters" with her father or her older brothers. The eloquent reports she penned from colonial Algiers testify to the quality of this education.

The Napoleonic wars affected this bucolic upbringing relatively little, although there is evidence of political tensions within Angé between those who supported the emperor and those who welcomed the return of the Bourbon king to the throne of France. Diverging political opinions introduced dissensions within the Berlau family between her royalist father and Bonapartist uncle; the latter was sworn in as mayor during Napoleon's brief return to power in 1815 but was quickly replaced by Zachari Breton. A year later Sylvain Berlau took up his pen to denounce all those in Angé who failed to support the king. While criticizing the absence of monarchist sentiment in Restoration Angé, he also emphasized Mayor Breton's illiteracy and hence inadequacy as mayor: "It is urgent, Monsieur le Préfet, to change the spirit in this commune. The means to achieve this is by changing the mayor and his assistant given that the former can barely sign his name and cannot read. . . . The assistant does not live in the commune and is not animated by a good spirit."[17] The singing competition Eugénie described between herself and a young lad during the hundred days of Napoleon's return to power shows that at age eleven she followed her father's political beliefs and supported the Bourbon royalty. Fifteen years later this was no longer the case.

In 1816 the restored Bourbon monarchy of Louis XVIII revoked the right to divorce, a decision the Berlau family probably did not register although later it would play a role in Eugénie's life. The change in government also brought a downturn in Sylvain Berlau's fortune, as the decision to stop land surveying brought an end to his employment as a first-class geometer. Then tragedy struck when Eugénie's brother Jacques died in 1817. His death brought an end to the family's rural lifestyle, as they sought distraction by moving into Montrichard, a decision Eugénie claims to have made herself. In town, Sylvain Berlau set up a small primary school in 1821 that also brought the family a small income to replace the surveying job he had lost.[18] The diocesan records indicate that he catered to young students, and by 1824 the curé reported that Eugénie also ran a class for girls in a separate room from the one where her father taught.[19] In these years before the Guizot educational law of 1833, village schools were relatively informal structures, and in small towns they often welcomed both boys and girls despite Catholic hostility to coeducation. In these circumstances, it was quite natural for Eugénie to take over the teaching of a small number of girls, thus supplementing the family income.

School teaching was, however, a precarious business, since teachers relied on student fees to survive. In 1824 Sylvain Berlau complained to the prefect that a young man had moved to town and was intending to open a boarding school to teach Latin, even though he was already a tax collector (implying that he already had a decent salary). In no uncertain terms Berlau argued that this school threatened his economic livelihood as well as that of the other schoolteacher in town, the elderly Jean-Pierre Gautier: "The town of Montrichard has a population of 2000 inhabitants, at least half of whom live in garrets and are unable to pay for the instruction of their children. That leaves, as a result, 1000 inhabitants who provide Gaultier [*sic*] and myself with thirty students a piece. What will happen to us, M. le Préfet, if the *sieur* executes his project? We will be forced to give up our profession and seek other means of living, which will be very difficult."[20] At age fifty-eight he was only eking out an existence with his thirty students, despite relatively favorable inspection reports about his instruction and morality. Arguing that both he and M. Gautier were too old to seek another employment, Berlau sought, unsuccessfully, to prevent the opening of a third school in the small town.

This familial context helps to explain Eugénie's parents' concern to find her a husband who could support her once she came of age. In the 1820s in France single women from her social background had relatively few options open to them if they wanted to maintain their social status. They either remained at home caring for their aging parents, got married, or entered a religious order. Teaching was also an option but a relatively risky business for women who did not have the financial resources to open a boarding school. Teachers of private primary schools, like her father's, had to rely on school fees and occasional municipal funding to survive, neither of which offered any financial security during these years (and even after Guizot's education law in 1833 school teaching offered only meager returns, particularly in small towns such as Montrichard). Eugénie's parents, as they reached the age of sixty, with two daughters still at home, had strong incentive to find husbands for both. Nor would Eugénie have had much to say in the matter, as her own retelling reveals. Once her young sweetheart had died, she had no reason to protest her parent's choice of a spouse, a young man whose career as a schoolteacher placed him in the same economic bracket as her father.

MARRIAGE AND MOTHERHOOD

Eugénie Berlau and Jacques Alexandre Allix were joined in marriage on 10 January 1826 in Montrichard. Not yet twenty-two years old, the bride was younger than the average of the time, as was her spouse at age twenty-three.[21] The marriage register listed his profession as "*instituteur, maître de pension*" (schoolteacher, boarding school master), living in Montrichard although the archives reveal no trace of his presence as a teacher in the town. More likely he was teaching in a neighboring village, and most probably he did *not* run a boarding school since no such school appears in the records. Teaching represented a form of cultural upward mobility for this young man whose father was a glassmaker in Chatellerault in the Vienne. We have only Eugénie's story about Alexandre's aspirations to enter the church; what we know for sure is that he spent most of his life either teaching or working as a clerk within various administrations, using his mind rather than his hands to earn a living. The professions of the witnesses at their wedding speak to the cultural proximity of artisans and teachers in the early nineteenth century: Alexandre's brother, Simon, was a painter from Chatellerault, and Ambroise Constant Rouilly was a friend and fellow schoolteacher at the *collège* in neighboring Romorantin.

Unlike his wife, Alexandre Allix had left his native Poitou after his birth in 1802, and during the years between his marriage and his death in 1845 he would move several times. In 1827, at the birth of his first daughter, he was working as a schoolteacher in Bléré, across the departmental border in the Indre-et-Loire (18 kilometers west of Montrichard). Three years later, he was still teaching in Bléré, but not for long. By 1831 both husband and wife had left Bléré for Vendôme in the Loir-et-Cher, 60 kilometers to the north. A subprefecture of the department, Vendôme was a regional hub with more than six thousand inhabitants. The town offered a far greater variety of employment possibilities than Bléré, which had less than half the population.

No sources beyond the tales of his wife conjure up a portrait of the elusive Alexandre Allix. Clearly, he was a relatively educated man, but without the commitment to teaching that Eugénie would demonstrate throughout her life. By 1836, having been abandoned by his wife, he was no longer a teacher, but rather a clerk in Vendôme, his home throughout the 1830s. Five years later, however, the population census reveals he was living and working in Compiègne, 85 kilometers north of Paris. This bustling industrial center in the nineteenth century had grown up on an ancient Roman site, becoming the residence of Merovingian royalty during the Middle Ages. The English took Joan of Arc prisoner there in 1430. At the time of Allix's death in 1845, he was a clerk in Compiègne's office of mortgages. This itinerary from Chatellerault to Compiègne, from teaching to clerking, tells us very little, however, about the man who married Eugénie and yet failed to keep her at home.

Their married life together was short, a mere six years, but during those years municipal records reveal that Eugénie gave birth to two daughters. Their first, Alexandrine Eugénie—known later as Marie—was born on 9 November 1827, exactly twenty-two months after her parents' marriage. Not surprisingly for the period, Eugénie had returned to her parent's home to give birth, leaving Alexandre in Bléré to tend to his school. Her father declared the child's birth with a cousin who was a policeman in Montrichard. A second daughter, Olimpe, was born almost two years later in September 1829 in Bléré. Less than a year later Eugénie, like many young mothers of the time, experienced the grief of Olimpe's death. The death register indicates that Eugénie had returned once more to her parents' house although it is impossible to tell whether this was a temporary move to deal with an ailing child or an indication of the marital problems she later confided to her British friends.

Superficially, the young married couple shared common interests and talents since they were both teachers. Shortly after their wedding in Eugénie's hometown, they settled a few miles west in Bléré, along the river Cher, where Alexandre began running a school. A half year later Eugénie followed suit, requesting authorization to open a girls' school. Curiously, the archives contain virtually no information about his stint as schoolteacher, whereas "Madame Allix" appears in a number of records. By January 1827 she had received authorization to open a school and had attracted a few students. In June 1831 Alexandre Allix no longer figured among the schoolteachers of the village. The "Femme Allix-Berleau"—a commonly found misspelling of her family name within the archives—was still on the lists of the committee of primary instruction for the canton of Bléré, but the clerk noted that she had closed her school and moved to Vendôme.[22] At the most, Eugénie ran her school for four years, probably just barely making a living, given the small number of families who could afford to pay for their daughters' schooling.

Elementary schools during this period were fairly rudimentary affairs run by men and women who often had no form of certification despite regulations in 1816 and 1819 requiring first male and then female teachers to pass exams.[23] Requirements for these exams were minimal: an ability to read, write, and cal-

culate, as well as proof of their good behavior. Teacher training was in its infancy, and no normal schools existed for women teachers before 1838. Prior to
the 1833 legislation that decreed one male normal school per department, few
men benefited from professional training either. As a result, teachers made do
as they could; most adopted the individual teaching method, dispensing their
lessons one-on-one with little pedagogical material to help them along. In the
early 1830s Inspector Prat for the Loir-et-Cher argued that most schoolteachers
were "without talent or training."[24] The Allixes' income was undoubtedly low,
since they received no aid from the town and depended on school fees from a
few dozen students who attended school on an irregular basis. During the summer months, when children worked in the fields, classrooms were deserted. As
a result, Eugénie may not have taught in the latter months of her two pregnan-
cies since both daughters were born in the fall. Years later, she told her British
friends that her husband took all of her earnings from her teaching; legally, he
had the right to do so, as married women did not acquire the right to control
their own earnings until 1907.

Given the sort of teacher and businesswoman Eugénie Allix became, it
seems likely that she found married life in Bléré constraining and unfulfilling.
Pregnancy and childbirth were dangerous and arduous experiences for early-
nineteenth-century women because of poor hygienic conditions and the absence
of anesthesia. Raising an infant while running a one-room school also would
have posed quite a few problems. With no family members in the immediate
environs, Eugénie would have had to rely on paid female help, an additional
cost she may not have been able easily to afford. Still, the religious lessons of her
Catholic youth would have taught her that women were expected to accept their
lot, bow their heads, and submit to their husbands. If her husband mistreated her
as she claimed, she had few options to respond, particularly given the abolition
of divorce in 1816. Among the aspiring middle classes, domestic disputes rarely
made their way into court, and only wealthy women could afford the procedure
of residential and financial separation (*séparation de corps et de biens*).[25] This was
not Eugénie's case, and so when her husband left Bléré to settle in Vendôme, she
followed him. But in 1831 the social and cultural climate had changed in France.
Following the Revolution of 1830 the urban working classes and the educated
lower middle classes felt increasingly empowered to protest against established
hierarchies. This context undoubtedly contributed to Eugénie's decision to question her relationship with her husband.

WOMEN, SOCIETY, AND POLITICS
DURING THE EARLY JULY MONARCHY

Eugénie Allix began her life as a mother and wife during the final years of the Restoration (1815–1830), with Charles X on the throne of France. These years were highly contentious ones, as mounting anticlericalism challenged the politics of the Bourbon king and Jesuit missionaries organized spectacular ceremonies throughout France. We have no way of knowing whether Eugénie participated in these mission celebrations or whether she found their messages appealing. Life as a teacher and young mother would not have left her much time for other activities. But like other women from her familial educational background, she undoubtedly continued to read.[26]

Neither Bléré nor Montrichard was large enough to have a *cabinet de lecture* (reading room), but books and newspapers circulated informally during these years before public libraries and the technological means of producing cheap books. And, of course, schoolteachers and their families had easier access to the printed word than other social groups. Despite press censorship during the late Restoration, newspapers contributed to the spread of liberal and even socialist ideas, which may have reached Eugénie's curious mind, although none of the local papers carried political news.[27] Certainly, she would have registered the Revolution of 1830 that brought Louis Philippe to the throne as King of the French rather than King of France and introduced broader manhood suffrage and new liberties of press and association. Her sister's husband, Jean Perdrier, directly experienced the effects of the revolution in municipal politics, as he lost his seat as mayor of Angé, only to recapture it in 1832.

On the face of it, the Revolution of 1830 that ushered in the July Monarchy affected men more than women, but the events of the early 1830s raised new questions about women's role in society, most notably among the Saint-Simonians. This group of what are now termed "utopian socialists" spread their ideas in newspapers, missions, and public lectures, using techniques that resembled those of religious missionaries. The group was originally inspired by the ideas of Claude Henri de Rouvroy, comte de Saint-Simon, and was organized first as a "school," then a "society," and finally, after Saint-Simon's death, as a "religion." Its leaders defended the principles of a more egalitarian society and appealed to Eugénie's generation of men and women, who had come of age during the reactionary years of the Restoration.[28] Among the leaders, Prosper Enfantin was the first to call for equality between the sexes and to develop a message that valued womanly characteristics and emotions. His feminist message was coupled with a vision of a new sexual morality requiring the "rehabilitation of the flesh." By the early 1830s, he had begun to attract a number of lower-middle-class and even working-class women who responded to his gender egalitarianism. Enfantin's call for a new world order of sexual equality represented a dramatic change for women, whose status in French society was markedly inferior to that of men. His female followers, such as Reine Guindorf, Suzanne Voilquin, and Eugénie Niboyet, focused their energy and writing on the material facets of women's inequality, especially their lack of education, their economic dependence, and their civil inferiority.[29] Jeanne Deroin in particular spoke angrily about how the education of girls shackled the minds and souls of the women they would become:

A woman's education is directed in such a way as to restrict her moral and intellectual faculties. Efforts are made to persuade her she is inferior to men and to ensure this odious supposition becomes a reality. . . . If she has an inquiring mind and studious habits, education compresses in her all that might bring her strength and moral dignity. It seeks to cultivate her frivolous tastes, suggests to her that the gift of charm and the art of pleasing should be her sole aim and the object of her wishes. . . . Even when she reaches a high level of knowledge and genuine superiority, all careers are blocked for her, she cannot enter public service, *lycées*, university faculties and educational academies.[30]

Although not many women were among the Saint-Simonians, their contribution to public debate raised issues about women's inferior status, particularly in marriage, that resonated in less radical venues. The ideal of the companionate marriage was gradually gaining sway among the middle classes, and the feminine press that developed during the 1830s and 1840s relayed this ideal.[31] An attempt to revive divorce in the 1830s testified to a current of opinion in favor of marriage as a dissolvable contract. During these same years women writers such as George Sand, Marie d'Agoult, Hortense Allart, and Delphine Gay de Girardin all wrote texts that questioned the gender hierarchies of their time.[32] Although no organized feminist movement existed in France at this time, there was a body of thought that challenged the idea that women's lives should be determined by the needs and desires of men and that women's place in society was mainly in the home.

There is no way to ascertain whether Eugénie Allix encountered any of these ideas in the early 1830s or whether her discovery of Saint-Simonian thought occurred only later in Algeria. Her native Loir-et-Cher was not a site of active proselytizing; but a few correspondents supported Saint-Simonian ideas, and by

September 1831, one of the papers most associated with the movement, *Le Globe*, was being distributed for free.[33] In Vendôme, the Allixes would have had greater opportunity than in Bléré to mingle with men and women who supported the more liberal ideals of the Revolution of 1830, and teachers were particularly likely to welcome these ideas. When yet another revolution ended the July Monarchy in 1848, the Loir-et-Cher was by then a hotbed of democratic and socialist agitation.[34] Who knows, however, whether either husband or wife mingled with the future revolutionaries and whether these encounters encouraged Eugénie Allix to throw off the bonds of marriage and motherhood. What we do know is that something happened to encourage her to abandon her husband, her daughter, and the proximity of her parents in search of another life.

She presented her flight as an escape from marital unhappiness, but that explanation fails to do justice to the radical choice she made. In the tale she told her British friends she said she could not afford the cost of separation. Certainly, the procedure was costly and complicated, as it required proving violence, cruelty, or serious offense of one spouse against the other; adultery of the wife; adultery of the husband if at the same time he maintained his concubine in the conjugal home; or the condemnation of either spouse for a serious crime. Women requested separations far more frequently than men because they allowed spouses to live apart and to divide their property; however, separations nonetheless maintained a relationship between husband and wife that was distinctly unequal for women. Separated women remained without legal capacity and were saddled with an obligation of marital fidelity; furthermore, the status of children was subject to the decision of a tribunal.[35] The decision to take to her heels rather than to the courts says something about the sort of woman Eugénie Allix was.

THE LURE OF THE UNKNOWN?

When Eugénie turned her eyes south to North Africa, the French conquest initiated by the Bourbon king Charles X in 1830 was in its very early years. Muslim notables would continue to wage war against the French well into the 1860s, although by 1848 the northern lands of Algeria, the Tell, were under French control. The city of Annaba, which the French renamed Bône, fell to the French in 1832 but remained primarily a military city for years. To the east of Algiers the city of Constantine along the coast fell to the French only after five years of combat between 1832 and 1837. Although Algiers had been "pacified," as the military put it, when Eugénie Allix first arrived, King Louis Philippe had not yet made the decision to continue restricted occupation (*occupation restreinte*) along the Barbary Coast; that decision was made in 1834.[36]

A decision to follow the military to a land renowned for the infamy of Barbary pirates cannot have been taken lightly in the early years of the French conquest. Eugénie told Bessie Rayner Parkes that she accompanied a family from her neighborhood, but the archives tell us nothing more. There are no traces of a request for a passport, no way of identifying the family who might have helped her in her flight. Nothing in her background would have paved the way for such a move. She did not travel in her youth, nor did she move in social circles for whom the northern shores of Africa would have been familiar. All this suggests a desire to start life anew, a desire for adventure.

The lure of the "Orient," which included at that time North Africa, may have played a role in her decision, as it did for the Romantics and the Saint-Simonians.[37] Saint-Simonian women, in particular, followed Enfantin to Egypt in 1834 and set up communities of forward-thinking men and women. Given what we know of Eugénie's life after her move, it is tempting to speculate on how the Saint-Simonian message may have given her the strength to cast off both the lessons of her Catholic childhood and the weight of conjugal and maternal obligations. Since the exact date of her departure is unknown, she may have followed in the footsteps of radical fellow thinkers, because as early as August 1833 a number of Saint-Simonians began their discovery of the "East" with an expedition to Algeria.[38] Perhaps she was tempted by the possibilities the new colony offered for making herself anew. What is certain, however, is that she left her husband and crossed the Mediterranean to ensure that he would not try to make her return to him.

The intellectual, social, and political effervescence of the early years of the July Monarchy offered the sort of historical context that makes Eugénie's decision more understandable. Her claim that she fled in the company of a neighboring couple undoubtedly would have given her a certain social legitimacy and shielded her from the suspicions surrounding young single women. Still, her decision to pull up roots for the Barbary Coast remains an exceptional one and all the more unusual for a woman from her background. This initial choice, which involved throwing aside the highly gendered duties and obligations of her youth in favor of adventure and the hope for self-fulfillment, is essential to the story that follows.

2 EARLY YEARS IN ALGERIA (1832–1845)

When Bessie Rayner Parkes described Madame Luce to her British feminist readership in 1861, she portrayed Eugénie Allix's move to Algeria as a means of escaping an unhappy marriage: "That Madame Allix three times returned to her father's house, and at last, with her father's consent fled to Algiers, then recently acquired by the French is enough to say."[1] Her readers probably shared my own impression that this explanation was not completely satisfactory. Why Algiers? Why without her daughter? In her private correspondence with Mary Merryweather, Parkes was a bit more explicit about the mechanics of the move, mentioning the existence of a family in the neighborhood whom Eugénie accompanied to Algiers. But the family remains unnamed, and no trace of official documentation about the move exists. It is unlikely we will ever know more.

Family memories were even more vague about Eugénie's decision to leave, as the following description by her great-granddaughter Jeanne Crouzet-Benaben shows: "A mere few years after the conquest, around 1840, a young widowed schoolteacher of *berrichon* origins [from the Berry region in central France], Madame Allix, established herself in Algiers. Following what events, what trials, did this audacious Frenchwomen form and then accomplish her plan to leave her country, alone with her little girl, her only child, to cross the sea—unusual and almost heroic act at that period—and to request the authorization to open a school in this barely conquered territory where virtually no Frenchmen lived aside from soldiers? I have no idea."[2] Nor in fact did she have a number of the facts right. Madame Allix probably arrived in Algiers in 1832, not 1840, and she was not a widow, but a wife fleeing her husband. And, contrary to the tale she told her family, she did not take her only child with her.

Eugénie's decision bears the mark not just of an independent-minded woman, but of an adventurous soul in these early years of the July Monarchy. The conquest of Algeria was a violent affair and far from accomplished in 1832. The French army presence in Algiers provided a certain security but not necessarily for a woman on her own. The government was not yet in the business of encouraging settlement in the new colony; those efforts developed only after

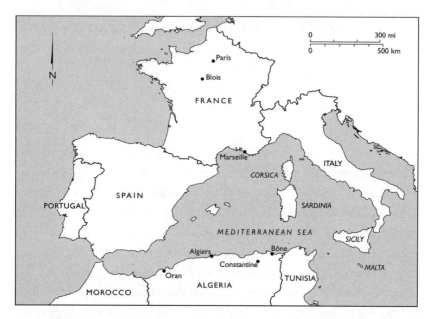

France and the North African coast.

1840. Rather, there was a concern to prevent the emigration of the urban poor, whose lack of financial means would then become a burden for the colony. As a result, Minister of the Interior Casimir Périer issued a circular in May 1831 giving metropolitan prefects the responsibility for issuing passports to Algeria.[3] The same procedure applied for movement between French departments and signaled the official intent to make Algeria French. Still, Eugénie's move from the Loir-et-Cher to Algiers required a great deal more initiative than the move that took her across department lines from Bléré to Vendôme.

The 1831 circular also specified the sorts of emigrants prefects should encourage, particularly merchants with trading interests in North Africa and people with the means and equipment to establish agricultural businesses. On no account were indigent and needy workers to be given passports. A month later the *Moniteur Universel* responded to procolonialist journalists by announcing that the government would provide free passage to Algiers "to families and to individuals from the working and agricultural classes who are capable of living from their own work and of taking to Africa some means of existence."[4] Emigrants still had to pay their own way to the port of departure and could not expect support from the government upon their arrival in Algiers. The departmental archives of the Loir-et-Cher have no records of Eugénie Allix's request for a passport. She, like many of the early settlers, probably left without going through the official formalities, perhaps purchasing a passport from the booksellers and traveling salesmen in Blois who worried authorities in 1832.[5] Given her status as a woman on her own and on the run, her story is plausible. Traveling with a local family would have given her a form of social respectability on the train to Marseille, during the five days at sea, and upon her arrival in Algiers, then known as El Djezaïr.

We have no trace of Eugénie's first impressions nor the hopes and expectations she carried with her as she placed the Mediterranean between herself and all that was familiar. Did she suffer from seasickness? Did she mingle with other passengers? Did her heart soar as El Djezaïr came into view? How did she envision making do once settled in the city? For the men and women who accompanied her on what was probably a military boat, Algeria was still relatively unknown. She would not have been alone, however, in hoping that it represented a new and better life. Still, as a woman without much in the way of financial resources, she must have realized that her decision involved real personal and social risk. Working women walked a precarious line in French society at this time, a reality that Eugénie Allix would have known as a provincial schoolteacher. It took guts and a certain insouciance about social propriety to flee.

Information about Eugénie Allix's activities in Algiers is sparse until the early 1840s, but we can flesh out the position that European women occupied in the city and show that their presence was more than anecdotal in the new colonial economy. Eugénie's gradual visibility within the archives can be directly traced to the relationships she developed with influential Saint-Simonian settlers. Her example reveals a hitherto untold tale of how radical ideas about gender relations crossed the Mediterranean into Algeria, not just into Egypt.

EUROPEANS IN ALGIERS IN THE 1830S

Algiers in the early 1830s was a bustling city, in stark contrast to the provincial towns where Eugénie had grown up and first plied her trade. European visitors to Algiers in the early years of colonization all commented on the shining white city emerging from the sea. Once on solid ground, most were struck by the frenzy of activity around the port and the variety of human types they encountered. The more ethnographically inclined observers commented on the mixture of races and their coexistence in the crowded streets of the upper city, or Casbah. Alexis de Tocqueville, better known for his writings on democracy in the United States, commented like many on the bewildering diversity he observed when visiting in 1841: "I have never seen anything like it. A prodigious mix of races, costumes, Arab, Kabyle, Moor, Negro, Mahonais, French. Each of these races, tossed together in a space much too tight to contain them, speaks its language, wears its attire, displays different mores."[6] Travelers were often fascinated by the city's women, who were draped in white linen and "hidden in their mysterious solitude," as Xavier Marmier wrote in 1847.[7] Not surprisingly, these early descriptions focused on the exotic rather than the familiar, so that Europeans, and European women in particular, were rarely the object of commentary.[8] So, was Eugénie Allix an unusual figure in the city of Algiers in the 1830s?

Not really. European women were a minority, but as early as 1833 they represented 27.6 percent of the European *civilian* population in Algiers (1,180 women).[9] In January 1833 another source estimated that the entire civilian population of the colony was 24,000, with 5,300 Europeans and 18,700 indigenous inhabitants.[10] Still, the large military presence, combined with the indigenous population, meant that the streets of Algiers were not particularly safe for single European women. This was all the more the case in that European women had an equivocal reputation in the city, given the sexual needs of the military population. Statistical tables from the outset of French colonization chronicled, alongside the number of schools, the number of women receiving treatment for venereal diseases, as well as the professions of both European and indigenous men and women. In 1840, 135 European women were registered as prostitutes, out of a population of approximately 6,900 women.[11] But it would be incorrect to imagine that prostitution awaited most single European women.

During the first two decades of French rule, Algiers was a fast-growing urban capital in a predominantly rural country. Many Europeans—French, Italians, and Maltese, in particular—flocked to Algiers in the early years of colonization, seeking employment and a better life. Their arrival changed the texture of the city and contributed to its increasing Europeanization. By 1846 Europeans outnumbered the indigenous population.[12] Demand for goods and services within this migrant population generated work for both men and women, while local artisanal production suffered from the disruptive presence of the French military. The European population represented a wide variety of social types, in both the colonial military and the settler communities. Educated Frenchmen staffed the colonial administration, which also attracted a host of interpreters, journalists, and scientists. These men (and a few women) had little in common with the poor fishermen or shopkeepers from Malta, the masons from Italy, or the prostitutes from Spain, nor did they share the same language. On the face of things, social experiences and economic capital radically separated wealthy merchants and consular families from agricultural workers or the urban poor, who made their way to Algeria despite efforts to keep them away. In colonial Algiers, however, social class played less of a role than race in the creation of hierarchies; this undoubtedly helped the young schoolteacher upon her arrival.

The boundaries between the European and native inhabitants of Algiers were physically marked in the city as it evolved during the early years of colonization. Urban projects divided Algiers between a lower city, which the French military administration and civilian populations occupied, and the upper Casbah, where the shrinking native population lived. Military preoccupations dictated the initial changes in the urban structure of this fortified city. The greatest occurred between 1830 and 1846 in what was known as the Marine Quarter, or the Quarter of the Ancient Prefecture, in the lower city along the waterfront where the Europeans settled. French military engineers began with the Place du Gouvernement in front of the Palace of the Dey; in order to create a space where the army could assemble, they destroyed shops, houses, and even mosques and enlarged the streets that converged on the new city center. The indigenous population was relegated to the upper Casbah where the network of narrow, sinuous streets was left largely untouched throughout the century.[13]

Eugénie Allix was not alone among female migrants in the early 1830s seeking another future in Algeria. The colonial imaginary that spurred many of these migrations had a strong economic dimension; most women came in search of work. Between August and December 1839 the newspaper *L'Akhbar* listed the arrival from France of forty-three women, many of whom were traveling alone: eight *rentières* (women with private means), nine proprietors, seven nuns, three women with their husbands, two *demoiselles* without a profession, seven shopkeepers, two artists, and five working-class women (such as seamstresses or laundresses).[14] As a schoolteacher Eugénie stood out, but she was not the only woman with professional skills beyond those related to sewing and cleaning. As early as January 1833, the *Annuaire de l'État d'Alger* listed three European midwives practicing in Algiers. Other women, particularly nuns, soon followed, setting up schools as well as hospices to care for the sick.

The Soeurs de St.-Joseph de l'Apparition were the first to settle in Algeria in 1835, under the dynamic leadership of Émilie de Vialar, whose brother, the baron de Vialar, was a major landowner and president of the Société coloniale, which was dedicated to promoting the settlement of the country. He employed the sisters in the civil hospital, where they had their hands full dealing with a devastating cholera epidemic that wreaked havoc as well in Europe and the United States in the early 1830s. The sisters quickly established a range of institutions mostly directed toward the European settlers: an infirmary, a pharmacy, three primary schools for girls (one boarding, one paying, and one free), a *salle d'asile* (nursery school), an orphanage, and a refuge for prostitutes. All this testifies to the fact that employment possibilities did exist for women in early colonial Algeria. For both material and symbolic reasons, however, it was clearly easier for women in religious orders to set up schools and run infirmaries than for individual laywomen. The Soeurs de St.-Joseph were imitated in the decade to follow by, among others, the Soeurs de la Doctrine Chrétienne de Nancy, who directed their attention to the European poor, and the Dames du Sacré-Coeur, who were more focused on the colonial elite.[15]

Whether Eugénie Allix imagined she would set up her own school upon arrival is impossible to tell. A few laywomen did indeed open schools, such as the Dames Lanneau (mother and daughter), who are listed in 1832 as running a boarding school for *demoiselles*. The *Annuaire* reported that the school compared favorably with schools in France in terms of both the teaching and the "good education" it offered.[16] Of course, the school was intended for European girls. A year later statistical tables indicated the existence of one "Christian" girls' school with thirty-four students.[17] In 1836 an Alsatian schoolteacher, Héloïse Hartoch, opened a school for Jewish girls that welcomed both European and indigenous students.[18] Still, girls' schools were not a top priority during the early years of colonization, and the religious orders were far better equipped to meet the existing demand than individual women. It is likely that Eugénie, when she first arrived at age twenty-eight, anticipated giving private lessons or acting as a nanny to wealthy settler families, rather than running a school, as she had in France. In reality, it appears that she was quickly confronted with a need to earn her living in a more menial fashion—washing clothes for the French military.

A FRENCHWOMAN ON HER OWN IN ALGERIA

Eugénie never spoke much about her early years in Algeria, and few traces of her remain in the colonial archives. Did she arrive with a mission, as she claimed later to her Saint-Simonian friends? Was she hoping to meet another man? Was she anticipating a more exciting life, given her new independence from marital and maternal obligations? Only a few sources offer any insight into the decade that followed her departure from Bléré in the Indre-et-Loire and her reemergence in Bône (present-day Annaba) on the Algerian coast. These sources tell, however, rather a different story than what she later claimed.

In 1857 she confided in Bessie Rayner Parkes, telling her "much of her private history." Notably, she admitted that the early years were difficult and that "she struggled on, giving lessons and when she had finished, going to the Military hospital to wash and mend the soldiers' linen for a franc a day."[19] While washing clothing clearly represented a downturn in Eugénie Allix's fortunes, the story rings true. It seems likely that private lessons in Algiers would not have afforded much of a financial cushion. The army offered employment for many of the single women in Algiers as laundresses, cooks, and servants and often attracted adventuresome women.[20] The story also rings true because Eugénie appears in the colonial civil register in 1835 as the mother of an illegitimate daughter, and here her profession is listed as "laundress."

The records provide the mere skeleton of a relatively familiar woman's story: an illegitimate birth, an unknown father, and the infant's death before reaching the age of one. On 21 January 1835 the Sieur Étienne Moreau, *officier de santé* (medical officer), aged thirty-four years, living at 288 rue Bab Azoun, presented an infant girl to the presiding official. The child was born on 19 January 1835 to *demoiselle* Véronique Eugénie Berlau, laundress, aged twenty-seven, living at 298 rue Bab Azoun. The father was listed as "unknown." Two witnesses testified to the exactitude of this information, Étienne Bernard, a nurse, and Jean Engel, a wig-maker. The child was given the names Césarine Victorine Eugénie Adeläide. Fewer than ten months later the civil register recorded the infant's death on 2 October 1835. Two men reported the death: Camille Jean Léon Philberty, a thirty-three-year-old merchant, and Clément Padovani, a landowner, aged sixty-two. Both men, as well as the mother, once again listed as laundress, are indicated as living at 6 rue Boutin in Algiers.[21]

These records offer some insight into Eugénie's life during these years beyond the obvious fact that she had sexual relations with someone, consensual or otherwise, and from this encounter a child was born. She appears in the record as *demoiselle* Berlau, reverting to her father's name and thereby hiding the fact of her marriage to Alexandre Allix. Perhaps this was a way to increase her anonymity in order to avoid any attempts her husband might have made to force her to return to France. Perhaps it also avoided sullying her married name. For whatever reason, she chose during these years to appear a single woman. Along-side the omission of her married status was an outright lie about her age: she stated that she was twenty-seven years old, but in January 1835 she was in fact thirty years old. Was this mere feminine vanity—a desire to appear a few years younger than her true age? Or was it a way to muddle the record a bit more?

In January, she was living on the rue Bab Azoun, a main thoroughfare that ran along the southern edge of the Casbah. Europeans lived in this area, which was socially mixed, as is partly evidenced by the men who served as witnesses in the civil act: the two men of the medical world, Moreau and Bernard, and the artisan Engel. Just a few streets to the north lay the Casbah, where the poorer indigenous inhabitants increasingly lived. An *officier de santé* at this time was a low-ranking medical man without the training, qualifications, or salary of a doctor; this was even more the case for male nurses. So all four of the individuals named belonged by their professions to the working or the lower middle classes, with Eugénie the least qualified in professional terms.

By October, however, Eugénie was living in a somewhat different part of the city with what appears to be more established middle-class neighbors or companions. The rue Boutin was located in the Marine Quarter, an area that would undergo considerable changes and house administrative buildings in the years to come. The two men indicated in the death certificate appear relatively established, since one was a property owner and the other sold goods. Was she living in a servant's room that belonged to the Corsican Padovani? Was she the lover of the younger witness, the merchant Philberty? Perhaps she was simply a neighbor in need. The registers offer no clear answers but suggest that during these difficult months, with cholera raging in the city, Eugénie either had the means to move or was provided with such means.

Illegitimate births were *not* noteworthy in early colonial Algiers, as early de-mographic studies show. The doctors Foley and Martin noted extremely high rates of illegitimacy in Algiers between January 1831 and December 1847: out of 10,173 births, 2,193 were so-called natural births (216 per thousand). In other words, more than one-fifth of all births were to unwed couples, whereas in France the rate was far lower (72 per thousand).[22] Eugénie's situation, then, was common and relatively tolerated during these years when single women were in short supply and the male European population was highly mobile. Signs of this tolerance can be seen in the high rates of paternal recognition of these ille-gitimate children, once again far higher than in France. The father of Césarine

Victorine, however, did not recognize his child, probably because the mother had no incentive to push him to do so. This would only have further complicated her situation as an adulterous woman illicitly living apart from her husband and bearing an illegitimate child under her maiden name.

The available material renders difficult any hypothesis about who the father was and whether he was more than a casual acquaintance. Was he one of the three men mentioned in the birth act? Or perhaps one of the men living with Eugénie on the rue Boutin at the time of Césarine's death? None of these men ever resurfaced in documents concerning Eugénie, and so her secret probably went to the grave with her. The daughter's birth, however, would have made the mother's daily life more difficult. With no family members on the African continent, she had the difficult task of juggling a need to work and the needs of an infant, although of course the father may have helped. She probably resorted to a network of women friends and possibly to a wet nurse to help her get by. A few years later a study of European demographics in Algeria noted the widespread use of Spanish wet nurses for the first eighteen to thirty months after the birth of a child; as in France, however, wet nursing was a risky business for the infant, since infant mortality rates were very high for children cared for by mercenaries.[23]

The only certainty in this story is that the baby was born and died within a year, an all too common fate for newborns in Algiers. In the first eighteen years of French colonization, one-third of all infants died in their youth (and this percentage excludes those who were stillborn).[24] During the same period in Paris and other industrial cities, doctors and hygienists deplored high rates of infant mortality as well, but these resulted "only" in the deaths of one-quarter of all infants. Poor hygienic conditions and a series of epidemics in Algiers explain the high rates, particularly among poor, ill-educated populations living in crowded sections of the city. Cholera in particular took a heavy toll and may have been the direct cause of the baby's death.[25] We cannot know what Eugénie felt at losing another daughter, nor do we have any way of knowing how she dealt during these often difficult years with the separation from her family and her daughter Marie, who in 1835 was only eight years old.

Life for Eugénie, *femme* Berlau Allix, went on, however, in the sort of historical obscurity that marks most individuals' lives, until once again her name emerges in the colonial civil register. On 20 February 1840, Mayor Fenech of Bône recorded the birth of another child, Louis Lucien Allix. The parents were "Sieur Alexandre, 37 years old, a teacher living in Vendôme, born in Chatellerault, department of the Vienne and dame Berlau, Eugénie, his wife, 34 years old, born in Montrichard, department of Loir-et-Cher, schoolteacher, living in Bône." The three men who testified to the birth were Louis Maljean, a thirty-two-year-old hardware dealer; Paul Boucheron, a thirty-year-old musician in the 26th regiment of infantry garrisoned in Bône; and Louis Auguste Napoléon Luce, a thirty-three-year-old music sergeant in the same regiment, who would become Eugénie's second husband. Did Mayor Fenech ponder the difficulties involved in the child's conception when thousands of miles separated the supposed father from the mother? Probably not. Given the fact that Louis Luce married Eugénie Allix in 1846, and the fact that the infant's first given name was Louis, it seems more than likely that by 1840 the two were a couple.

The birth declaration sheds some light on Eugénie's circumstances eight years after her arrival in Algiers. To begin with, she had left that city for a smaller and more recently conquered one. In 1832 the French captured Annaba, which relatively quickly became a settler city, as the native population fled, and was renamed Bône. First a military and then a civilian European population settled in this ancient Roman port city to the east of Algiers. Near the site of Hippone, where Saint Augustine lived in the Middle Ages, Bône attracted a wide variety of adventurous capitalist souls who eagerly bought up land and forests and mined the rich minerals available in the area. By 1838 three thousand Europeans lived in Bône, although far more men than women; in 1843 European men still outnumbered women two to one.[26]

What prompted Eugénie's move to Bône? Well-to-do patrons may have attracted her, in particular A. Marion, the Saint-Simonian justice of the peace in Bône. This is probably where she met Louis Luce, who had arrived in Bône in 1837 with the 26th infantry regiment.[27] Certainly, by 1840 Eugénie appears to have been living in somewhat less difficult circumstances and aspiring to a more respectable status. With Louis Allix's birth she chose to register her son under her French husband's name, unlike her declaration five years earlier, and she was listed as a schoolteacher rather than a laundress. Once again, however, she shaved a year off her real age, indicating that she was thirty-four when in reality she was thirty-five.

And once again, Eugénie's infant died, six short months after his birth. The probable father did not appear at the town hall; rather, two official witnesses—the town hall secretary and a police officer—signed Louis Allix's death certificate. In a span of thirteen years, then, Eugénie gave birth to four babies, three of whom died within a year. Certainly, infant mortality rates were high, but it is conceivable that her mothering skills and instincts were not highly developed and that her priorities were not in ensuring her children's survival. The decision to leave her first daughter, Marie, in France reflects, at any rate, an ability to distance herself both physically and psychologically from the responsibilities of motherhood. The few remaining traces of her life in these years suggest that she had other issues on her mind.

SAINT-SIMONIAN FRIENDSHIPS

The civil registers offer tenuous insight into Eugénie's social network during her first decade of life in Algeria. They highlight in particular her mobility both within and between cities, as well as the social range of her acquaintances within the civilian and military populations. European immigrants made do, moved around, mingled, and made love during these years of conquest, and the French schoolteacher appears to have been no exception. She had, however, higher ambitions that echoed those of the Saint-Simonian military officers, engineers, scientists, and intellectuals who were an active and visible presence in Algeria during the first four decades of colonial rule.[28]

From the outset, the French colonization of Algeria combined greedy material objectives with more ideological aims. Christophe Louis Léon Juchault de Lamoricière was one of the more visible officers whose Saint-Simonian inclinations influenced his attitude toward the French presence in Algeria. This future minister of war (appointed in 1848) wrote in 1832 that he saw the French conquest as an apostolate and as "a powerful means of importing ideas."[29] Saint-Simonians used this sort of missionary language to describe their vision of a new society, which they sought to enact in the "Orient." In the 1830s, a number of Enfantin's disciples made their way to Algeria, including two women from Lyon, referred to only as Mesdames Bocarnel and Gregoria, who in 1835 briefly ran a school in Algeria before leaving for Egypt, where a larger group of Saint-Simonian exiles were gathered.[30] Eugénie Allix was not alone among Saint-Simonian women in linking travel, mission, and schooling in her concern to improve women's lot.[31] But she expressed her ambitions only when Enfantin himself came to Algeria.

In 1840 Enfantin requested and was granted a place in the scientific commission that explored Algeria between 1840 and 1842.[32] For 500 francs per month he was placed in charge of "works concerning ethnography, history, morals and institutions."[33] During his travels in Algeria he spent time in Algiers with various disciples, including Auguste-Alexis Lepescheux, who was director of public instruction. And when he visited Bône, he met and befriended Judge Marion. In particular, he encouraged the latter to publish in 1842 a *Lettre sur la constitution de la propriété chez les Arabes* (Letter on the Constitution of Property among Arabs), which argued that private property existed in Algeria only in and around cities. This theory, of course, provided grist for colonizers, who as a result could dispose of tribal lands as they wished, according to Marion.

Marion was also a friend of Eugénie Allix, and as a prominent landowner and Saint-Simonian, he had the sort of cultural and economic clout that later would prove indispensable to helping her achieve her plan to educate Muslim girls. In the fall of 1840, following the death of her baby son, he also facilitated her encounter with the charismatic Enfantin.

Eugénie Allix never openly proclaimed her Saint-Simonian sympathies, probably because it took unusually daring women to declare their belief in the new social and sexual society Enfantin sought to implement. In France, Saint-Simonian women drifted away from Enfantin's call for free love in the mid-1830s. They started their own newspapers and mounted feminist campaigns to improve the legal and civil status of women.[34] In Algeria, traces of Saint-Simonian women are few and far between; they appear mostly in existing histories as lovers, rather than visionaries. One such woman was Hortense Jourdan, who declared her passion for Enfantin while he was living with the Jourdan family in Algiers in November 1841.[35] Eugénie may have been a lover as well, but she also harbored a radical dream that drew its inspiration from Saint-Simonian ideals and distinguished her from the other women migrants in Algiers. Her audaciousness was tempered with caution, however, so she never openly announced her ties to Enfantin when writing to the colonial administrators known to share the Saint-Simonian social vision. As a result, the only conclusive evidence of her commitment to Saint-Simonian beliefs is contained in four surviving letters addressed to the Père Enfantin between November 1840 and May 1846. These years also show the way she moved from romantic imaginings of how she might contribute to a better world to putting these imaginings into action.

This correspondence strongly suggests that her interest in Saint-Simonianism began in France and may have been the motivating force behind her decision to pull up roots and leave her family. Here is what she wrote from Bône on 6 November 1840 upon learning that Enfantin was in Algeria:

A liberated (*affranchie*) and independent woman who is perhaps the only woman to have understood your grand and noble mission, a weak and timid woman whom you have inspired with an energy and courage which has never flagged over the past nine years. This woman has just learned that you are here, you to whom she owes all of her worthy inspirations, you to whom she owes a daily life of which she is proud; for indeed she feels strong and powerful in her independence and so she could not resist the desire to testify her thankfulness for all the work you have undertaken, convinced as she is that if you had been better understood, this work would now be accomplished. But I have faith that better times will come, although in the distant future.

Please receive, Monsieur, the sincere feelings and the eternal gratitude of your devoted E. Allix[36]

This curious missive written mainly in the third person testifies to the loving enthusiasm Enfantin was capable of inspiring, an enthusiasm that bolstered Eugénie through difficult years when employment was scarce and her finances scanty. Was teaching the daily life "of which she is proud"? Certainly, other Saint-Simonian women channeled their convictions into educational projects designed to produce a more egalitarian world. This was the case in France, but also in Egypt around such women as Suzanne Voilquin and Clorinde Rogé. The two women wrote earnestly in 1834 about their desire "to attack through a variety of means the stultifying ignorance of women in this country, which transforms them into automates rather than living beings."[37] Schools were the solution, they believed, as did Eugénie. More strikingly, this letter emphasizes notions of liberation, independence, strength, and courage that all characterized Saint-Simonian women's writings. Particularly the use of the term *affranchie* signaled how Enfantin's ideas allowed Eugénie to move from being an enslaved to a liberated woman.

Whether Eugénie's relationship with Enfantin was purely spiritual is hard to determine. A second letter, written seven months later from Algiers in 1841, hints at a closer relationship, which would not be surprising given Enfantin's history of amorous adventures with his female followers. In this letter we learn she has moved from Bône to Algiers, that she is waiting for him to visit her, and that she is counting on him to find her some form of gainful employment in order to make her apartment less "miserable." She writes that "no one here knows my true position except for you," and she closes: "I will not tell you the feelings I have for you, they are too saintly, too sacred; putting them into words would only desecrate them. My heart keeps them for itself. Adieu, père adieu!"[38]

While it is not apparent what Eugénie means by her "true position"—her faith in Saint-Simonian ideals?—it seems clear that Enfantin's ethnographic insights about colonization in Algeria echoed some of her own. He argued for the importance of gaining the natives' trust by respecting their customs and institutions while gradually transforming them.[39] Above all, however, the encounter with Enfantin inspired Eugénie to move forward with her project to found the first school for Muslim girls. In a long letter to Enfantin dated 10 December 1845 she described the steps that had led her to act: "Since your departure from Algeria [in November 1843] a single idea has haunted and consumed me like a fever!" Her dream of founding a school for Muslim girls led her to study Arabic in order to communicate with the families of her future students. She then rented and equipped a house for the school, bought material to clothe the poor students, and hired a "Moorish" woman to teach religion and a "Negress" to care for them. But all of this cost money, which she did not have. However, Providence answered her prayers, she wrote, because her husband died in July 1845 ("inspiring no regret"), allowing her at last to return to France after "thirteen years of exile and all sorts of tribulations." She claimed the inheritance and her now-seventeen-year-old daughter Marie. This reunion with her daughter helped her to forget "her long years of suffering," and the money from the inheritance made up for all of her sacrifices. This letter also confirmed her friendship with Judge Marion: "Monsieur Marion whom I see occasionally, welcomed my ideas with enthusiasm because he understands generous natures."[40]

Enfantin's influence on Eugénie Allix appears most clearly in a final undated and rather enigmatic poem included with her letters in the Saint-Simonian archives.[41] Here she adopted the heavily romantic rhetoric of other Saint-Simonian women to celebrate her idol:

My father! Oh! For ages, my soul was rocked!
By a name so sweet
Another name now stills my tongue
With respect to you
I called your name when my soul was broken
And yearned for you
I called your name when my thoughts
Turned to you
In this name, you know, lay all my hope
All my faith
In this name, you know, was a faith
Sweet faith for me

When this name came

The name alone gave me force and courage

For the future

When this name pulled me from slavery

I was going to die

This hymn to the "name" illustrates the sort of passion Enfantin could inspire and his ability to infuse men and women alike with the energy and confidence to overcome their difficulties. Like other women, Eugénie associated her earlier status with that of slavery, and her letters and poem speak of her emancipation. The poem also suggests, however, that circumstances have changed, since her "tongue is now stilled" by the existence of another name—Louis Luce perhaps? Since the poem is undated, the only firm evidence it offers is the devotion she felt for Enfantin, at least for a time.

The somewhat more prosaic letters show that Enfantin played more than just an inspirational role in Eugénie's initial decade in Algeria. Throughout their relationship he provided both counsel and forms of material aid. This encouraged her in May 1846 to turn once more to him, recounting her financial difficulties as well as the death of her mother: "Are you in a position, Monsieur, to associate yourself with the dream that I pursue by helping me in my extremity?" she queried.[42] It is unknown whether Enfantin responded favorably to this request, but this archival cache of letters clearly reveals a side of Eugénie that explains in part the passion she directed toward schooling Muslim girls.

FAMILY MATTERS

By 1845 Eugénie Allix had acquired the confidence, the funds, and the social network that allowed her to pursue her vision of establishing the first school for Muslim girls in Algeria. For the next sixteen years she would remain very much in the public eye. Behind this public façade, however, she was also a daughter, a wife, a mother, an adulteress, and then a widow. What importance did she attach to these tags, which normally weighed heavily on women in French society? Did family matter to her?

Her flight from France in 1832 was a flight from both husband and family. By December 1845, however, her situation had changed, as she indicated in her letter to Enfantin. Her husband's death in July of that year gave her "at last the liberty to return to France. . . . What happiness for me to unite again with my family and a charming young girl, whose education leaves nothing to be desired.

I have brought her with me to Africa because I still had to achieve my great work here and four to five thousand francs inheritance allowed me at last to undertake the task."[43] As this letter hints, family did indeed matter on a variety of levels.

In 1845 when Eugénie returned to France to settle her husband's estate, she expressed no regret at his premature death. On the contrary, it was clearly a relief, allowing her to reclaim her daughter and see her mother. Her father, however, had died in 1836, leaving a pittance for the family. As we have seen, during Eugénie's adolescent years in Montrichard, Sylvain Berlau had moved from land survey-ing into teaching, running a small primary school without any specific teaching credentials. Eugénie never said anything about her father's later years, once she had married and then left for Algeria, perhaps because these years clearly rep-resented a period of social decline. When he died at the age of seventy, he was still working as a schoolteacher, but no longer in his hometown.

In November 1834 Sylvain Berlau had been appointed the public school-teacher in the village of Pouillé, 10 kilometers to the southeast of Montrichard along the river Cher.[44] The school he ran in this rural village of 560 inhabitants took in both boys and girls because Pouillé had no school for girls in the 1830s. The inspector reported that Berlau had ten paying boy students and six girls in the winter, alongside sixty students whose parents were too poor to pay any fees. As a result, his salary was meager: the base salary of 200 francs accorded by the Guizot Law of 1833 reached 300 francs total in the year, thanks to the paying students. The inspector also listed the books he used in class, *La morale en action* (Morality in Action), reading and arithmetic tables, and a catechism. Overall, the school was poorly noted—"Mediocre direction, little capacity, the amount of zeal that his [Berlau's] age allows"; however, the inspector wrote that Berlau "is highly respected."[45]

During these years when Eugénie was struggling as a laundress and giv-ing birth to an illegitimate daughter in Algiers, her father was struggling as a schoolteacher in a village where school absenteeism was rife. While his learning brought him a degree of social esteem in this agricultural community, it had not brought him any financial security, as the decision to apply in his late sixties for a position as public schoolteacher indicates. In order to get this position, he passed the most elementary teaching exam (the *brevet élementaire de capacité*) in January 1834 and started teaching in February 1835.[46] He died at the end of the summer on 31 August 1836; the two men who witnessed his death were peasants unable to sign the civil register.

Berlau's testament confirms the precarious economic status of rural French schoolteachers at this time. Five descendants were listed in 1837 when his material possessions were dealt with: his eldest son, Sylvain, and four daughters, Marie, Agnès Rose ("Louise"), Eugénie, and Olimpe, all indicated as either married or widowed. The value of his property was estimated at 190 francs, a sum that would not cushion either his widow's or his children's lives.[47] It is impossible to know whether or when Eugénie learned of her father's death; she certainly did not return for the funeral.

Nine years later, however, she did return to France to deal with her husband's death. She had several reasons to make the trip in that summer of 1845. In June she had made her initial request to open a school, and the director of the interior, after consultation, had authorized the existence of such a school on 10 July, "at her risk and peril."[48] Four days later she sent a letter to the queen of France requesting her aid in her plan to "improve the morals and assure the happy future" of the indigenous population.[49] Another four days later, on 18 July 1845, her husband died in Compiègne, leaving their daughter, Marie, on her own. Shortly after receiving this news, Eugénie left for France to recover the inheritance that would allow her to make her school a reality, reuniting in the process with Marie.

Alexandre Allix, only forty-three years old, knew he was dying because he drew up a will six days before his death, indicating that he was "of good mind but sick in the body." His legitimate daughter, Eugénie Véronique Alexandrine, known as Marie, was designated his residuary legatee, and she inherited 5,286.35 francs while his wife received the same sum, which constituted her half as usufructuary.[50] The will reveals no sign of the bad blood that undoubtedly existed between the couple and had led Eugénie to flee to Algeria. Rather, he bequeathed a tidy sum of money that not only left his widow considerably better off, but also helped provide for his daughter's future. Clearly, his material situation had improved since his life with Eugénie in Bléré.

In 1845 Alexandre Allix was no longer a schoolteacher; instead, he had been working in various administrative positions for a decade. By 1841 he had moved from Vendôme to Compiègne, where the population survey indicated that he was a clerk in the mortgage office living with his daughter, aged fourteen.[51] By the time of his death he had reached the position of head clerk and had accumulated a modest fortune. The will testifies as well to his efforts to offer his daughter the trappings of a middle-class culture, since among the debts he left at his death was the sum of 39 francs to Madame Rossignol, a boarding school mistress in Compiègne. In these years of expanding educational offerings for girls, lay schoolmistresses opened boarding schools throughout the French urban landscape, catering to the educational aspirations of an increasingly visible middle class.[52] Allix's decision to place his daughter in such a school signifies his desire that she should receive, in the company of her peers, a modicum of general culture. There was a certain irony in Eugénie's pride concerning her "charming" daughter, "whose education left nothing to be desired," as she had written to Enfantin, since this education was none of her own doing.[53] Having abandoned her daughter in childhood, Eugénie could only thank her own parents and her husband for this education. She could also thank her husband for accumulating enough money before his premature death to enable her to develop her school for Muslim girls in Algiers.

The widow Allix returned to Algiers with her daughter in the fall of 1845, precisely at the moment when the colonial administration was debating the future of her school. Marie's reunion with her mother brought a great deal that would have been strange for a provincial boarding school student: the move to Algiers; the discovery of a forceful and determined mother; and life in a Moorish-style home with a surrogate father, Louis Luce, the soldier-musician her mother was living with. The strangeness of her new circumstances may have encouraged her rapid courtship with and then marriage to a suitor she scarcely knew in early 1846.

On 17 January 1846 Marie Allix wedded Félix Belly, a man some eleven years her senior. The witnesses at their wedding testify to the widow Allix's social positioning in Algiers fourteen years after her migration. A property owner, Brunemaire, and Judge Marion served as witnesses for the groom; and a Doctor Dru and another property owner, Fabas, witnessed for the bride. These men of substance were Eugénie Allix's and Louis Luce's friends, not Belly's. Marion and Dru were part of the Saint-Simonian power nexus within Algiers at the time; Dru was also a relative of Louis Luce.[54] Their presence highlights the couple's rise in status as Eugénie mobilized her networks in support of the school she had opened three months earlier. Marie's marriage was undoubtedly convenient since it meant Eugénie could focus her attention on her own projects. Whether the marriage was initially a love match remains a mystery. We do know, however, that it was not a success. In giving her consent to the marriage of her underage daughter to Félix Belly, Eugénie once more abdicated her maternal responsibilities.

The son of a Napoleonic general, Félix Belly was a political journalist and somewhat of a hothead, as the future would show. A fervent supporter of Louis Napoleon, who was elected president of the newly born Second Republic in 1848, he set off for Nicaragua in 1857 and devoted several years of his life to the project of the Panama Canal. In October 1870 he published a text advocating the creation of an armed battalion of Amazons and later fought on the side of the Communards.[55] From the outset, this energy and commitment to political projects left him little time to care for his wife. He never spent much time in Algeria although he was there enough during his first year of married life to impregnate Marie. She gave birth to a daughter eleven months after their marriage on 21 February 1847. The birth certificate indicates that Félix was absent at the birth of Marie Augustine Eugénie Sabine Belly, known through her life as Henriette, and that his wife was still living at home in her mother's school on the rue du Diable in the Casbah of Algiers.

Writing more than a century later, Félix's granddaughter, Jeanne Crouzet-Benaben, would describe him as "a remarkably intelligent man, but with a violent and bizarre character, inclined toward misanthropy and pessimism, with whims and terrible fits of passion."[56] While she had kept in her familial archives the book he had written about the Panama Canal, she clearly felt his familial influence had been largely negative: "This driller of isthmuses, this captain of Amazons, this reformer of constitutions was, in private, a quirky and insufferable husband. . . . I believe I heard that one day [his wife] fled and took up a new life in another family. But those around me never spoke about this and the details remain obscure for me; all I know is that she died relatively young, worn out from sorrow."[57] In 1847, however, Marie Belly was still a young mother, adjusting to life in Algiers with her forty-three-year-old mother and the musician Louis Luce. In fewer than two years she had lost all that was familiar to her, as her father's death was followed several months later by the death of her maternal grandmother, who had raised her. In the place of these family members, she now had her mother, a stepfather, an absent husband, a baby daughter, and the novelty of life in Algiers. Unlike her mother, she had not chosen this new life, and she never thrived in this environment.

Eugénie, on the other hand, was coming into her own during these critical months between the fall of 1845 and the summer of 1846, when the authorities finally decided to support her imperious requests for public funding. Her husband's death was indeed providential, offering her both the financial means to launch her new school and a timely release from her marital ties. Although she emphasized the importance of the money in her letter to Enfantin, the freedom from marriage was almost as important for her plans because as a school director she could ill afford to continue living with a man to whom she was not married.

THE MAN IN THE SHADOWS

Information about Napoléon Louis Luce, Eugénie's second husband, is far more difficult to uncover than for his articulate and strong-willed companion. The circumstances surrounding their encounter and romance have left no trace in the archival record. Born 5 March 1806 in Versailles, Luce came from a more humble background than his future spouse: his mother is listed on the birth certificate as Hyacinthe Elisabeth Luce; no father is mentioned. Both of the witnesses were young military men, strongly suggesting, as does his first given name, that the father came from the military as well. In 1828 he was incorporated into the army since, like many lower-class men, he did not have the means to pay for a replacement.[58] He spent the next nineteen years in the army, gradually advancing to the rank of *sergent major* bandmaster within the 26th infantry regiment, which was based in Algeria. His military records indicate that he was 1.70 meters tall with an oval face, gray eyes, blond eyebrows, a well-formed nose, and an average mouth. While these records do not allow us to know whether he was physically attractive, they do suggest that his skills were appreciated by his superiors since he was decorated as *chevalier* of the Legion of Honor seven months before leaving the army in November 1847.

His path probably crossed Eugénie's in Bône in the late 1830s when his regiment arrived in North Africa. By the spring of 1839 the army musician and the schoolteacher were certainly lovers, as their son was born in February 1840. In the fall of 1845 they were living together in Algiers, learning to behave as parents to the young Marie, while Eugénie continued to write letters and visit Muslim families in order to attract support and students for her school. Louis remained in the army for two more years, but his encounter with Eugénie decisively changed his life, wedding him to a life in North Africa, which he might not otherwise have had. Alexandre Allix's "providential" death in July 1845 opened possibilities for the couple to envision a more respectable lifestyle and future together.

On 2 May 1846 the army authorized Louis Luce to marry the widow Allix, who is listed as living in Paris at the time. In February 1846, shortly after Marie's wedding to Félix Belly the month before, Eugénie had left for France in order to press her case for her school more personally (see Chapter 3). This time in France was momentous in familial terms as well. Her mother died on 14 April 1846 in the small village of Monthou-sur-Cher at the age of eighty. We will never know whether Eugénie arrived in time to offer any comfort or help after almost fifteen years of absence. We do know that she quickly traded mourning garb for a wedding dress, since a month later she traveled to Paris to marry Luce. Her widowhood had lasted ten brief months.

At the time of his marriage to Eugénie on 19 May 1846, Louis Luce was living at the Popincourt military barracks.[59] The witnesses at their wedding testify to a certain degree of social mobility characteristic of careers within the army; on the marriage certificate the four men present are described professionally as an employee, a doctor, a merchant (one of Eugénie's cousins), and a musician-artist. It seems clear that Eugénie Allix was the more ambitious of the two, and Louis followed her back to Algiers without question. He appears to have easily accepted his secondary role both within the family and within colonial politics. In her memoir Jeanne Crouzet-Benaben describes him as "an exquisite being, all devotion and goodness, a true artist . . . he and Maman Luce formed the perfect couple, their union was cloudless, a circumstance I hasten to emphasize given the contrast with the future generations"—and, she might have added, in contrast as well to Eugénie's first marriage.[60]

Marital happiness tends to leave fewer traces than marital discord. As a result, we know little more about this newlywed middle-aged couple in the spring of 1846. Nor do we know much more about the musician Luce whose life marked the pages of history less than that of his wife. He left the army shortly after his marriage and devoted himself to teaching music. He appears periodically in the colonial archives as the music teacher in Auguste Depeille's Arab-French school in Algiers.[61] When not teaching in classrooms, he kept busy in the city's first musical societies, which he helped to create.[62] He was also active in efforts to make military music more popular, participating in the *Journal de la Renaissance des Musiques Militaires*.[63] Although he received the Legion of Honor, his dossier has vanished from the archives, and his public record is difficult to assemble. Historian Annie Rey-Goldzeiguer describes him as a freemason, but there is no trace of his name in the Algerian lodges.[64] The difference in the couple's careers explains in part the contrast in the surviving archives. As a teacher, Eugénie plied her pen with enthusiasm, exposing her projects and her ambitions. Louis Luce played musical instruments and wrote little.

During his lifetime he was clearly a central figure in the musical events that played such an important role in the social life of Algiers. His music could be heard in processions, in local concerts, at the opera, and at mass. In 1856 he published a little book about musical theory that indicated he was the director of the local music school in Algiers.[65] In 1860, when Napoleon III first visited the city, the educational circles gathered to honor him, and the musicians who played for the occasion performed a piece written by Luce. In 1871 high school students gave a concert in the Salle des Beaux Arts under his direction.[66] As composer, music teacher, and musician (he played both the viola and the double bass), he shared with Eugénie an appreciation for Arab cultural forms and participated in his way to the French civilizing mission. Music was an important aspect of this vision, and musical societies were seen as promoting the desired fusion of the races.[67] In this context Luce acquired modest local fame adapting Arab music for European ears. Commentators, including the *Journal des Demoiselles* in 1860, frequently praised his creation "Dani-Dan," "a charming Arab quadrille, composed of five of the most popular tunes among Arabs today."[68] At Luce's death in 1872 the newspaper *L'Akhbar* noted his passing without writing an obituary, and *L'Algérie Française* indicated that he left vacant a chair in music teaching at the *collège* in Algiers.[69]

This "exquisite being," as Jeanne Crouzet-Benaben wrote, remained, however, very much in the shadows of his wife's ample frame, and the family left no pictures of him. Once married, they did not have another child together although Eugénie, at age forty-four, was probably still fertile. But at this point, she had other plans, and within months, she also had an infant granddaughter at home with her.

By the summer of 1846, Eugénie's familial situation had changed considerably, allowing her to envision the future with greater equanimity. With both parents and her first husband dead, she now had sufficient funds to become the mistress of her fate. Her marriage to Luce, while rendering her once more dependent on a husband's will, gave her the social position she needed for the school she had already established. If Luce offered respectability, love, and harmonious companionship, her daughter's presence was a visceral connection to her French past and youth, a past she never turned her back on despite her move to Algeria. Did she feel guilt about having abandoned her young daughter at age five? Perhaps. Raising her granddaughter was an opportunity for her to atone for her flight of 1832; family did indeed matter. In Eugénie's ascent from impoverished schoolteacher and laundress to being the head of Algiers's only school for Muslim girls, she emphasized publicly her determination, her vision, and her skills. She appears in the colonial archives as very much an independent woman. In reality, the *men* in the shadows, both Alexandre and Louis, made a difference. The first motivated her move to Algeria, and the second may have encouraged her to stay. Both shaped her life in ways the biographer can only imagine.

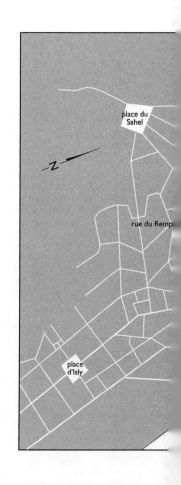

PART II

Women in the Civilizing Mission

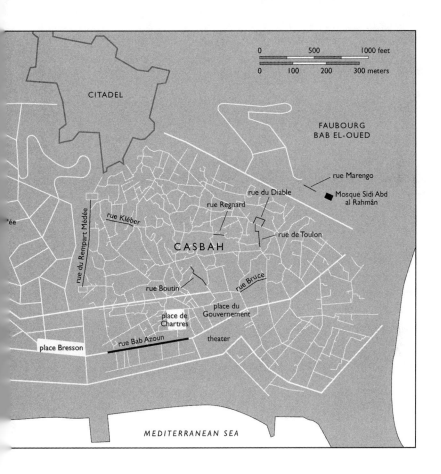

Previous page: The Casbah and the Marine Quarter in Algiers. The heavy lines indicate the streets where Madame Luce lived between 1835 and 1875: rue Bab Azoun, rue Boutin, rue du Diable, rue Regnard, and rue de Toulon. Mlle. Chevalier's school was located at rue Kléber; Henriette Benaben's workshop, at rue Bruce from the mid-1880s until 1895. Benaben then moved to rue du Rempert Médée and opened a second establishment on rue Marengo.

3 A MISSION TO CIVILIZE (1845–1850)

Woman is the most powerful of all influences in Africa as in Europe, but even more
so in Africa. If you convert to our civilization 100 young native girls in all classes
of society and in all the races of the Regency, these girls will become, in the nature
of things, the privileged wives of the most important men of their class; they will
become our guarantee of the country's submission to our authority, as well as the
unimpeachable pledge of its future assimilation.

Letter from Madame Allix to members of the Administrative Council of Algiers,

31 January 1846

Written some six months after Eugénie Allix first opened her school for Muslim
girls, this letter to the Administrative Council of Algiers gives a good sense of
the rhetoric she used to persuade colonial authorities that they should support
her initiative. Her arguments echoed those of other Saint-Simonians who believed in the transformative power of French civilization to integrate the colonized populations of Algeria into a greater France. The difference, however,
was her insistence on *girls'* education as the key to effecting a "fusion of the
races." Her goal, she claimed in this same letter, was "to change native morals,
prejudices and habits, as quickly and as surely as possible, by introducing the
greatest possible number of young Muslim girls to the benefits of a European
education." These young girls would leave school grateful to the French state,
which had allowed them access to this education, and one day they would become "the mothers of a new generation, veritable intermediaries in the fusion
of the two races."[1]

Eugénie Allix was undoubtedly the loudest female voice in the mid-1840s
asserting women's role in the civilizing mission. Education held an important
place in the French colonial discourse, and this enterprising schoolteacher in-
tegrated her vision into a broader policy in order to win support. The story of
her school for Muslim girls highlights, however, the significance of colonial
sexual politics for women seeking a public role. Eugénie's aggressive demands

for money, as well as the discovery in the summer of 1846 that she was living out of wedlock with Louis Luce, durably affected her reputation within the colony. Although she managed to mobilize support on her own behalf, she clearly left a lingering impression that she was not quite as disinterested and as morally pure as she pretended to be. It is all the more remarkable that she did win public support and that her school became a model for the Arab-French schools for boys and girls created in 1850.

THE FRENCH "APOSTOLATE" IN ALGERIA

Although the colonization of Algeria involved brutal warfare, many of the military officers saw the French conquest as an "apostolate" and believed this could be achieved only through a form of moral conquest. As the Arabist Charles Richard wrote in 1846, "When one seeks to conquer a country, in the true sense of the word, one must accomplish two forms of conquest: that of the terrain, which is the material conquest, and that of the population, which is the moral conquest."[2] For Richard and others, the costly commitment to the process of colonization could be justified only through the spread of cultural civilization that would allow institutions and structures in Algeria to become more like those in France. Although historians continue to debate whether the ideal of assimilation or association guided colonial policy in Algeria, all recognize the weight of the French "civilizing mission"—in discourse at least.[3] The colonization of Algeria involved, then, not just the pacification of the native population, but also efforts to introduce that population to French civilization, notably through schools.

The Saint-Simonian officers and administrators who saw Algeria as a testing ground for their experiments in social engineering encouraged the creation of a range of institutions intended to rally the indigenous populations to the French cause. They opened schools, libraries, and hospitals and promoted efforts that would contribute to the development of industry and agriculture. Although no single doctrine existed on the subject of Arab schooling, a number of influential actors during the early years of colonization argued for using the French language as an instrument in the process of colonization. Auguste-Alexis Lepescheux, who later became the director of public instruction, repeatedly insisted on the importance of spreading French among the local populations during the early years of conquest: "The Arabs, Moors and Jews will only become civilized by the use of the French language; they will not be useful to us, and will not be sincerely gained to our cause until our idiom has become familiar to them."[4] The Saint-Simonian newspaper *L'Algérie. Courrier d'Afrique, d'Orient et de la Méditerranée* also emphasized the importance of reciprocal training in language so the populations in contact would get to know each other.[5]

This particular intellectual context helps to explain the importance attached to schooling, since schools were seen as an indispensable vector for the promotion of the French language and civilization. As early as June 1833 a school of mutual education that taught French and Arabic was opened for both European and indigenous students. Although the school attracted two hundred students, Arab students were not among those present. Rather, from the outset, French initiatives proved more attractive to indigenous Jewish, not Arab, families.[6] The choice of mutual education nonetheless says something about the understanding the French had of the local terrain. In France liberals supported the development of mutual education, notably through the Society for the Improvement of Elementary Education. Often known as the Lancasterian system, the mutual school method had English origins and was tailored to teaching large numbers of poor students. Schoolteachers divided their classrooms into small groups and appointed older student monitors to teach these groups. Blackboards and slates alleviated the need for schoolbooks and papers. The system had the advantage of being cheap, because school monitors cost far less than regular teachers and school supplies were limited. The method was also seen as pedagogically innovative compared with the "individual method" used in most schools. The latter involved teaching students one-on-one, so at any moment most students were unsupervised and unoccupied.

Although mutual education had a foreign accent in France because of its English origins, in Algeria it corresponded to existing traditions in schooling. In 1830 A. Perrot noted:

There are a number of public schools [in Algiers] where children from the ages of five or six learn to read or write. The method used in this country seems to be at the origins of mutual teaching; every student has a slate upon which he writes with chalk. A verse from the Quran is copied out by one, and then copied by the others, who both give and receive successively the different lessons, which deal not only with explaining the texts but also forming the characters. The lessons are then repeated out loud in front of the teacher who crouches in a corner with a long rod in his hand to maintain order and discipline.[7]

According to Perrot, such schools existed for both boys and girls, the latter run by women teachers, thus debunking a widely shared notion that girls' education in Algeria was nonexistent before the arrival of the French.

The concern to educate indigenous students in French persisted throughout the early years of French colonization, encountering relatively limited success. In September 1834 a *collège franco-arabe* was opened catering to Arab students. Only a handful of students attended until 1842 when Auguste Depeille took over and gradually more students came, thanks to a policy of paying families to send their students to school.[8] In 1839 the government made the decision to create a *collège* for the sons of elite Muslim families in Paris. Inspired by a similar institution in Egypt, the Collège Arabe de Paris was not as successful in attracting the sons of native elites. Between 1839 and 1847, 25,000 francs were spent to educate a total of eleven students, clearly an expensive and relatively unsuccessful effort to inculcate an understanding of French "grandeur and power."[9] All of these creations testify to a cultural climate in these early years that attributed importance to schooling in the civilizing mission.

But these schools were aimed at boys, the presumed future allies of the occupying forces. The authorities made no efforts on behalf of indigenous girls, leaving initiatives up to private individuals. Most of the women schoolteachers, however, directed their attention to other Europeans. In 1838 the first statistics noted the presence in Algiers of five elementary schools for girls (compared with only three for boys). Nuns dominated the market, educating 162 students; three private schools welcomed 113 girls; and Héloïse Hartoch's school for Jewish girls included another 68.[10] The appointment that same year of Bishop Dupuch, who actively encouraged the arrival of teaching sisters, did little to change this situation, as they directed their attention to the migrant Catholic poor. The provincial superior of the Soeurs de la Doctrine Chrétienne argued that before turning to Arabs, "it is important to focus on regenerating as much as possible the European, and especially French, populations who come here seeking to make a fortune."[11] The indigenous populations were not the only ones in need of "civilization."

French administrators expressed concern as early as 1842 that so little was being done for Arab girls. In a long report about Arab language teaching for the French and French language teaching for the indigenous population, Inspector General Nicolas Louis Artaud devoted several paragraphs to the "education of Moorish girls."[12] He noted that in the past, several schools for girls existed but that at present only one still operated, under the direction of a woman named

Souna, the wife of Bou Serwâl: "She has six or seven students to whom she teaches reading, writing and some sewing. She writes herself very poorly and has no book knowledge, which remains as a result inaccessible to women." He went on to state that people who knew Algeria well believed that it would be possible to create a girls' school in Algiers and that it might even thrive. His report continued:

For such a school, we would need a woman who spoke a bit of Arabic who could teach [the students] to read, write, calculate, sew, embroider, etc.; parents or their slaves would accompany the girl students in the morning and bring them back in the evening. They would bring their own food or a Negress would cook at the school. M. Bresnier [one of the prominent French Arabists in Algeria], among others, gave me the names of four young girls whose parents would send their daughters in a flash to a French school and he has no doubt that other families would follow their example.

Although the government did not follow up this suggestion, Artaud's report shows that the idea of offering a "French" education to indigenous girls was in the air in the 1840s. The inspector concluded his report by stating that for mutual language training to progress between the two populations, the government would have to demonstrate a strong will and perseverance. Four years later, on a tour of Algeria, Minister of Public Instruction Narcisse Achille, comte de Salvandy, similarly supported the creation of schools and language teaching, noting that "the most serious obstacle to the pacification of native people generally stems from differences in language."[13]

The concern to encourage France's civilizing influence became more systematic in these same years as institutional structures developed and the European presence grew. The European population doubled between 1842 and 1846, increasing from 20,982 to 42,635. In response to this demographic pressure, the French set up schools, hospitals, and courtrooms to address the needs of migrant Europeans, as well as the extremely diverse local population. For all of Algeria, the Bureaux Arabes, or military administrative units, were formalized in 1844 to serve as links between the French central government and indigenous leaders. The administrators saw themselves as "interpreter[s] of the conquering nation's thought and institutions," as well as liaisons between the European and native races. In Algiers, the Central Directorate of Arab Affairs oversaw and coordinated the activities of these institutions in relation to the Ministry of War.[14] Saint-Simonians were prominent within this military administration, bringing to their task a conviction that the benefits of technology and science as well as the ratio-nal management of human problems would inaugurate a new and better world.

EUGÉNIE ALLIX'S MISSION:
THE FUSION OF THE RACES

Eugénie Allix shared with the Saint-Simonians the belief that education was the key to pacifying and improving relations with the populations now under French rule. Like European missionaries, her rhetoric was imbued with notions of cultural superiority that mark her as a woman of her times. But her cultural arrogance in pursuit of what she described as her "great work" was leavened with a genuine concern for indigenous women that led her to question the govern-ment's management of colonization—though not without a sense of humor.

In the same letter to colonial administrators that argued for women's role in Algeria's future assimilation, she questioned the cost-effectiveness of French colonial policy in the fight that continued against Arab warlords. Specifically, she noted that the French state was willing to pay annually for the upkeep of some four thousand to five thousand Arab prisoners, "whose hatred [of France] develops during their captivity," while it refused to pay the far cheaper cost of schooling one hundred, two hundred, or even five hundred young girls—a cost, she noted, that would allow them over the course of ten years to reduce the numbers of the French Army by nineteen twentieths, or 95 percent. Her letter is filled with figures detailing the sums the government was prepared to spend on armies or even boys' education when in reality, she argued, girls' education would be a far more efficient means of ensuring the moral conquest of an entire people. She concludes: "Now, Messieurs, I ask you, what Government willing to spend annually 100,000 francs for a Collège Arabe which has never had more than 10 students, would refuse to spend 33,000 francs for a model institution, filled with at least 100 young indigenous girls? . . . What Chamber would refuse such a modest sum to accomplish the conquest of an entire people by pacific and conciliatory means?"[15] By framing her project in this fashion, Eugénie showed she understood the dual priorities of the colonial government, which sought to pacify through both might and persuasion, and she made a strong argument for inserting women into the equation.

Her arguments, honed over the winter in 1846, insisted on the moral transfor-mation she sought to effect. Like other religious or lay teachers, she insisted that her school transmitted a variety of lessons that transformed first students and then their families through the introduction of good eating habits and sewing skills and the immeasurable benefits of a "French" education. But this emphasis on transmitting the moral dispositions of domestic motherhood was infused with a highly political message. As mothers of a new generation, her students were expected to transmit a sense of gratitude to the French and act as "intermediaries in the fusion of the two races." Interestingly, her arguments frequently emphasized the effects of this education on the individual girls themselves, "whose joyous faces full of life and animation, whose good health is more and more apparent as the days go by, and whose unmitigated contentment renders them almost unrecognizable to their parents."[16] Not only would the French authorities appreciate her efforts in reducing misery and prostitution, she suggested, they also would reap the benefits of the well-being her school produced in her students. Although it took more than a year of such missives to win her case, Eugénie ultimately succeeded in persuading the authorities to finance her school. Her path to success reveals not only how French women played a role in the cultural politics of these early years, but also how gender shaped these politics.

Eugénie Allix's efforts to establish and finance her school have left ample traces in the colonial archives. Not only did she write frequently and persuasively, but she also recopied earlier missives and reports so that the authorities were fully informed of her efforts and investments. Chronologically, her letters begin on 14 July 1845 with a letter to the queen of France requesting financial support for her school. Eighteen months later, in January 1847, she was finally paid 4,000 francs and her institution became officially subsidized. In between these dates, she sent lengthy letters and reports to officials and men of influence, in both Algiers and France, returning to France between February and May 1846 to further her cause.

Her ultimate success can be attributed to a number of factors. To begin with, the Saint-Simonian sensibilities of some of her interlocutors, particularly Director of Public Instruction Lepescheux and General Lamoricière, undoubtedly helped her cause. Although they did not themselves write or speak about native women, they were sensitive to an argument that providing Muslim girls with some education and professional skills in sewing would help prevent them from falling into prostitution. Eugénie was also extremely adroit in gaining the support of individuals or institutions with clout, such as the Catholic Church or the queen of France. But above all, she was able to persuade the comte Eugène Guyot, the person in charge of the civilian aspects of colonization, both that her school was a useful addition to the French colonizing efforts and that she was the only person capable of making it a success.

The voluminous dossier concerning her efforts to gain official support testify to her perseverance and to her skill in mobilizing people who could speak in her favor. That her project took eighteen months to come to fruition is also testimony to its unusual character and the suspicions it generated. Undoubtedly, her familiarity with Algiers, her knowledge of Arabic, which few European women spoke, and her social network of both local French and Muslim elites gave her requests for money some authority. In her initial plea to the queen of France she presented her project as one that would allow the "improvement of morality and the happy future of a people which now must become one with that of France."[17]

The comte Guyot supported her project with more sociological arguments, defending the need to educate young girls:

The life of Moorish women has been until now a life of idleness. The ideas and customs among Moors are opposed to the idea that their wives and daughters exercise any honest work, aside from the ordinary details of the household. Rendered incapable of any serious occupation by their education and not having been raised in the principles of morality or modesty, which serve in Europe as the first base of girls' education, they are led early into debauchery. As a result, we are beginning to see that they constitute the main body of prostitutes in Algiers; anything that is done to change this morality and these ideas, and to moralize the population is a useful and meritorious enterprise that deserves the encouragement and support of the Government.[18]

These arguments were convincing to Thomas-Robert Bugeaud, the governor general of Algeria, but his approach was to wait and see how the school managed before committing funds.

These hesitations stimulated Eugénie Allix to new rhetorical heights as she penned missives throughout the first six months of 1846 to the Administrative Council of Algiers, the governor general of Algeria, the minister of war, and her firmest supporter, the comte Guyot. Running at times to more than twenty pages, these letters and reports insistently emphasized the money she had spent herself to set up the school, her own special qualifications to run the school, and the higher ideal she was serving: "Having devoted my life to teaching and being welcomed into the intimacy of many Moorish families, I was better placed than any other European woman to attempt this perilous project. Moreover, I was intimately convinced, given the nature of our interminable warfare, that civilization would achieve nothing unless it penetrated the interior of the family; I felt I had the courage to render this service to my country at the cost of some personal sacrifice."[19] She reiterated frequently her belief in France's civilizing mission and that her goal coincided with that of the French as her school would lead indigenous women to support the French conquest thanks to their recognition of "the benefits of a European education."[20] In March 1846 she printed an "Explanatory Note" that detailed the nature of these benefits:

To teach them the tasks which are the exclusive prerogative of womanhood: needlework, household chores, grooming. To inspire them with love for what is beautiful and good, the habits of cleanliness, moral well-being, and the instinct of refinement [typical] of their sex. Later, to establish with these regenerated young women genuine workshops for sewing, embroidery, drapery and lingerie; to make them appreciate the value of labor by placing in their hands the returns of their day's work. In this fashion to keep the majority of them out of the prostitution which poverty infallibly would lead them toward; and to return them to their grateful families one day as accomplished women, hard working, orderly, familiar with all that constitutes physical and moral well-being, precious for all these reasons in the eyes of the men of their nation, and thus the natural intermediaries for the civilization that has conquered them, and the mothers of a new generation that will belong to us by heart and by mind.[21]

Although her rhetoric here focused on the shaping of hard-working domesticated womanhood, she relentlessly pursued this argument by emphasizing how such women constituted a vital link in the French civilizing mission.

In defense of her project Eugénie took care to note the eclectic nature of the support she had: men within the colonial administration, the bishop of Algiers, not to mention Muslim elites who entrusted her with their daughters. This trust is what encouraged her in January 1846 to move to a larger building and hire a woman to teach Arabic who had, she argued, the reputation of being the most educated woman in Algiers. This woman had been a teacher in the house of Hussein Dey, the last dey of Algiers, whose insult of the French consul had supposedly set in motion the French invasion in 1830. Thanks to Eugénie's ceaseless energy for the cause, and particularly the individual visits she made to Arab homes, "accompanying each of her visits with a gift, a small favor, a generous act of courtesy" as well as the assurance of her "respect for the religion of the country," students began to appear and her school to take shape. All this had a financial cost, and by the end of 1845 she noted she had spent 2,000 francs, exhausted her resources, and had only thirteen pupils to show for her efforts.[22]

Despite the support of Guyot and Lepescheux, Eugénie's requests for money were sufficiently high that the government hesitated. In January 1846 she estimated she needed a total of 37,500 francs for the year, a sum that included the salaries of five teachers and two servants, as well as the cost of twenty-six boarders and seventy-five day students. Lepescheux responded that an annual sum of 8,600 francs should suffice. His budget covered the salaries of only two teachers, one servant, and one hundred day students. The battle of sums undoubtedly contributed to a certain amount of suspicion, as marginal annotation in her reports indicate. In the twenty-page document she sent on 28 February, one of France's leading Arabists, Alexandre Bellemare, an official in the office of political affairs, noted, "the woman who has written this letter is a *maîtresse femme* [a masterful woman] if indeed she is the author. Unfortunately she appears more motivated by her own concerns than that of her project."[23] Léon Blondel, the director of finances, similarly noted that a desire for financial solvency seemed to predominate over charitable instincts in Eugénie's reports.[24]

Throughout the early months of 1846, she hammered home her argument that her school represented an unprecedented way to include Arab women in the French civilizing mission. But the local administration's hesitations led her to close the school and return to France, apparently the better to barrage the minister of war with her missives. She claims on this occasion to have pawned plate, jewels, and a gold thimble to pay for her transport in mid-February 1846.[25] Her "Explanatory Note" of March 1846 described the "serious question" she was seeking to address: "It is civilization itself, inoculated in Algeria through pacific means; it is the fusion of the races, a problem heretofore considered insoluble, which is resolved affirmatively through a new institution; it is, in addition, such an unexpected success and it so decisively counters indigenous prejudices, that once the first step is taken one can reasonably and without presumption hope for everything in the future."[26]

Eugénie Allix did not limit her requests for money to the government but knocked on a variety of doors while in France between February and early June 1846. In May the *Journal d'Éducation Populaire* reported that "Madame *veuve* [widow] Allix, founder of an institution for poor Muslim girls in Algiers, requests that the Society [for elementary education] encourage her efforts through a grant for a school purchase for which she has sent the bill." Antoine François

Demoyencourt, who was vice president of the society and the director of the Collège Arabe in Paris, spoke favorably about Madame Allix, and accordingly her request was granted.[27] During the same month, she also wrote to Enfantin explaining her financial difficulties: "Of the 8000 francs at least that I have spent on my institution, I have only received 3000 francs in support. I sent 3000 francs via Mr. Marion to pay the most urgent bills in Algiers. The cost of my trip and stay in Paris has been paid, but when I return to Africa I will have no money left and I will be assailed by my creditors. I need funds to function a month without the support of the administration." She asked Enfantin whether he was in a position to associate himself with her work and to help her out in her hour of need.[28]

She also turned to the church and the curate of Algiers, the Abbé Pelleteau, who gave her some financial aid and continued to patronize the school by sending cloth for the students to sew. The comte Guyot also helped out privately from his own purse as well as from public sources. Eugénie told her British friends that one day he gave her a small bag of money, left by King Louis Philippe's son, the duc d'Aumale, when governor general of Algeria. Guyot explained that the money was initially destined for a journal that had by this time "ceased to exist." As a result, she could use whatever sum it contained; Madame Luce opened the bag and found 250 francs, "and this money," she said, "appeared to me to come from Providence."[29] In late 1846 Queen Marie Amélie of France offered to pay for the schooling of several pupils, although this promise was not kept and the Revolution of 1848 soon swept her from the political scene.[30]

But Eugénie's grandiose claims, associated as they were with heavy financial demands, gave officials pause for thought. Throughout these months the comte Guyot defended her requests for money, while various bodies in Algeria and France debated the cost of including boarders, the cost of daily lunches for students, and the number of teachers and their salaries. Then, just as she seemed to be on the verge of getting the money she requested, discussions ground to a halt in June 1846. At this point the local administrative council requested an investigation into Madame Allix's moral character, stating that there was evidence of moral "misconduct" on her part.[31] It would appear, they argued, that Eugénie Allix was not the person she claimed to be.

NEGOTIATING COLONIAL SEXUAL POLITICS

Anxiety about teacher morality was not unusual in France and the colonies, given the weight of moral lessons in primary education. All French schoolteachers had to submit proof of their good conduct signed by the mayor of the town where they lived. There is ample evidence that in France issues of morality affected the careers of both men and women. But the administration seems to have sanctioned only men for various "moral affairs"; women offenders were treated differently.[32] Indeed, it seems likely that "affairs" concerning schoolmistresses had less to do with student-teacher relationships than with the reputation of the female teacher. In the colonies, where the social constraints of French village communities were loosened, this was particularly true—teachers had to watch their step, given the responsibilities they were seen to hold.

In Algeria schools for European girls were predominantly concerned with inculcating appropriate behavior, which meant habits of discipline and work and demure ways of being. These schools had multiplied since Madame Lanneau and her daughter had opened the first one in 1832. It was important that the daughters of settlers or the single women arriving in the colonies not slip into immoral behavior, especially prostitution. As a result, religious teachers in particular opened schools and orphanages for the needy poor. For Eugénie Allix, winning over the colonial administration inevitably involved not just convincing them of her capabilities and the intrinsic merit of her project, but also proving her personal moral integrity. Administrators such as Guyot supported the school precisely because they believed that offering Muslim girls the benefits of French civilization through the study of language, the experience of discipline, and the inculcation of work habits would prevent Muslim women from sinking into debauchery through contact with the French military. Inspector Lepescheux argued along the same lines that Eugénie's school represented "an enormous step forward for the intellectual culture and the moral improvement of indigenous women."[33] Naturally, such an institution required a teacher of impeccable morality herself, or at least that is what the administration argued in the summer of 1846 when a scandal erupted concerning Eugénie Allix's private life.

Guyot explained the nature of the scandal in a letter to Governor General Bugeaud in August 1846:

Madame Allix, in the early months of her stay in Algiers, encountered the sieur Luce, a musician in the African regiments and lived conjugally with him for a time. The Moors whose daughters attended the school thought the sieur Luce was the legitimate husband of Madame Allix and so his presence in the school was not a source of surprise. Then the legitimate husband, M. Allix, died in Paris. The widow hurried back to collect the inheritance and returned from France in widow's garb, which revealed that she had deceived the public about the nature of her relations with sieur Luce. In another trip to Paris, she hurried to repair her fault, marrying the sieur Luce who now lives with her.[34]

Naturally, this discovery generated a certain amount of alarm in colonial circles, as living outside the bonds of wedlock could hardly be considered exemplary moral conduct for a woman. Fortunately, the fact of Eugénie's two illegitimate births did not come to light. It seems, however, that it was her deliberate act of deception that most disappointed Guyot, who continued nonetheless to support her. In her defense he included her second marriage certificate as well as a number of certificates of morality from both France and Algeria, although he recognized that many of these were, by then, a bit dated. In his view, her second marriage showed her good faith, and he argued more pragmatically that the administration was unlikely to find another European woman who could speak Arabic and run a school such as the one she had opened.

Over the next five months Eugénie's school and her behavior were the object of more reports and letters. Governor General Bugeaud, who was hostile to civilian colonization, was clearly opposed to her appointment, arguing that one could not place at the head of a school "a person whose antecedents would always represent an obstacle for the honest mother seeking to leave her daughter in responsible hands."[35] The members of the Administrative Council were similarly unwilling to entrust such a delicate task to a woman with moral stains on her character. A vote in early October showed that although a majority of administrators still approved the existence of such a school for Muslim girls, only two of the eleven members were prepared to keep her as its director; five voted to keep the school and replace Allix, and four wished to see the school vanish from the colonial agenda.[36]

The determined and newly remarried Eugénie Luce was not prepared to accept this unfortunate turn of events without a fight, although retrospectively one wonders why she was so foolhardy as to advertise her widowhood in a location where no one had ever known her husband. Three weeks after the vote that signaled her disgrace she wrote an explanatory letter to Minister of War Alexandre Moline de Saint-Yon in which she argued that her relationship with Luce had never been a source of scandal. Indeed, she pointed out, he had left Algeria two years before she had started her school. Above all, though, she justified the abandonment of her first husband and argued for her own moral rectitude as evidenced by her good name. Her letter began by stating that fifteen years earlier she had fled her husband after seven years of mistreatment on his part. She claimed not to have the money or the desire to create a scandal by asking for a judiciary separation and so she left for Algeria where she devoted herself to teaching: "As in France, the parents who asked me to teach their daughters have always held me in high esteem; among your honorable deputies there are fathers of my students. I have always been admitted into the interior and shared the meals of families who honored me with their confidence, highly ranked families, who could, if necessary, provide witness to my character."[37] This missive did not have the intended effect, however, as neither Governor General Bugeaud nor Minister of War Saint-Yon was swayed. In early December, then, she shifted gears and began a campaign to be reimbursed for the money already spent—a whopping total of 15,000 francs, according to her calculations. Writing directly to the minister of war, Madame Luce accused the local colonial administration of retaliating against her because of the actions of her son-in-law, Félix Belly, a hotheaded journalist for the opposition whose articles in *L'Afrique* were highly critical of the government's orientations.[38] Recognizing, however, that her accusations coupled with her demands for money might irk rather than pacify the authorities, she concluded her letter in more feminine tones:

I have tried to have him [Félix Belly] abandon this career. . . . Politics is not my concern, me, a poor woman, who only dreams of her institution, of raising Muslim women from the state of abjection in which ignorance keeps them. Never mind, I must suffer, thanks to this newspaper, from the hatred that my son-in-law has provoked due to certain articles, which I have not read, articles directed against an administrator, who to satisfy a desire for revenge, seeks to have my institution fail, although it could accomplish such good; make no mistake, with my disgrace the institution will founder.[39]

This "poor woman," however, was able to count on the support of both Lepescheux and Guyot, who, although irritated by her conduct and the tone of her missives, nonetheless continued to believe she was the only person likely to succeed with such a school. On 16 December 1846 the comte Guyot sent off to Governor General Bugeaud a series of testimonials on behalf of Eugénie Luce, arguing that she should be kept on temporarily or else the school would close.

The men who wrote in her favor were local French notables whose support undoubtedly tipped the balance in her favor. Ponton d'Amécourt was president of the court of justice in Algiers, and he wrote enthusiastically about the lessons she had given his daughters over the previous three years. Casimir Jobert, a landowner and founding member of the Colonial Society for the State of Algiers, similarly indicated that his daughter had received her lessons with profit over a period of two years; he arrived in Algeria at the same time as Eugénie Allix, but whether their relationship stretched back to the early 1830s is not apparent. Finally, A. Marion, the Saint-Simonian judge who had helped Eugénie Allix in her hour of need, wrote a powerful letter testifying not only that she had taught writing, French, history, and geography in Bône, but also that she had experience running a school for young girls that had an excellent reputation. He noted, moreover, that this project for Muslim girls had been years in the making, suggesting in this fashion that her school was not an opportunistic whim.[40]

On 22 December 1846 Governor General Bugeaud gave up the fight and wrote Minister of War Saint-Yon that, much to his regret, Madame Luce needed to be kept on as the head of the school.[41] She had won her first battle, but as the future would show, not without cost. Her good name was clearly besmirched by the news of her relationship with Louis Luce, despite their marriage. And she also had gained a reputation for being an avaricious adventurer, since her missives had been accompanied by requests for money and detailed accounts of all that she considered the government should pay her. This twin association of illicit sex and greed for money defined her character for the officials with whom she dealt. Although the administration supported her school for the next fourteen years, local officials did not forget.

GOING PUBLIC: MADAME LUCE
AND THE POLITICS OF MUSLIM SCHOOLING

By the time Madame Luce's school was finally up and running with official subsidies, the educational landscape in Algeria had changed considerably since the first colonial creations in 1832, although the most important changes would come at mid-century following the educational surveys of 1847 and 1848. Untangling the nature of the French commitment to education in these years remains a complicated task, since individual and official attitudes varied considerably and evolved over time. The decision in 1848 to establish academies within Algeria and set up inspections as in France was an effort to impose order, but from the outset it encountered the resistance of the men within the Bureaux Arabes, who defended their special knowledge of the terrain. Lamoricière, the Saint-Simonian minister of war, pushed through an executive order in August 1848 that instituted a clear separation of power between the Ministry of Public Instruction in charge of education for the European and Jewish communities and the Ministry of War responsible for the education of Muslims. The Bureaux Arabes, with their cadres of Arabists, were placed in charge of the curriculum, surveillance, recruitment, and evaluation of Muslim students.[42]

This distinction between structures responsible for European Christian, Jewish, and Muslim education was a response to realities on the ground. The numbers of European students, both boys and girls, had risen steadily since the French occupation began in 1830. The arrival of Catholic religious teaching orders in particular had stimulated growth in the number of both schools and students. In 1837 the first surveys had found 22 French schools and 1,047 students; by 1847 there were 108 schools and 7,571 students (girls represented 43 percent of this total), and numbers rose steadily during these years of heavy immigration.[43] The statistical tables distinguished structures according to student origin and commented on the difficulties posed by the presence of such diverse populations. Indigenous Jewish students were from the outset perceived as more open to the civilizing influences of French schools, although this was truer for boys than for girls. The education of Muslims, however, clearly posed another set of problems as the army's Arabists uncovered the existence of a network of native schools for boys that the French occupation threatened. Should the French encourage the reconstruction of these schools? Should they seek to unify them under the control of the military? Should they modify the nature of the education proposed, inflecting it with French culture and ways of thinking?

In the end, the educational laws of 1850 cemented a two-tiered approach to Muslim schools, in which the Ministry of War controlled and inspected traditional Arab schools but also created a series of Arab-French schools. France's leading Arabists, and particularly the Muslim convert Ismaÿl Urbain, supported the latter to promote their vision of Franco-Muslim association. These schools introduced Muslim students to the French language in the hopes of creating an "elite" of educated boys and girls whose knowledge of French would foster closer economic, social, and cultural ties with the occupying forces.[44] The inclusion of girls in this cultural experiment bears special notice and testifies to the ways that Madame Luce had succeeded in drawing attention to the plight of Muslim women. Above all, she managed to convince civilian colonial authorities that Muslim girls' schooling, and her school in particular, represented a model deserving of imitation.[45]

Reports during the three years following the official recognition of Madame Luce's school and the creation of Arab-French schools in July 1850 testify to the rapid success of her institution. From the outset visitors and inspectors were impressed by what they saw. This was the case at the very first visit before the administration had decided to finance her. On 17 January 1846, the comte Guyot and Inspector Lepescheux were agreeably surprised by their inspection of the school situated in the Casbah at 10 rue du Diable. A newspaper reported the following: "A vast and well-lit room situated on the terrace served as a classroom for the students whose numbers increase daily, in almost frightening fashion. At the time of the visit, 32 students were present and six others absent, probably because of the visit. Seated, or rather crouched, on cushions arranged around the room, uniformly wearing a red *sérouel* [sirwal, or typical baggy Arabic pants] and a blue scarf, the visitors were immediately struck by their picturesque and gracious appearance. M. the comte Guyot had hardly expected such an advanced organization."[46] The school was closed shortly thereafter, however, when Eugénie left for France, and did not start up again until early 1847. In January a survey of primary schools in Algeria indicated that her school had fifty-nine day students.[47] Lepescheux continued to praise the school, arguing, "We will never really conquer the Arabs until, through knowledge of our language, we can train the ideas and spirit of the generations born under our control." He noted in this report that the schoolteacher was already looking for another location because the rue du Diable was considered a relatively infamous neighborhood associated with prostitution.[48] A year later she was settled with 120 students at 10 rue Regnard, another street in the Casbah, but one with a better reputation.[49] Ismaÿl Urbain also viewed the school favorably, writing in the fall of 1847 that "a school for Muslim girls in Algiers has attracted over one hundred students, testifying to the inaccuracy of those who claim that the Arabs are repulsed by all that we offer."[50]

Although the rector of the newly created Academy of Algiers, Charles-Lucien Delacroix, was not officially in charge of schools for Muslims, he nonetheless viewed them with the same sort of enthusiasm that characterized people such as Lepescheux and Guyot once the quarrels about financing had been resolved. In April 1849 he noted that Madame Luce had 137 students and that the school was "prosperous." Moreover, Delacroix supported her desire to admit a few French students as a way of facilitating the teaching and especially the pronunciation of the language: "The French families who request the admission of their daughters to the Muslim school are not rare. We could choose those who already know how to read and write moderately well, in order to use them as monitors. Naturally they would be required to participate in all of the school exercises, notably the lessons of the Arab *sous-maîtresse* [assistant teacher]."[51] There is no evidence that French girls were admitted to the school at this time, but by the early 1850s a few French names were on the student lists, suggesting that Eugénie Luce had managed to create sufficient confidence in her institution that even French families would send their daughters there.

THE CREATION OF ARAB-FRENCH SCHOOLS AND ADMINISTRATIVE RECONFIGURATIONS IN ALGERIA

The years between 1847 and 1850 were critical for establishing the school's repu- tation and generating the sense that girls' education deserved pride of place in France's civilizing mission in Algeria. These years were also tumultuous in po- litical and military terms. On 23 December 1847 Abd al-Qadir had surrendered to the French; by February 1848 he was being held prisoner with his extended family and a large suite of retainers in the château d'Amboise near Tours. In France, economic and political crises precipitated the Revolution of 1848 that installed the Second French Republic and resulted in the election of Louis Na- poleon as president in December. These events had repercussions in Algeria where no fewer than eight military commanders and governors general suc- ceeded each other, at times remaining a mere month in the position. In March 1848 the provisional government declared Algeria an integral part of the French domain, and measures were drawn up to assimilate the colony administratively. Finally, in November 1848 constitutional amendments declared Algeria a terri- tory of France; its provinces were transformed into departments with their own general and municipal councils. French Algerians became eligible for election as representatives to the National Assembly.

In educational matters, these years also brought a number of institutional and legislative changes. A series of measures granting greater authority to ad- ministrators in Algeria had already established a municipal regime for Algiers in September 1847 whose voice would make a difference in discussions about public schooling. In August 1848 the public instruction portfolio and those of religion, justice, and finance were attached to their respective French ministries, and on 1 September 1848 the Academy of Algiers was created.[52] A rector under the orders of the minister of public instruction and assisted in his tasks by the Academic Council headed the academy. This new educational organization cre- ated two inspectors for the Academy of Algiers as well as primary inspectors for the province who were in charge of inspections. Unlike in France, where prefects were in charge of primary education, the rector of Algiers had control over the appointment of schoolteachers and the authorization of French schools.[53] It was in this context that the Bureaux Arabes struggled successfully to maintain their control over indigenous education, convinced that their own expertise was far greater than that of civilian authorities. Lamoricière's executive order of August 1848 clearly indicated that the Ministry of War, rather than the Ministry of Public Instruction, was responsible for the education of Muslim students.[54]

Two years later a presidential decree formalized a system of Arab-French schools that drew upon the experiences of Luce and her male colleague Auguste Depeille, who had run a boys' school since 1842. The decree of 14 July 1850 announced the creation of five Arab-French schools for boys and four for girls, as well as adult schools in three cities.[55] Given the existence of Luce's school for girls and Depeille's school for boys, the decree represented an effort to spread a certain type of education that was seen to bear promise for the future. In essence, these Arab-French schools were laboratories for cultural experimentation, while the authorities were far more cautious with the traditional Muslim schools. The inclusion of girls' schools was not a forgone conclusion, however, since the early projects for these schools mentioned only boys. An amendment of the original project was introduced in January 1850 in order to include girls.[56] The discussions around this amendment clearly show that Madame Luce had convinced authorities both in Algiers and in Paris that girls' education was the key to future change: "the germ of an intellectual and moral revolution."[57]

The decree was surprisingly egalitarian in its treatment of boys' and girls' education. For both, schooling was free and composed of lessons in the reading and writing of Arabic and French, aspects of the French language, and arithmetic. Gender differences in the program spoke directly to the future lives envisioned for the students of these schools; for boys this meant learning the legal system of weights and measures, useful for careers in the French administration, and girls learned to sew. The governor general appointed a French director and an indigenous assistant to each school, following the prefect's proposition. The schools were under the jurisdiction of the prefect, not of the cities, in which the schools were located. The decree did favor boys more than girls by creating more schools for boys, and the male directors earned 1,200 francs to the female directors' 1,000 francs (the assistants earned 600 and 500 francs, respectively); still, compared with the situation in France, the female personnel were remarkably well-paid, and all categories of personnel earned a great deal more.

In September 1850 Madame Luce sent a seventeen-page report to the prefect of Algiers that summarized her achievements since her school's initial authorization in July 1845.[58] Generated in response to the prefect's request, this document offers precious insight into how she positioned herself in the French civilizing mission and the role she attributed to her school in this mission. She also made clear that she saw herself participating on an equal footing with her fellow Frenchmen in their collective endeavor to assimilate the indigenous population. As a result, her report concludes with a number of suggestions about how to improve the existing situation. Clearly, she saw the presidential decree as a form of personal vindication, and she emphasized that she saw her institution as superior to the three other Arab-French schools for girls that the decree announced.

Following a series of general remarks about her own courage in pursuing her dream, Luce's report detailed what had been accomplished. Over the previous five years (between 10 July 1845 and 31 August 1850), 245 girls had attended her school. Of this number 108 were no longer in the school: 8 had married Moors from Algiers; 9 had married Arabs from the interior; 11 had left the school at age sixteen, knowing how to read, write, and sew and lived "honestly" with their parents; 23 had left Algiers with their families, knowing French, some writing, and how to sew; 9 had died, including a young student who had been sent to act as interpreter for the mother of Abd al-Qadir in Amboise; 17 had been expelled; and 31 had been written off the lists because of frequent absenteeism. These figures were clearly intended to impress, showing as they did that a considerable number of girls had been exposed to French culture and that they had gotten married or lived good lives within their families after leaving the school. The high number of students who had been expelled or written off the lists (48 of 108) showed that Luce exerted her authority over those students who did not take their education as seriously as Luce took her task to educate them.

Luce estimated that the 90 to 120 students welcomed each day were roughly divided into three age categories: one-third were between the ages of six and nine; one-third were aged nine to twelve; and one-third were aged twelve to fourteen. Although none of her students came from wealthy families, she argued that over time families from all classes of Muslim society had sent her their daughters. The students studied "classical subjects," that is, French, in the morning; but from the outset, she emphasized more vocational training, devoting the afternoon hours (12:30 to 5:00) to sewing and embroidery, under the guidance of a sewing mistress whom she paid from her own pocket. The students were authorized to keep the money earned from the sale of the objects they produced. In Luce's opinion, her school had contributed to the assimilation of a "considerable number" of young girls who had received an education that allowed them to function in European society or to act as assistants within the schools that the government might see fit to create throughout Algeria. She was, however, particularly satisfied with the vocational training of her students, which gave them the means to eke out an honest living, rather than resorting to "the odious resource of prostitution."

Despite her satisfaction with her successes, Madame Luce took the opportunity in this report to the prefect to suggest a number of changes that would set the tone for the debates about girls' education in the years to come. To begin, she highlighted local resistance to "intellectual" education; for the Moors of Algiers, she wrote, her school was seen as a House of God, given that she gave out alms and distributed bread, clothes, and food to her students. In order to merit such a vision of her institution, she argued that the prefect should create a *salle d'asile* (nursery school) for young children, a workshop for girls between the ages of fourteen and twenty, and a hospice for old women. In order to accommodate such projects, she needed a bigger building. Unfortunately, she argued, there was a tendency in Algiers to see her school as a commercial venture and hence to cut financial corners, rather than to treat it as an institution for public welfare.

She concluded her report with a similarly political argument about the importance of her school with respect to the new Arab-French schools inaugurated with the presidential decree. Naturally, she wrote, the new decree could not apply to her institution in Algiers, which was far more than a primary school. She argued that it was also a welfare institution in addition to being a nursery, a sort of normal school that would produce the indigenous Muslim schoolmistresses who would later be called to spread the moralizing principles of French civilization among their fellow believers. By positioning her own institution above the new schools, Luce clearly sought to avoid coming under the authority of the prefect and to defend her existing salary of 1,500 francs (the women directors of Arab-French schools received only 1,000 francs).

This report, like the many Madame Luce had penned during the first years of her school's existence, set the tone for her relationship with the men in charge. While integrating the cultural arrogance of the French civilizing mission, she insisted on her own special contribution to this mission, thanks to her long experience in Algeria, her knowledge of Arabic, and her social network. Unlike other French schoolteachers, she was familiar with Muslim customs; and as a woman, she was able to communicate with Muslim women, who remained un-touchable to the male civilian population and military leaders in Algiers. Her report also shows her business acumen in her dealings with the administration. She kept records about her school and kept a close eye on expenses. Her final comments about salaries show that her own investment in this school was far from disinterested. Her early years in Algeria had taught her about poverty as she struggled, giving lessons and washing clothes. In addition to alleviating the poverty of the Muslim girls she educated, she meant to maintain her status as the well-paid headmistress of the only school for Muslim girls in Algiers. Her commitment to the ideals of the French civilizing mission came with a healthy dose of economic pragmatism not unlike that of her Saint-Simonian friends. Undoubtedly, this contributed to her success in the years to come.

4 SCHOOLING MUSLIM GIRLS (1850–1857)

Writing about Madame Luce in 1857, the British feminist Barbara Bodichon recounted Luce's success in persuading colonial authorities to fund her school:

At length, in January 1847, the storms were weathered; the school was formally adopted by Government, and received its first visit of official inspection, at which Count Guyot was present. The inspector declared himself more than satisfied with the condition of the children, not thinking it possible that so much progress could have been made in instructing Moresques. On this occasion the gentlemen were received by thirty-two pupils and the Arab sub-mistress *unveiled*, which Madame Luce considered a great moral triumph. She always works against the use of the veil, thinking, and truly thinking, as it seems to us, that it is far from conducive to true modesty of bearing, which should be simple and straightforward, of that purity which "thinketh no evil." Since 1847, Madame Luce has pursued her path of usefulness. The school numbers at present 120, of all ages between four and eighteen.[1]

Within a decade Eugénie Luce had succeeded in anchoring her school within the Algerian educational landscape, drawing in students, inspiring imitations, and attracting outside attention. This included attention from British feminists who were similarly engaged in promoting women's rights through education in their home country and in British colonies.

This success was partly testimony to Madame Luce's chutzpah and her persistence in pursuing what she described as her "oeuvre" in the face of administrative obstacles and moral opprobrium. But it was also the product of a favorable intellectual climate in these years of consolidation of the French presence in Algeria. Although revolts and fighting continued sporadically until the final great uprisings in Kabylia in 1870–1871, by December 1847 the Arab leader Abd al-Qadir had surrendered and been exiled to France. On 12 November 1848 the constitution of the Second French Republic incorporated Algeria into French territory, making the Province of Algiers one of three new departments in France—no longer a colony on paper. Although the military remained in charge of relations between the French and the local Algerian populations through the Bureaux Arabes, this

same military contained many Saint-Simonian officers who shared Luce's interest in improving relations between the indigenous populations and the French.
Naturally, profound inequalities durably marked the French "civilizing mission"
of these years; the French operated as conquerors and set the terms of the discussion with Muslim leaders, but in this discussion hopes for a more respectful
relationship between the races existed and opened the way for unusual social
and cultural experimentation, such as that proposed by Eugénie Luce.

Madame Luce sought to promote a form of dialogue between the cultures
through the education of girls, albeit a dialogue that emphasized in no uncertain terms the superiority of French civilization. The years between 1850 and 1857
represent the heyday of her success, when the colonial authorities largely silenced
their early misgivings about this aggressively entrepreneurial schoolteacher and
instead used her school to showcase their commitment to improving the status
of indigenous women through education and the inculcation of useful vocational
skills. The attention Madame Luce garnered in Algeria, in France, and within British feminist circles masks, however, the degree to which her girl students remain
within the shadows, both within the school and afterwards in their adult lives.

MADAME LUCE AND THE
ARAB-FRENCH SCHOOLS FOR GIRLS

Debates about schools were rife between 1848 and 1850, testimony to the political
weight the French attached to educational matters. In both France and Algeria
the issue of religious schools and their degree of independence was at the heart
of these discussions. In Algeria a series of measures were passed in 1850, beginning with the creation of Arab-French schools for boys and girls described in the
preceding chapter. This presidential decree of 14 July 1850 also included provisions for instruction in French for indigenous adults. A decree of 30 September
1850 then established guidelines with respect to traditional indigenous education. It set up a loose system of inspection over *zawiyas*, or Koranic schools, and
the creation of three madrasas, or institutions of higher learning.[2] The hope was
that native establishments would gradually integrate the Arab-French schools
as the process of cultural assimilation progressed.

The year 1850 was an important one in French educational politics as well.
In March, the government instituted the Falloux Law, which required villages
of eight hundred inhabitants or more to open a public primary school for girls.
Passed by a conservative government responding to the social upheaval of the

Revolution of 1848, the law also opened the door to the church's increasing influence within the school system, with members of the clergy and religious orders acting as inspectors and teachers. The measure unquestionably encouraged religious teaching orders to open girls' schools, since women religious were not required to have a teaching degree like their lay counterparts. The schools promoted religious values, but they also contributed significantly to rising literacy rates among women.[3] Madame Luce's school in Algiers similarly promoted conservative social values, but its significance within the colonial context was completely different given the absence of other opportunities for indigenous girls' schooling at mid-century.

The decree of 14 July 1850 theoretically established Arab-French schools for boys in Algiers, Constantine, Bône, Mostagenem, and Blidah and schools for girls in Algiers, Constantine, Bône, and Oran. However, this remarkable concern to provide almost as many schools for girls as for boys did not develop as intended. In reality, only the girls' schools under the direction of Madame Luce in Algiers and Madame Parent in Constantine lasted long enough to have an effect on the local urban environment, while the boys' schools multiplied in the years to come.[4] Born in 1802, Parent was Luce's contemporary and had a diploma from the Sorbonne authorizing her to teach in nursery schools. Her dossier reports that she spoke Italian, English, and Arabic.[5] Parent was less vocal than Eugénie Luce, so her school in Constantine, which opened in 1853, encountered less criticism. It continued to function, primarily as a workshop, until the late 1870s, but it never attracted the same sort of public attention as Luce's. In December 1850 Ursule Robin de Montmain was authorized to open an Arab-French school in Blidah, a city that initially was slated to have only a school for boys. However, this school does not appear to have lasted for any length of time.[6]

Haggling with Authorities

The government's support of Arab-French schooling for girls did not immediately end the sparring match that characterized Madame Luce's relationship with male authorities. Following the decree of July 1850 the Ministry of War oversaw the organization of these schools, dealing most notably with questions concerning the rental of appropriate buildings, the cost of school supplies, and money for prizes and food. In these discussions, Luce intervened loudly, seeking to maintain her independence and arguing that the July decrees could not be applied to her institution in Algiers because she saw it as a form of normal institution, providing teachers for the other girls' schools. This effort to remain outside the framework of the Arab-French schools failed, however, and soon she was involved in endless haggling with the prefect who had authority over the schools.

Madame Luce's clearly stated demands in both financial and organizational terms were a source of frequent friction, just as they had been five years earlier when she first appeared in public life. But in 1850 she was in a far stronger position to bargain, since her school existed and was by all reports, and especially her own, successful. After a full year of discussions, the prefect felt the need to signal her "bad behavior" to the minister of war, writing, "She takes pleasure in denigrating the smallest measures [of the administration] and she has adopted the same system of slander that she used against the town hall, when the latter sought to oversee her school more carefully. . . . Madame Luce is among the most recalcitrant members of my administration."[7] This "bad behavior" led the minister of war to recommend in January 1852 that she be severely reprimanded.[8]

The nature of this "bad behavior" is not completely clear although a number of issues emerge in the archives as sources of tension. To begin with, Luce wanted more money for her school than the prefect was prepared to give her, more than twice the sum that the minister of war ultimately granted. She wanted this money in order to pay a second assistant teacher, a Frenchwoman who specialized in sewing; to finance the functioning of a sewing workshop for older girls and the cost of renting a larger building; and to distribute prizes and cash rewards to her students. The issue of money was a particular thorn in the side of the prefect, and considerable correspondence went back and forth on the subject. The annual budget for Madame Luce's school was decided only in February 1851, and although the sum was not what she requested initially, she ended up winning most of the organizational battles. That is to say, she remained in charge of both the school and the workshop, which she had created alongside her school, and she was given money to pay for a second sewing mistress, a woman who taught in both the school and the workshop. The total sum allocated was 11,250 francs; Auguste Depeille's boys' school received only 4,390 francs. This difference stemmed from the decision to feed the girl students—considered an added incentive for parents—but not the boy students. Luce's salary in this budget was 1,000 francs, with a 500-franc "indemnity" and an additional 800 francs based on an estimated number of 150 pupils. She could count on a minimal salary of 1,500 francs, and as much as 2,300 francs, which was the equivalent of a salary for a captain, a judge, or a male secondary school teacher in metropolitan France.

Although all colonial salaries were higher than on the mainland, Luce's salary was indeed handsome for the time, particularly for a woman.

Money was not the only source of friction with colonial authorities; the joint direction of the school and the workshop also generated debate. Some feared moral problems that might result from contact between younger students and the older "workers" within the workshop.[9] Others hinted at the amount of influence Madame Luce had over the indigenous female population. Ultimately, however, the Ministry of War's reprimand may have had little to do with the school or workshop in Algiers but rather with colonial politics on a larger scale. During the final months of 1850, the prefect asked Eugénie Luce to send three of her more advanced students to France to act as interpreters for the women of Abd al-Qadir's family.[10] At this point, the emir and his retinue of more than seventy people had been held prisoner in the chateau d'Amboise in the Loire Valley for more than two years.[11] Government officials sought in various ways to make his forced sojourn a little less disagreeable, and apparently they believed that the students from Madame Luce's school could help make a difference through their ability to communicate in both French and Arabic with the emir's wives. Following a suggestion by Captain Laurent-Estève Boissonnet, who was the French interlocutor for the Arab chief in Amboise, General Eugène Daumas, who was in charge of Algerian affairs in the Ministry of War, authorized three students to make the trip to France; they were granted the sum of 300 francs for their services. Madame Luce was unable, however, to find three families who would allow her to send a daughter off to France, so in the end only two young women went: Nefissa Bent Ali, who was fourteen years old, and an orphaned girl, Aziya Bent Yahia.[12] The girls arrived on 6 January 1851, but within a few months rumors that one of the girls was planning to convert to Christianity brought the government's leading Arabist, Ismaÿl Urbain, into action, insisting the girls be sent rapidly back to Algeria. His correspondence with Boissonnet argued that the "moral and political consequences" of such a conversion would be "enormous" and that news of this affair would promptly ruin the French efforts to "civilize" through such Arab-French schools. Captain Boissonnet was ordered to edit his report to the ministry: "No mention should be made of the effort to convert, but rather it should specify the minimal usefulness of the young Muslim women's stay in France." He concluded: "[See] in what a bad way Madame Luce has led us."[13]

It seems a bit unjust to blame Madame Luce for the behavior of her students in Amboise, especially given the official decision to place them with Catholic religious sisters, but Urbain was undoubtedly correct in imagining that news of such an event would have had negative repercussions on the French effort to improve Franco-Arab relations through schooling. Urbain's correspondence emphasized the need to keep the affair hushed up and expressed clear irritation with both Madame Luce and the Soeurs de la Présentation de Tours, who had served as hostesses to the Muslim girls. Eugénie Luce recounted the story somewhat differently years later: "Attempts were made to convert them to Christianity, and the parents, hearing of it, were so indignant that it became necessary to recall the girls."[14] Neither the government nor Luce said anything publicly about the efforts at conversion. Still, upon the girls' return, the administration, as a sign of their displeasure, boycotted the prize ceremony she had organized.[15] The correspondence of the period shows that the incident contributed to making Madame Luce a political actor in the French colonization of Algeria, and in the process, she had made herself unpopular in certain quarters. Still, she had become the unavoidable interlocutor for the government with respect to the schooling of Muslim girls.

Lessons in the Schoolroom

In 1853 the rector of the Academy of Algiers, Charles-Lucien Delacroix, reported favorably to the governor general on Madame Luce's school, which had moved the previous year to a larger building at 5 rue de Toulon, where it remained for thirty years. Bessie Rayner Parkes, who visited in the late 1850s, described the school as an old Moorish house "in the heart of the compact labyrinth forming the Corsair city":

> The little narrow steep streets, which often break abruptly into regular steps are wholly inaccessible to any vehicle. . . . In one of the steepest, darkest, and dirtiest of these streets, a very handsome arched doorway leads into the oblong vestibule where servants—and in the olden day, slaves were supposed to wait. From this we emerge into the square court of two stories, open to the sky. The classrooms are both above and below, and the quaint little figures which linger about the doors are the scholars for whom Madame Luce has fought so severe a battle.[16]

Delacroix noted in 1853 that the schoolrooms were now sufficiently large for the existing 130 students. True, the inner courtyard was too small to allow all of the students to play at once, but otherwise they had at their fingertips the necessary texts and school materials; mural maps were painted on the walls for geography lessons. "I need not remind you of the sacrifices the State has accepted in order to attract Muslim girls to the school," he wrote. "I can only say it will not regret it if it succeeds in transmitting a taste for work, orderly habits and a sense of duty to these poor, abandoned, and exposed children." Such habits, the rector continued, would give the students the means to survive and resist the moral lapses provoked by hunger and poverty. In his view Madame Luce had succeeded in this task. Her students were relatively weak in academic subjects, but they knew how to sew, knit, and embroider and would be able, if necessary, to sew their own clothes, those of their children, and some of their husband's. When need no longer threatened, embroidery work would chase away boredom and the dangerous promptings of idleness, Delacroix argued.[17]

This portrait of Madame Luce's school suggests the weight of manual work and moral lessons within the classroom, although it would be an error to think that lessons in literacy were quickly forgotten. Trimester reports between 1853 and 1856 allow us to judge the nature of the schooling offered and the care that was taken to observe the program theoretically put in place.

The program Madame Luce established resembled in many ways that of the French elementary schools at the time, except of course that French children did not learn Arabic and Muslim girls did not learn the Christian religious lessons that permeated French infant and primary schools. Like infant schools, Parisian girls' schools, and Arab elementary schools, the Arab-French schools adopted the monitorial system of education, which allowed one teacher to manage large numbers of students thanks to the use of older students who were placed in charge of small groups of less advanced students.[18] Madame Luce divided the total student body into eight different levels for each subject; as a result, students did not progress by class, but rather by level within an individual subject.

Madame Luce gave lessons in reading, writing, and arithmetic as well as in French grammar for the more advanced students. In any given trimester, the number of students engaged in the arduous study of French grammar ranged between 10 and 26 out of an average student population of 127. Virtually all of the students studied reading and arithmetic, with fewer learning to write. Learning to read French and learning to calculate were considered more useful skills for these students than writing.

Although the school always promoted lessons in both academic subjects and manual skills, the former had pride of place during the early years. In 1853 Rector Delacroix considered this emphasis misguided, noting that it would always be difficult for the students to learn French because they heard it spoken only in the classroom by their mistress, not to mention parental suspicion about acquiring such language skills. In his view, Madame Luce's desire that her school should train assistant teachers for the other Arab-French schools had led her to overemphasize the academic aspects of the schooling experience. To this end, she had called in outside teachers to give lessons to her student monitors: Madame Merz gave lessons in grammar and geography, Monsieur Muller gave lessons in mathematics, and Louis-Jacques Bresnier taught Arabic. The latter, Algiers' leading Arabist, was part of the Saint-Simonian nexus and the author of the first textbooks for teaching Arabic in the French schools in Algeria.[19] Delacroix noted, however, that Luce's ambitions had lessened with the years and the realization that the use of male teachers was likely to raise suspicions among families. Given the weak demand for trained women teachers, these lessons were on the verge of ceasing when he wrote in February 1853. With only two existing Arab-French schools, aspiring teachers were better advised to learn needlework than the intricacies of Arabic.

A ruling dated 17 September 1851 specified the organization of the school day: during the winter months between October and April, students had three hours of lessons between 8:00 and 11:00 a.m. These hours were spent learning Arabic (one hour) and then the different subjects taught in French. For part of the morning, Madame Luce ran a special class in French for the student monitors. The afternoon was spent doing more manual activities—sewing and embroidery—but during these hours certain groups received lessons in the French language, and younger students studied mathematics.[20] Naturally, the program was very elementary, but more advanced knowledge was transmitted in the writing and reading lessons—in particular, basic ideas about history, geography, and the natural sciences.

Expenses for the school show that Madame Luce purchased schoolbooks, but it seems likely that the books remained mostly in her hands or in those of her student monitors. Still, the prize-giving ceremonies (described below) were an opportunity to hand out schoolbooks to the best students. Evidence from these ceremonies shows that the school was using instructional material and textbooks common in France twenty years earlier during the heyday of mutual education there. In this way French educational ideals moved from the school into Muslim homes. A comparison of the books purchased for the boys' and girls' schools shows very little difference except for the presence in Madame Luce's school of a book of fables by a contemporary Protestant Frenchwoman, Madame Alida de Savignac: *Petites fables d'après nature*. This prolific author of children's stories contributed to the development of this genre for girls, notably through articles in the *Journal des Femmes* and the *Journal des Demoiselles*, two journals that appeared in the 1830s as the commercial press developed.[21] Otherwise, students learned to read using the textbooks found throughout rural France, except of course for the presence of Depeille's textbook for learning to read Arabic.

Writing books and slates were available in large numbers at the school, as was common in mutual schools. Here students learned the flowery gestures that characterized French nineteenth-century calligraphy. Handwriting samples, which were frequently included with the school records, suggest the similarity between learning to execute an attractive cursive and the movements necessary for stitching embroidery.

Writing sample exhibited at a prize ceremony for Eugénie Luce's Arab-French school for girls, 1854. Such elaborate handwriting and ornamentation were common in French schools of the time. Centre des Archives d'Outre-Mer, GGA 22 S/2.

In an 1854 report the inspector commented: "Reading has made noticeable progress. Writing which at first had made little progress has begun to improve more and more. The use of the Carbonnel transparencies [which allowed students to copy patterns in handwriting, much as they copied patterns in embroidery] is very advantageous in these large classes. Needlework continues to progress steadily; they are just beginning indigenous embroideries (using silk and gold)."[22]

A particularly detailed report at the end of 1855 offers a clear picture of studies at the time.[23] Ninety-two students were enrolled in the school; of this number the inspector considered that twenty were able to read easily and twenty-four were studying French grammar. Students learned to read using the popular Peigné method, which the Society for Elementary Instruction promoted in France during the early 1830s as public primary education developed.[24] It involved teaching children to read words and sentences through a phonetic method that associated letters and groups of letters. In arithmetic, the first four of eight classes were devoted to learning to pronounce and write numbers; the following three classes focused on the four arithmetic operations, and the final most advanced class (with four students) studied the metric system.

In Arabic the first seven classes learned to read and write using Depeille's textbook, while the seven students of the final class were given a book of fables and dialogues by Jean-Honorat Delaporte, the *Phraséologie* of Auguste Cherbonneau, and the anthology and elements of calligraphy of Louis-Jacques Bresnier.[25] All of these textbooks were produced by French Arabists between 1835 and 1851 and reflected modern French thinking about how to teach Arabic. Luce's Arab-French school mimicked Depeille's school for boys in its approach to the study of Arabic. Rather than learning verses of the Quran by heart, students learned to read with Arabic characters that adopted a system of conventions to facilitate reading without transcription into the Roman alphabet. Only the most advanced students in Luce's school recited the first chapters of the Quran. In this fashion, historian Alain Messaoudi notes, the Arab-French schools participated in creating Arabic as a modern national language, but with less success for girls than for boys.[26] Indeed, the inspector noted relatively little progress in the study of Arabic in Madame Luce's school, contrary to what he observed in Depeille's school.

The overall impression that this 1855 report gives about the curriculum in Madame Luce's school is not very different from what one might get at a midcentury rural primary school in France, except that the Algerian school welcomed far more students. Most of Luce's students were grouped in the lower classes, with little probability that they would grapple in any depth with French grammatical rules. Still, all of the more advanced classes had students, most probably the student monitors, who ensured that the school operated smoothly. In 1855 there were twelve such students with a relatively solid background in the basics. At this point the indigenous teaching assistant, Nefissa Bent Ali, relied on textbooks produced by French Arabists for the study of Arabic. She, at least, had acquired a sufficient mastery of both French and Arabic to use the texts.

Lessons in Needlework

Needlework was an essential aspect of the school's program because it taught a useful skill and inculcated work habits. Sewing classes were divided into two divisions, according to age. In the first division, the youngest students learned "all sorts of knitting,"[27] producing everything from garters to lace. In the second division, students were introduced to sewing, tapestry work, and embroidery. The 1855 inspection report noted that fifty-nine students alternated lessons in these more difficult skills, which received high praise from the inspector. Eugénie Luce's concern to develop students' sewing skills explains her long struggle to keep her sewing mistress, Marie Antoinette Dufraisne, permanently on the colonial payroll. By 1856 she had achieved this task, and Dufraisne was assured of receiving 900 francs a year for her services.[28] A contemporary of Luce, Dufraisne probably had no professional training herself but clearly had sufficient knowledge to teach a wide variety of handiwork to a generation of students.

Prize-giving ceremonies offered testimony to the skills students learned, as students themselves crafted most of the clothing distributed at these occasions. In June 1855 fifty-three students received prizes for their success in their studies or for their hard work, sewing, or good behavior. In the table adjoined to the description of the ceremony, Luce recorded the objects distributed and their monetary value. With the exception of the five French students, all the others, including Fatima, the black woman who cleaned the school, left the ceremony with various pieces of Arab clothing varying in value from 5 francs for a shirt or pair of pants to 41 francs for an embroidered vest (*djabadouli*).[29] The more common prizes were aprons worn over dresses, shawls, pants, or shirts, all the product of student handiwork. The value of this clothing came to a total of 491 francs. Luce's decision to award both practical and more festive clothing to her students says a great deal about the priorities of the school. In France, students traditionally received books as prizes, although mutual schools during the Restoration at times also gave out clothing.[30] Rather than reinforcing the academic side of the classroom, the distribution of pieces of clothing emphasized the relationship between femininity and needlework, success in school, and pride of presentation. In June 1854, for example, the governor general gave to the school 145 meters of Indian cloth, which the students then transformed into forty *djellaba*s (long loose-fitting robes) that were distributed as prizes.[31]

Inspection reports reveal that well before the creation of a sewing workshop the students were kept busy knitting and sewing shirts, pants, scarves, socks, ties, and even curtains for the classroom. Some of these objects were intended for the city's poor, whereas others were made for the students themselves. In the space of four months, the inspectors noted the production of 88 shirts (of various difficulty) and 147 *caracos*, or women's loose jackets, at a time when the school had 135 students. This did not include the objects produced for the school's annual lottery, which in June 1853 earned 4,166 francs through the sale of objects made by the students.[32] The cost of buying material and thread was 3,467 francs, so the lottery netted 699 francs, which was given back to the students either through the purchase of clothes or by the deposit of money in individual student savings accounts. As this organization reveals, Eugénie Luce was using needlework to teach students the principle of charity by donating clothes to the city's poor, the monetary value of work through the sale of student handiwork, and the virtue of thrift by establishing student savings accounts.

The savings accounts (*livrets sur la caisse d'épargne*) are mentioned for the first time in an 1853 inspection report and deserve notice for several reasons.[33] To begin with, the accounts very concretely gave value to the educational experience, even if the archival record makes it difficult to chart the results for more then a few students. Between March 1859 and March 1860, Luce noted that students had earned 2,745.40 francs; in the space of six months, between April and October 1860, twelve of her students alone had earned 1,122.45 francs. These included Nauourine, who was the highest wage earner, with 250.85 francs; followed by Houssine, with 213.75 francs; and then Nefissa, with 129.50 francs. The youngest student recorded was only nine years old, and she had earned 38.80 francs.[34] Such sums represented a considerable amount of money for indigenous women, given that the sewing mistress in another school earned only 100 francs per year. Perhaps more significantly, they anticipate later developments in France and suggest the ways that the colonial terrain provided opportunities for experimentation. Although some primary mutual schools in France had set up such student accounts in the 1830s and 1840s, the development of school savings accounts (*caisses d'épargne scolaires*) occurred only in the 1870s in the context of widespread educational reforms.[35] The vast majority of French primary girls' schools in the 1850s and 1860s emphasized the importance of sewing both as a household skill and a potential source of livelihood, but the lesson was not reinforced with student savings. It should be noted that no similar initiative existed in the Arab-French boys' schools, in part because the nature of manual work for boys was more indeterminate and less obviously lucrative, but also because the emphasis on book learning took clear precedence. In Depeille's school in Algiers, students had lessons in geometric drawing and even music, thanks to the services of Louis Luce, but neither skill produced objects for ready sale.

Madame Luce's decision to set up such accounts for the students in her school testifies to the wide-ranging objectives of her educational project despite the seemingly modest nature of the school's program. Lessons in the academic rudiments, coupled with training in various methods of handiwork, were expected to fashion young women who would be good wives and mothers, emissaries within the family for the French civilizing mission, but also thrifty workers who appreciated the monetary value of work, thanks to their savings. Well before the transformation of Luce's school into a workshop, Madame Luce defended the importance of teaching native girls skills that would be useful in the home but were also a potential source of income.

Moral and Physical Education

Madame Luce's school, and the others founded on the same model, had grander ambitions than simply teaching students to read, calculate, and sew. As an inspector noted in 1856, the school sought not just to develop instruction: "it sought to ennoble sentiments and to substitute honest habits for traditions which are contrary to religion and morals."[36] A few years earlier Rector Delacroix had argued that moral education should predominate in these institutions, inculcating habits of "order, obedience and work."[37] These institutions were part of the French desire to effect the "moral transformation" of the conquered populations thanks to the presumed influence of women within their future families. As a result, the teachers in the school focused not just on lessons, but also on instilling both mental and physical attitudes that were consonant with the French civilizing mission. This meant in practice learning respect for hierarchies in both religious and political terms, learning the value of work and punctuality, and learning habits of good hygiene through the school's careful monitoring of cleanliness, health, and eating habits. Attention to these aspects of girls' schooling is shown clearly in the trimester inspections throughout the 1850s.

The surviving reports from 1853 to 1856 all begin with the results of the "medical and hygienic inspection" of schools, which constituted a new priority for French educational administrators of the period.[38] On the whole, inspectors were enthusiastic about this aspect of Madame Luce's school, as noted in 1853: "As with the boys' school, great praise should be directed toward the woman director for the cleanliness and the care given to the students of the school. In medical terms, nineteen young girls were treated [for various illnesses] and nineteen were cured. The most serious infection was a passing fever."[39] These compliments were repeated in succeeding reports. The nature of medical ailments was frequently mentioned, most of them being common problems arising from crowded living spaces: ringworm, canker sores, or scrofula (a form of tuberculosis affecting the lymph nodes). A few students died, indicating the existence of more serious infections. In 1854, for example, four of thirty-four students left the school for health-related reasons: two died, a third had smallpox, and a fourth suffered from an unspecified sickness. Two years later an outbreak of smallpox among students led to the decision to vaccinate all of them.[40]

Good health was strictly associated with hygiene and cleanliness, as the inspections reveal, and there are signs the girls were encouraged to exercise and move around outside in the playground that Madame Luce took pains to sand and plant in 1853. The school building itself was washed twice a week and whitewashed to chest level, and every evening the servant swept the building carefully. Upon arrival in the morning, girls wearing dirty clothes were sent home to change them. After meals, students washed their faces and hands.[41] Commenting on the Arab-French school for girls in Constantine, the inspector there conveyed the administration's concern that French standards of cleanliness be instilled with respect to body and clothes: "Cleanliness is not one of the virtues of the indigenous population and we have extreme difficulty imposing it on our students. . . . In the middle of winter many girls arrive barefoot at school. We had to buy them the shoes they needed."[42] This concern for students to wear shoes was a clear sign of the school's efforts to change native habits, since footwear was not common among the urban poor.

Healthy eating habits were another concern, and the issue of food for the morning and afternoon meals was a frequent topic of often acerbic debate between Madame Luce and the Bureaux Arabes. From the outset, she had encouraged families to send their daughters to her by giving them a sum of money and then by providing food at school. This gesture of hospitality toward the students was considered an important but costly incentive in school attendance (the annual budget allocated almost half the total for food—5,400 out of 11,250 francs).

The cost of providing student meals explains in part the frequent debates on the subject, but finances were only part of the story. Clearly, the authorities considered the girls as future mothers and wives who should learn the importance of eating a well-balanced diet, not only for their own health, but for the health of their future families. In June 1854 a second girls' school opened in Algiers, run by Noémie Chevalier, Luce's former assistant teacher. Chevalier adopted a new method with respect to the morning meal. Rather than preparing the meal for the students at school, parents were asked to provide a meal using a portion of the sum they were paid to send their daughters to school. The departmental Bureau Arabe inspected the school weekly to ensure the quality of this food. To the authorities' gratification the parents were not stingy, providing bread, soups, couscous, berkoukes (a North African dish similar to couscous), kebab, fried fish, fava beans, artichokes, potatoes, and even some oranges, dates, figs, and apples for dessert: "Health, gaiety and especially the appetite of the children were most satisfactory on every occasion."[43] A year later Madame Luce was asked to put the same policy in place and to respect the provisions of an *arrêté* (administrative decree) of 16 March 1855. This measure involved giving parents 4 francs per month but requiring in exchange that they provide a meal for their daughter. Families were then docked 15 centimes for every day of unauthorized absence or for meals judged inadequate. As a result, Madame Luce was obliged to keep strict records, sending to the prefect every evening a list of absent students or those without a meal.[44]

The daily inspections of students' cleanliness and the careful attention to their health and the quality of their food paralleled concerns expressed within primary and nursery schools in France at the time. Underwriting these concerns in Algeria, as in France, was the conviction that lower-class families exerted a bad influence on their children through slovenly habits and poor hygiene, so part of the schooling experience involved changing these habits. In late 1851 the minister of war even contemplated opening a female boarding school in Constantine, given the "bad advice" that students' families gave them.[45] Naturally, however, such a decision was a weighty one for both financial and cultural reasons. In the end, the French attempted such total means of changing native habits only within orphanages after the establishment of civilian rule in 1870.[46]

Another testimony to the moral underpinnings of this schooling experience can be seen in the constant concern to ensure students' punctuality, regular attendance, and habits of work through daily sewing lessons. Naturally, the latter had more vocational objectives as well, but in general the French sought to combat what they perceived were slothful habits among Moorish women. If sewing kept students busy, Eugénie Luce also tried to instill a serious attitude toward academic studies. In 1856 she refused to grant four of her student monitors their monthly bonus because they had shown "nonchalance in their homework."[47] This punishment was intended to warn others of the dangers of not working hard, while prizes helped stimulate good behavior.

The inspections do not detail the percentage of students who attended regularly versus those who did not, but they comment on the issue, generally noting that attendance was "satisfactory." When attendance was unsatisfactory, students were expelled. In 1854, for example, thirteen students left the school in the second trimester, eleven of them "expelled for the absence of punctuality and prolonged absence."[48] Clearly, Luce attempted to maintain standards of scholarly behavior, even though she had a financial incentive to leave students on the books.

Finally, the school reinforced traditional moral values through daily religious lessons and through the encouragement of charity. Inspection reports had no specific entry for moral issues, probably because the French were very careful to emphasize their respect for Muslim religious values. The Muslim assistant teacher offered lessons in reading and writing Arabic in addition to lessons on the Quran. For the authorities this attention to the religious sensibilities of the student body was far more than a nineteenth-century nod toward political correctness. Attracting students depended on convincing parents that the school would not engage in any form of religious proselytism (although cultural proselytism flourished). In deference to the school's clientele, the school adopted a calendar that respected Muslim holidays, closing school, for example, for the festivities of Eid el Fitr, which marked the end of Ramadan. Students enjoyed within the schoolroom an environment that did not clash with their religious beliefs and were encouraged to engage in the sort of charitable activities that characterized French lay and religious schools alike. In 1856, for example, the students raised 73.80 francs to send to France to succor those in need following flooding of the Loire River.[49] And as already mentioned, proceeds from the sale of needlework were frequently distributed to the poor within Algeria. In practice, moral lessons for girls differed little in Catholic France and Islamic Algeria.[50]

In many ways the attention to all nonacademic aspects of schooling paralleled the advice that inspectors showered on teachers in the French rural countryside, with an important difference: the messages inextricably inculcated a package of gender, class, and especially racial hierarchies that positioned the Muslim girl students very differently from their peasant or working-class counterparts in France. This positioning emerges most clearly in Madame Luce's elaborate prize-giving ceremonies, which were first and foremost a way for French authorities to showcase the generous underpinnings of the civilizing mission.

SHOWCASING THE EDUCATION OF MUSLIM GIRLS

Despite the French awareness that women in Algerian society were expected to lead secluded lives, Madame Luce's school for Muslim girls received widespread public attention. In particular, she organized with support from the local authorities biannual prize-giving ceremonies, beginning in October 1851, in addition to opening her school to passing photographers, journalists, painters, and visiting lady travelers.[51] She also actively promoted the products of her student workshop, sending examples of student embroideries to exhibitions in both Algeria and Europe. Although these efforts to publicize the school undoubtedly contributed to Luce's personal fame at the time, they were orchestrated with the explicit benediction of colonial authorities, who saw the school as a way to testify to their good faith in wishing to spread the fruits of French civilization to both local men and local women.

Prize-Giving Ceremonies

The organization of elaborate prize-giving ceremonies had a long tradition in French school culture for boys and girls alike. When Madame de Maintenon opened her famous school for noble girls at Saint-Cyr in 1686, she took pains to publicize the school through ceremonies that attracted the French aristocracy, most notably through the production of Racine's plays *Esther* and *Athalie*. Although French school authorities frequently deplored the lavishness of such public ceremonies, particularly in the nineteenth century, they remained an integral aspect of secondary school life that spread to primary schools, notably through mutual schools. The decision to stage such ceremonies in Algiers borrowed clearly from metropolitan practices, but the ceremonies took on additional meanings within the colonial context. They offered Luce an opportunity to restate publicly the educational and moral goals of her school, to attract broader support among both colonial and local notables, and, of course, to reward girls for their good behavior and intellectual achievements. The ceremonies were also moneymaking events for the school, since Luce organized a lottery for the woven goods and embroideries that her students produced.

Detailed descriptions of these ceremonies exist for the years between 1851 and 1854 when the school attracted the most attention. In general, Eugénie Luce began the festivities with an opening speech addressed to the students that paid careful attention to the presence of visiting dignitaries. In 1852 Luce insisted that the presence of military officers, civil servants, and other colonial dignitaries was testimony to the French concern to protect, encourage, and help young Muslim women to play their roles with dignity within poor families, as mothers and wives and occasional workers. "Persevere and rest assured that everywhere that a French sword gleams," she told her listeners, "a supporter and a protector will be there for womanhood, the oppressed and the weak."[52]

These stirring words were then followed by dialogues recited by the more advanced students capable of speaking the flowery prose that Madame Luce wrote for the occasion. These dialogues reinforced the message that her students should feel grateful to the French for providing them with a knowledge of French, the courage to work, and both moral and physical protection. At the same time, she did not hesitate to mention the more problematic aspects of the French conquest, notably the deaths and impoverishment that many faced. And yet, better to be poor and orphaned under the rule of the French than under the rule of the Turkish dey, as she had one of her students proclaim in a dialogue titled "The Past and the Future": "Yes, our father died a fighter, but one could not fall into the hands of a more generous victor. Rather than the infamy and shame generally accorded the vanquished and the feeble, witness the refuge into which we have been welcomed. . . . Here we experience the legitimate self-satisfaction, the supreme pleasure one always finds in useful work and the efforts of the mind and heart to work toward good." The young woman who took the opposing viewpoint in the dialogue, emphasizing French cruelty and oppression, was represented as an idle woman incapable of spreading happiness around her. In contrast, the young orphan's defense of the French civilizing mission argued that work, knowledge, and good taste would allow them future happiness in an Algeria filled with "gay and peaceful villages, easily accessible thanks to the roads built by the French army." The most eloquent speaker in this dialogue, Nefissa, was also the most successful of Madame Luce's students, and after this ceremony she was hired as a teaching assistant in the school.[53]

These elaborately choreographed occasions lasted in general about two hours and offered Madame Luce the opportunity to invite local notables, in addition to the parents of her pupils, to hear these speeches and admire the results of her students' academic and manual work. The actual numbers of guests present are difficult to ascertain. Whereas the boys' prize-giving ceremony took place in the central courtyard of the grand mosque, the girls' ceremony took place within the school itself, thus limiting the numbers who could attend. Reports indicate the frequent presence of Governor General Jacques-Louis Randon and his wife the Countess Randon, the rector of the Academy of Algiers, and the wives of high-ranking dignitaries, such as Madame Lapaine, the wife of the secretary general to the prefecture of Algiers.[54] But clearly, only a few of the parents could fit within the school, given the obligatory presence of 150 pupils. To enable these parents to follow the proceedings in 1854, Luce's granddaughter Henriette Belly, a student in the school at the time, translated from French into Arabic the fables that her Muslim peers recited.

The events were overtly propagandistic in their concern to demonstrate French generosity in spreading instruction.[55] To this extent they were clearly directed toward adults both in Algeria and in France. Reports on the ceremonies were reproduced in such venues as the official *Moniteur de l'Algérie* and the *Journal de l'Éducation Populaire*, as well as in almanacs.[56] But they were also special days for the students, who were placed on a stage, given roles to play, and received prizes of various sorts. Both the ceremony and the prizes distributed at the end (books and clothing) testify to the ways the school promoted both book learning and practical skills, and, of course, to the ways a moral dimension imbued both learning and sewing. A few book titles give a sense of the messages that the book prizes sought to convey: *The Angel of the House*, *Orphans or the Fruits of Education*, *One Should Never Lie*, and *The Little Mother*. In June 1854 the head student monitor, Hanisa bent Khelil, received three volumes on filial love, in addition to a history of the Ottoman empire in French and a book of conversations about religious holidays. The student monitor of the first class, Khera Bent Braham, received a volume called *Beauties of Christian Morality*, a rather surprising choice in a school that took such pains not to offend Muslim religious sensibilities. Such books were also used as prizes in metropolitan French schools.[57] Most students, however, went home not with books, but with pieces of clothing.

Displaying Goods: Local and Universal Exhibitions

Madame Luce's school probably achieved its greatest fame through the embroidered and woven cloth her students produced. By the mid-1850s, she not only used the afternoon school hours to teach her students how to sew, but she had established the workshop where older girls pursued these skills under the guidance of her French sewing mistress, Madame Dufraisne. This issue of opening a workshop was the object of much official discussion because the administration was convinced that religious orders and orphanages had basically cornered the market on these activities for women.[58] Although the authorities authorized the salary for a sewing mistress only in September 1855, inspectors spoke casually about the sewing workshop from early 1853 on, and it seems to have functioned almost from the outset of the school's existence. In June 1854 it was situated in a neighboring house, where women from the Turkish elite lived, the dames Omar Hassan Pacha.[59]

This workshop provided students with the opportunity to learn techniques in indigenous embroidery, gave ex-students an opportunity to earn a small livelihood through the sale of the products they produced within the workshop, and generated income for the school and its students.[60] Although the French authorities initially supported book learning over vocational skills, European women actively promoted the workshop and the Algerian goods produced within it from the beginning. On 4 January 1853 the school and its workshop were placed under the protection of Governor General Randon's wife, the Countess Randon, who acted as a patron for Luce throughout these years. Like the Empress Eugénie in France, who defended the cause of girls' education and professional opportunities, the Countess Randon also set in motion charitable activities to support Madame Luce in her efforts to promote the status of Muslim women. When the enterprising schoolteacher decided to organize a lottery to raise money for her school from the objects produced by her students, the countess offered her logistical help and her connections to make the event a visible success. The emperor's entourage bought up three hundred tickets, and Prince Napoleon purchased another five hundred. More importantly, the countess helped organize the exhibition of the goods for sale within the main salon of the governor general's residence.[61]

Discussion of these initiatives extended far beyond Algiers, thanks to a detailed article on the subject on 28 May 1853 in the popular illustrated monthly *L'Illustration*. The images reproduced in this article depict not just Madame Luce's school—which was described as a nursery school—but also the exhibition in the governor general's residence, where elegantly dressed European women are shown exploring the Algerian embroidered fineries.[62] Although the article is unsigned, the author mentions the artist's name: Charles Camino, who visited Algeria in 1853 and 1854. Wealthy Parisian and American collectors appreciated his line drawings and his miniatures. His drawing of Eugénie Luce is probably the first visual representation we have of her. She appears stern and distant, dressed in European clothing, overseeing the activity of a great number of young girls clothed in Moorish attire. The drawing of the lottery focuses more on the objects than on the visitors, with Horace Vernet's portrait of the emperor when he was president of the Second French Republic occupying the center background. The setting for Luce's school's lottery speaks eloquently for her visibility and her clout during these years.

Madame Luce achieved another degree of notoriety through her participation in the early universal exhibitions. The French organized the Exposition Universelle of 1855 in Paris following the Crystal Palace Exhibition in London in 1851. Like the British, who had included the manufactured productions of their empire, the French showcased their colonies at this exhibition.[63] Not surprisingly, given Madame Luce's effort to promote her school and workshop, she worked actively to have her students' handiwork present at the exhibition. Within the industrial division, 728 exhibitors from Algeria (representing both local and French artisans) presented objects weighing more than 7,563 kilos and worth

Drawing of Madame Luce's school in the early 1850s. The artist, Charles Camino, makes Luce the central character and highlights the diverse student body and the variety of activities taking place. Some girls are reading, others are listening or are involved in needlework activity in a setting that is clearly quite different from that of a French school. From *L'Illustration*, no. 1 (28 May 1853): 340.

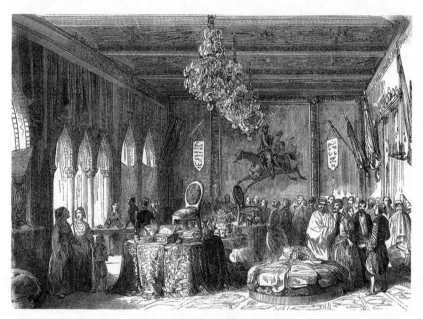

Lottery for Eugénie Luce's school in the Palace of the Governor General. The artist, Charles Camino, depicts European men and women as well as indigenous men and some children admiring the handiwork. From *L'Illustration*, no. 1 (28 May 1853): 340.

51,200 francs.[64] Men far outnumbered women among the Algerian exhibitors, but this did not deter Madame Luce, who presented the embroidery and lingerie of her Arab-French school for young Moorish women in the XIXth Section, entitled "European Industries and Industrial Arts," as well as pieces of indigenous embroidery in the twenty-third class.[65] In the latter category she won a second-class medal for her Arab-style embroideries, and she received a first-class medal in the twenty-fifth class of light clothing.[66]

Once again, *L'Illustration* used the Exposition Universelle as an opportunity to write about Algeria, the "prodigious fecundity of the African land" and the beauties of its artisanal productions. In the description of the Algerian products within the Ministry of War, Frédéric Lacroix—an ardent Arabophile, ex-prefect of the department of Algiers, and friend of Saint-Simonians—highlighted the elegant embroideries produced within Madame Luce's school and then described a visit to her institution and urged his readers to support it through the purchase of embroideries:

The Luce institution admits only indigenous students; it has existed for over ten years and has already harbored several generations of girls. At the moment she has 150 stu-

dents, Arabs, Kabyles, Negresses, etc. . . . The author of this article remembers with pleasure the moments he spent amidst this mixed population that Madame Luce directs
with such skill, his surprise the first time he heard the students speaking French with
incredible ease and the progress he saw among all these young minds in all aspects of
their studies. But when I visited, the school had not reached the degree of excellence
it now has in embroideries. We exort our women readers who have the means to be
charitable to go satisfy their desire for luxury by buying the magnificent scarves. . . . In
addition to adding an elegant and unusual object of apparel to their wardrobe, they will
also accomplish a good deed, because the product of the sale is then distributed among
the workers.[67]

Three years later, a former chief of the Bureaux Arabes, Ferdinand Hugonnet,
published another article about the Arab-French schools in Algeria in *L'Illustration*.
The images he selected emphasize a very gendered representation of colonial
schooling. In the boys' school, Auguste Depeille is drawn as an imposing presence
gesturing before a blackboard with the following sentence written in French: "My
children love France your new country." On the other hand, Luce is seated in a
corner while her students sew. True, a blackboard signals the existence of other
sorts of lessons, but the text on the board is in Arabic, not French. Boys, then,
are shown learning civics while the girls perfect more traditional skills and are
not encouraged to envision citizenship.[68]

Auguste Depeille, the head of Algiers's Arab-French school for boys, is represented here teaching
male students how to read French. This drawing comes from a photograph taken by Félix Jacques
Antoine Moulin in 1857. From *L'Illustration*, no. 1 (1858): 297.

Ecole de jeunes filles mauresques dirigée par Mme Luce (alger)

Sewing class in Eugénie Luce's school. Notice the map of North Africa as well as the use of blackboards typical in mutual schools. The students are grouped by their level of expertise in sewing or embroidering. Eugénie Luce sits in the corner with a student. The other adult Frenchwoman is Madame Dufraisne, the sewing mistress. The older Arab student sitting on the floor with students at her feet is probably Nefissa Bent Ali. Photograph by Félix Jacques Antoine Moulin, 1857. CAOM, 8 Fi/427/29.

L'Illustration reproduced drawings from photographs taken by Félix Jacques Antoine Moulin, who toured Algeria between 1856 and 1857. Thanks to an official letter of recommendation from the minister of war, Moulin produced some of the first official photographs of Algeria's local celebrities. His photos, which then appeared under the title "L'Algérie photographiée," focused on the indigenous populations but also included portraits of the governor general, the archbishop, and the military hierarchy present in Algeria at the time. In these early days of photography, the technology required that Moulin stage his portraits, with his subjects placed within spaces enclosed by wall hangings.[69]

Moulin took at least three photos of Luce's school in the course of his visit, representing three distinct moments in the school day. The first (p. 111) shows Madame Luce in her role as teacher. She points at a large map on the wall, and an older student monitor stands in front of a blackboard with the following proverb written on it: "The principle of wisdom, is the fear of God." Although not a realistic portrayal of a school day, since the girls are clustered on benches or sitting on the ground around Madame Luce rather than divided into small groups, it is nonetheless clearly an image of a school. The second picture shows a male inspector in the school, with student monitors leading various activities and an arrangement that seems more realistic within a monitorial school. The third picture, already mentioned, shows the girls sewing, and it seems noteworthy that this is the image that circulated most widely at the time. Luce's students are the only images in his collection that represent indigenous *school* girls. Unlike Moulin's other photos of women, which tended to exaggerate their exotic otherness, these photos show a wide variety of girls being shaped to resemble more closely Frenchwomen. The girl students are very much on show, however, as in the prize-giving ceremonies. The contrast between this visibility and the surviving knowledge about these students merits closer attention.

Lesson in Eugénie Luce's school. The older student in front of the blackboard is a monitor teaching a moral lesson in both French and Arabic. Photograph by Félix Jacques Antoine Moulin, 1857. CAOM, 8 Fi/427/28.

ELUSIVE GIRL STUDENTS

Between 1845 and 1861, 1,035 students attended Madame Luce's school for some period of time. The regular inspections have left information about numbers as well as the occasional name and the reasons why a student left the school. Prize-giving ceremonies also often recorded the names of those who received prizes, including the student monitors, about whom there is slightly more material than for other students. Visitors sometimes described the students, as did Bessie Rayner Parkes in 1861:

They wear full trousers and jackets; their hair is twisted into long pigtails behind and tightly bound with green ribbon, on the crown of their heads are little velvet caps embroidered with gold thread; their nails are tinged with henna; their legs, from the knees to the ankles are bare, and are then finished off with anklets and slippers. They talk rapidly in an unknown tongue, and sit writing French exercises and doing sums on black boards, or sit under the trees of a sunny yard at the back, sewing frocks and towels and dusters, like any other school-girls all the world over.[70]

Although this description certainly catches the atmosphere for the outside observer, it does not tell us much about the girls who attended the school and what they got out of their schooling.

At the moment when her school became part of the network of Arab-French schools, Madame Luce sent the authorities a summary of her early results. In the five years between July 1845 and August 1850, 245 girls had attended her school, with approximately 90 to 120 present each day.[71] In the following years, her school steadily attracted more students, in part because of the attention it garnered and the financial incentive parents received to send their daughters there. The regular reports between 1852 and 1856 show numbers ranging from a low of 88 students in February 1855 to a high of 161 in the first half of 1854. On average, Madame Luce had a full house even after the decision to create a second Arab-French school for girls in Algiers in 1854. These numbers also explain Luce's decision to move into a larger house on the rue de Toulon in 1852. But numbers shed little light on who these girls were, and the information about what they became is frustratingly limited.

Poor Girls or the Future Wives of Elites?

From the outset, Madame Luce had presented her school as a charitable response to indigenous poverty but also as a means of influencing the wealthy. She wanted her school to welcome all classes of Muslim society, she wrote. In reality she acknowledged in several reports that wealthy families were reluctant to enroll their daughters despite her having recruited as her Arab mistress a woman of recognized good birth and educational qualifications. This woman, Zhéra Bent Braham, was the daughter of a Turk and the former teacher of the children of the last dey of Algiers, according to Dr. Auguste Warnier, who wrote admiringly about Madame Luce's school in 1851.[72] It was not surprising, however, that Madame Luce had difficulty attracting daughters from elite families. The same situation prevailed in France, where elementary schools catered almost exclusively to the poor, with the wealthy either educating their daughters at home or placing them with social peers in boarding schools. In 1851 a report on Luce's school confirmed that "almost all [students] come from families who have fallen into complete destitution," so that every year the authorities spent between 1,000 and 1,200 francs to purchase books and clothes for the school.[73] Although the majority of students probably came from poor families, scattered evidence suggests that the school welcomed a mixture of students in terms of both ethnicity and class.

The photographs taken in 1857 show students who represent a range of ethnic origins and ages. A number of the girls appear very light-skinned and possibly European; others are clearly black Africans or of mixed race; and a majority seem North African. During this period French statistics divided the population into relatively imprecise groups: Moors, Arabs, Jews, Negroes, and Koulouglis (a Turkish term designating the offspring of local Arab women and Turkish men).[74] For contemporaries, the term "Moor" referred to urban inhabitants whereas "Arabs" and "Kabyles" came from rural areas. Given the school's location in Algiers, Moorish students would have predominated, and this explains why it was often described as a "school for Moorish girls." The school lists often state specifically, however, that a student was a "Kabyle," a "Turk," or a "Negress." Presumably, the others were "Moors" or Arabs. A British visitor in the late 1850s noted the presence of Jewish girls: "There were several little Jewesses squatting most amicably among the Mauresques, conspicuous only by their simpler robe of colored stuff and a conical cap of red velvet, tipped with gold lace, with a little gilt tassel depending from it, that was most coquettishly on the side of the head."[75] The same visitor also noted the range of student ages, which he judged to be between five and fifteen years.

Somewhat more unexpectedly, Eugénie Luce also had a few French students, whom she argued helped in the teaching of French, just as French boys attended

Depeille's school. Seven European students appear on various lists, including Henriette Belly, Luce's granddaughter, and Ernestine Dufraisne, the illegitimate daughter of Madame Dufraisne. Alongside these two, five other European students attended the school: Camille Maille, Émilie Salvador, Joséphine Ventre, Marie Allix, and Maria Robert. The latter, the daughter of an employee for the military, was born in Mustapha in 1848. Her name appears on a list of students receiving prizes in 1855, when she was seven years old and had recently lost her mother. It seems likely that her father knew Madame Luce and felt more comfortable placing his daughter in her school than in one of the numerous schools for European girls in Algiers. Still, such European girls were a rarity within a school where Arabic predominated.

Groups of sisters attended the school, but it is difficult to know more than that about their origins. The students are identified for the most part as "daughter of" ("bent"): Zohra Bent Mohammed or Mimi Bent Abd el Kader, for example. A few are listed as Negresses or Mulatto, testimony to the ethnic mix revealed in the photographs. From the beginning Madame Luce took in orphaned girls who were sent to her at times from afar. In August 1847, for example, she welcomed three orphans from Constantine: Aïïka, Seheia, and Zora Mohammed. In 1861 Bessie Rayner Parkes reported that Aïïka, now a widow, had become submistress of needlework in the school in Constantine and had taken Zora under her custody; Seheia had been adopted by a family in Bouzareah.[76] When a second school for Muslim girls was opened in 1854, Luce sent seven orphaned students from her school to attend the new institution. These girls came from the Maison de refuge, an orphanage next to the new school.[77] As in other colonial contexts, orphaned children were prime candidates for cultural experimentation since they had no families to protest. The school lists also indicate the presence of girls whose physical disabilities left them in a precarious social position. In 1853 three students were described as "deaf and dumb." Despite this significant handicap, one of them, Khadoudja Himmi, was awarded a prize for her sewing skills in the most advanced class in 1855.[78]

Luce's greatest success story concerned the orphaned girl Nefissa Bent Ali, who was among one of her first students in 1847. Her skill in mastering French explains why she was chosen in 1851 at the age of fourteen to go to Amboise to act as an interpreter. A year later she received the school's prix d'honneur, and in 1853 she was earning a salary as the indigenous teaching assistant in the school. Under Luce's guidance she became the first Muslim woman to pass successfully the exams for the French teaching diploma, the *brevet de capacité*, on 16 April 1856. Sadly, however, her teaching career was cut short when she died of consumption in the spring of 1861. Her obituary appeared in both the newspaper *L'Akhbar, Journal d'Algérie*, and the *English Woman's Journal*. The latter wrote: "It was grievous to see her on her bed of sickness, above which was a shelf of French books of all kinds—strange sight in the room of an Arab or a Moresque—which she could never use more." This homage emphasizes her exceptionality and testifies to the impression she made as one of the first "professional" Muslim women.[79]

Whereas the authorities had the impression that Luce's school attracted primarily the very poor, archival sources reveal a certain degree of social mixing. Inspection reports indicate that some students left the school to marry. The husband's profession offers some insight into the social connections the school provided for young women. In 1853 thirty-four students left the school, eight in order to get married. Half wedded workers of some sort: two girls married agricultural laborers from the plain, and two others remained in Algiers, marrying a sailor and an unidentified "Moor from Algiers." The other four married artisans, property owners, or small shopkeepers: a mason, a café owner, a man who worked in the public baths (*maître de bain*), and the owner of a silk-weaving business in Blidah. These professions show that some of Luce's students found husbands among men who were not destitute, although clearly she had a vested interest in letting this be known. In 1854 Fathma Hammed, for example, married a grocer in Algiers and Zohra Moh'ammed married a gardener at an agricultural school.[80] Still, by the 1850s Madame Luce's earlier affirmation that she sought to educate the daughters of the rich and poor alike was clearly inaccurate. The decision to pay the families of students to attend the school encouraged the very poor and discouraged the local elites.

As a result, Eugénie Luce and Auguste Depeille both made a plea to the authorities in 1853 to create a separate school for students from the "superior classes." Just as in France, they argued, elite families hesitated to place their children with those of the poor, so they wanted to set up school in a different location and charge families a sum of money rather than paying them. The prefect of Algiers supported this project, writing, "It is essentially by modifying the intelligence and the unfortunate tendency to do nothing among young Muslims that we can hope to effect the fusion which has begun to make itself felt." Still, he worried that charging money for such an education went a step too far, given "Muslim stinginess."[81] The minister of war, the maréchal Armand-Jacques Leroy de Saint-

Arnaud, however, was firmly opposed to such an innovation: "It is completely counter to the spirit of this administration and the interests of the indigenous population and the necessary economy that must preside over public expenditures to create a special institution for rich children, to sanction in this fashion a division of the inhabitants into two classes while setting them up side by side and imposing on the local and municipal budget sacrifices in favor of families who are considered wealthy."[82] The minister did not disguise the financial considerations that argued against such a creation at a time when the numbers of students in the Arab-French schools were steadily rising. Despite his opposition, Governor General Randon, whose wife knew Madame Luce well, continued to push for the creation of such a school, arguing that the special relations between the school director and local families served as a guarantee for success. The minister of war, however, was not prepared to try.[83]

Although Madame Luce's school continued to flourish and attract attention during the second half of the 1850s, this unsuccessful bid to create a school for the daughters of the indigenous elite was a sign of events to come. In 1854 the authorities decided to pursue their efforts with respect to the poor by opening a second Arab-French school for girls along the same lines as Luce's school. This was a clear attempt to reduce the influence—and salary—of Madame Luce, since she received money for every student over the number of one hundred. The appearance of a new school immediately reduced her student numbers and created a potential source of competition. The epistolary exchanges testify to Luce's hostility to the project, and once she realized she could not successfully prevent its opening, her concern shifted to ensure her influence over the new director. The prefect had recommended the appointment of Madame Parent, the director of the Arab-French school in Constantine, suggesting that Noémie Chevalier, Luce's assistant teacher, take over the school in Constantine. Luce, however, supported Chevalier's appointment in Algiers as the lesser evil, given her influence over the young woman, a relative, whom she had recruited in France a year earlier. Luce successfully resisted the prefect's efforts to appoint Parent and placed her young family member as director of the new school on the rue Kléber. The school lasted only four years, perhaps in part because of Luce's efforts to denigrate it. The prefect complained in particular that Luce described the new school as "a reform house where students would be poorly treated and very poorly fed."[84]

The arguments surrounding this new school, as well as the suggestion that Luce's students were only from the poorest families, paved the way for more pointed criticisms that would arise during the late 1850s. It seems clear from the reports concerning the Arab-French schools for girls that the inspectors had difficulty reading local social categories and were somewhat unclear about the role of women within indigenous families. Were women the "slaves" of their husbands within the home, or sensuous, languid creatures caged within a harem? In 1854 the inspection of Parent's school in Constantine highlighted such uncertainties: "The time has not yet come to declare definitively the significance of these institutions. Peevish minds claim that the young girls only find pleasures and the sort of knowledge that allows them more easily to be seduced. Better to think the contrary, that they leave school with orderly and studious habits that render them useful; moralizers tend to give women a role that they do not yet occupy within Arab families."[85] In the years that followed, the conviction that the French civilizing mission should include indigenous women increasingly came under attack. Observers began to question whether the schooling offered to Muslim girls really brought the sort of benefits that Madame Luce claimed. Did poor girls acquire industrious work habits and recognize the moral underpinnings of the civilization being taught? Or were they led astray, seduced by the pleasures that French culture offered? By the end of the 1850s, as the tide in favor of the education of Muslim girls turned, these issues emerged with new intensity.

5

FROM BOOK LEARNING
TO EMBROIDERY

Reorienting the Civilizing Mission
(1857–1875)

The years leading up to Napoleon III's declaration in 1865 that he envisioned Algeria not as a colony but as an Arab kingdom signaled a downturn in Madame Luce's political fortunes. The whiff of immorality that had plagued her from her early dealings with colonial officials heightened in the late 1850s and spread to her students. Administrative reports suggested that her students were not raising the moral tone of Muslim families; rather, they were becoming concubines for Europeans or mere prostitutes. Journalists dwelt on the dangers of *déclassement*: too much education pulled young women from their social milieu, making them unattractive marriage prospects, an argument used throughout France to limit educational achievements for lower-class Frenchwomen. These criticisms from within the military and civilian administrations were a partial response to shifting power alliances between the French military, the growing settler constituency, and the indigenous populations that had a visible effect on the educational policy being pursued in Algeria.

The Saint-Simonian Ismaÿl Urbain directly influenced the emperor's conversion to an Arabophile position, which led him to propose measures granting greater political and economic rights to the native populations. Like his advisors, Napoleon III did not lose sight of ethnic hierarchies and saw these measures as an effort to mold Arabs "to our laws, accustom them to our domination and convince them of our superiority."[1] And in reality the various reforms promulgated during this period, such as the Sénatus-consulte of 1863 on land tenure or the first attempt at naturalization with the Sénatus-consulte of 1865, had ambiguous effects for the native population. Racial tensions and increasingly vehement debates between Arabophiles and Arabophobes also marked the 1860s, influencing the legislation that was passed. Less recognized, however, is the way gender played into these struggles, notably around the issue of polygamy that so troubled the legislators in their discussions about the naturalization of Muslims.[2] During these years as settlers and officers jostled for power, Muslim women increasingly disappeared as autonomous subjects of discussion, their plight tied up with their degraded status in a polygamous society.[3]

This is the necessary context for understanding the vicissitudes of Madame Luce's institution. The voices that questioned the wisdom of educating Muslim girls were increasingly dominant, including within the General Council of Algiers that funded her school. The decision to withdraw this funding in 1861 signaled an important change in cultural politics: winning women over to the civilizing mission was no longer seen as a priority in the grand colonial project. For the girls themselves, these changes meant that book learning ceased to become a goal for schooling. In its place, needlework and the training necessary to pursue a trade took on a new importance. From this point on, Madame Luce would be recognized not for the dialogues her students recited in prize-giving ceremonies, but for the oriental-style embroideries her apprentice workers produced for sales and exhibitions.

Madame Luce's institution sat within the more general context of debates about educational policies in Algeria. The juxtaposition of a wide variety of schools—European schools, "traditional" schools run by Muslims, and the Arab-French schools run by the Bureaux Arabes—produced an institutional complexity that contemporaries had trouble clarifying—as have historians since. Within this complexity, historians have often neglected to trace the fate of indigenous girls' schooling. I highlight how gendered debates at the time determined the withdrawal of support for Luce's school and erased the figure of the Muslim girl pupil from the colonial agenda. In her place emerged the embroiderer who had no pretensions to becoming French, but who nonetheless was an indigenous woman with a useful skill.

GENDERING THE POLITICS OF EDUCATION IN COLONIAL ALGERIA

Eugénie Luce's influence with respect to indigenous schooling waned in the late 1850s as the French sought to consolidate their presence throughout Algeria. In the process colonial politics with respect to schooling came once again under scrutiny. These politics varied considerably from the mid-1840s until the end of the nineteenth century; positions ranged from a wish to achieve a form of fusion through the Arab-French schools, to a theoretical commitment as of 1867 to "assimilation" of the Muslim population through schooling in écoles mixtes (mixed schools), to a generalized hostility to anything but practical training. These debates about the nature and goal of the civilizing mission in Algeria took on a particular importance during the second decade of Napoleon III's rule in France. Not only did the emperor take a specific interest in Algeria, following two visits in 1860 and 1865, but he also surrounded himself with men who had strong opinions about the role of education in a modernizing society, most notably Ismaÿl Urbain for things Algerian and Victor Duruy for things French. One of the ironies of history is that the man who proclaimed himself emperor and manhandled public liberties from 1852 until 1870 nonetheless encouraged the development of schooling both in France and in Algeria. Duruy, his minister of public instruction (1863–1869), promoted lay secondary courses for girls and less elitist secondary schooling for boys, mandated the spread of primary schools for girls along the same terms as for boys, and offered the first serious encouragement to professional education for both sexes. Although Duruy had little direct influence on educational initiatives in Algeria, he declared himself "Algerian in his heart" and was clearly receptive to the Arabophile Saint-Simonians, who saw Arab-French schooling as a means of conquering the hearts and minds of the indigenous elites.[4]

The concern for developing schooling, however, encountered a changing social reality in Algeria, notably the growth of a French settler community with its own educational priorities. By 1861 the French civilian population had acquired demographic clout and represented almost 60 percent of a European population totaling almost two hundred thousand inhabitants. Moreover, this population increasingly demanded greater civil rights while contesting the administrative sovereignty of the military regime.[5] The growth of an Arabophobe settler population, as well as the massive 1864 revolt of the Awlad Sidi al-Shaykh (a confederation of Muslim brotherhoods) in western Algeria, testified to the failure of efforts to reconcile the different populations in Algeria. As a result, both settlers and the indigenous population offered resistance to official policies.[6] In this context, the debates about schooling took on an explicitly political tone, pushing indigenous girls into the background. The heady experimentations of the early years of colonial rule gave way to increasing dogmatism as ethnic and gender hierarchies hardened in a context of increasing colonial exploitation.

Schooling European Boys and Girls in Algeria
Historians have primarily focused on indigenous schooling since it represented a critical and often criticized aspect of the civilizing mission. But the educational

landscape and the debates it generated were in reality more complex, particularly if one includes girls. From the outset, Eugénie Luce operated in a context in which the schooling of girls had a different cultural valence than that of boys. As a result, understanding the reorientation in her institution requires a recognition that for her contemporaries her institution was positioned alongside European schools or workshops.

In France, opportunities for girls' schooling soared during the years between the Falloux Law of 1850 and the fall of the Second Empire in 1870 despite the conservative political climate. Although religious teaching orders ran a majority of the new schools and offered lessons that emphasized feminine obedience and docility, not independent thinking and the virtues of autonomy, they nonetheless taught rural and working-class girls to read and to write, offering a means for some to question the class and gender codes so prevalent in France. Among the more interesting evolutions of the 1860s was the emergence of a debate about vocational education and the creation of schools that offered more practical "professional" training. For example, in 1861 the Congrégation de la Mère de Dieu altered the educational program they offered at the schools of the Legion of Honor in order to teach vocational skills, recognizing in this reorientation that women needed the skills to allow them to work.[7] At the same time the Saint-Simonian Élisa Lemonnier created the Société pour l'enseignement professionnel des femmes (Society for the Professional Teaching of Women) and opened a vocational school for girls in Paris. Although her program more radically challenged gender norms of the period than that of the teaching nuns, what she offered in terms of vocational schooling was quite similar. More generally, the 1860s represented a moment in French schooling when issues of vocational training for both boys and girls were raised. These debates inevitably crossed the Mediterranean along with the schoolteachers who accompanied the settler population.

In Algeria the numbers of schools for Europeans increased steadily as the authorities sought to stabilize the migrant population. The government published official statistics in 1862 that confirmed the growth of educational opportunities for the school-age European population. In primary education, 470 schools offered instruction to 33,065 students almost equally divided between boys and girls (16,872 boys and 16,193 girls). Religious orders educated 72.3 percent of female pupils.[8] Here, as in France, they were in the forefront of this expansion, following settlers as they extended their authority over the territory and opening schools throughout the country. The Soeurs de la Doctrine Chrétienne de

Nancy alone ran fifty schools educating 8,510 female pupils.[9] Officials bragged about these figures, arguing that schooling per inhabitant in higher, secondary, and primary education was higher in Algeria than in France (1 student per 6.7 inhabitants compared with 1 per 8.7 inhabitants, respectively). But these figures concerned only European girls and boys.

Adult schools, secondary institutions, and higher education also expanded during these years. For the middle classes, a *lycée* in Algiers, four *collèges*, and one private school run by Jesuits existed in 1864 catering to 1,109 students, a figure the authorities deemed "satisfactory."[10] In 1859 an École préparatoire de médecine et de pharmacie welcomed its first students, including five indigenous students. This was the first step in the creation of what would become the University of Algiers. The emergence of a network of institutions from nursery schools to higher education changed the setting in which authorities debated indigenous schooling.

Schooling Indigenous Boys

Historians agree that during the Second Empire the numbers of traditional Muslim schools decreased dramatically, even if hard figures are difficult to come by.[11] This was a product of a number of forces, among them the support of the Bureaux Arabes for Arab-French schools in military territories. These schools were seen as "the most powerful means the Government has to push the indigenous populations on the path to progress and civilization."[12] The brief period when the office of the Government General was abolished and absorbed into the new Ministry of Algeria and the Colonies (1858–1860) was followed by a restoration of military rule and the heightened sovereignty of the Bureaux Arabes as the privileged interlocutors between the indigenous populations and the French. As Osama Abi-Mershed has shown, the most aggressive phase of the French commitment to Arab-French schooling for boys occurred between 1856 and 1867 when forty-eight of the sixty-one dual schools were founded.[13]

In the wake of the French defeat of the Kabyle uprising of 1857 and the return of military rule in 1860–1861, the Bureaux Arabes renewed their commitment to Arab-French schools and encouraged their creation beyond urban areas, although only for boys. These schools, however, did not exist in an institutional vacuum, and the debates surrounding them were inevitably linked to the existence of indigenous schools, be they traditional *zawiya*s or the madrasas created in 1850 to train Muslims for different functions in the colonial administration.[14] As the years passed, it became increasingly clear that the indigenous population was not enthusiastic about the Arab-French schools and viewed them as a burden, like forced labor.

As the French struggled to find the appropriate instruments to enact their "moral conquest" of Algeria, a number of new institutions appeared. On 14 March 1857 Governor General Randon responded to Saint-Simonian pressure and founded the Collège impérial arabe-français in an attempt to spread French values among an Algerian elite.[15] Created at the same time that the decision was made to no longer pay students to attend the elementary-level Arab-French schools, this institution represented an effort to form an intermediary category of colonial personnel. As in French secondary institutions, the Collège impérial offered boarding possibilities for the indigenous students, who also could apply for scholarships. The program of study followed that of special secondary education in its more scientific and practical orientations, but its objectives remained firmly anchored in the civilizing ideal.[16] As officials in the Bureaux Arabes argued, the study of French, Arabic, mathematics, and mechanics should bring about the union of the East and the West. But from the outset the institution suffered from suspicion, not only within indigenous circles, but also from the civilian educational authorities. Rector Delacroix, for example, thought that indigenous elites should send their sons to the *lycée*, not to this new creation, which only reinforced the separation between the indigenous and the settler populations; the fact that he had no control over the Collège was also undoubtedly a factor in his hostility.

Dr. Nicolas Perron, the erstwhile director of the school of medicine in Cairo, was placed in charge, while Auguste Depeille, Luce's equivalent in the boys' Arab-French school, took responsibility as his assistant.[17] Despite the long professional experience of these two Arabic speakers, the Collège impésrial had difficulty from the outset attracting both teachers and students, even though fellowships existed for Arab students. It opened in January 1858 with fifty-five indigenous boarding students and sixty European students; in the early 1860s the Europeans continued to outnumber the indigenous students. Above all, however, the school failed to produce a significant number of cultural intermediaries. After seven years of existence, it boasted ninety-nine indigenous graduates, but a mere handful had continued their education or careers in French military or colonial institutions: seven entered military academies, two entered training schools, and three entered the colonial administration. Not surprisingly, the civilian regime that came to power in Algeria in 1870 ended this experiment in cultural assimilation that had achieved such meager success, and a decree of 28 October 1871 ordered the students of the Collège imperial to join those of the French *lycée*.[18]

For the advocates of assimilation, the lack of bilingual teachers significantly limited efforts to promote Arab-French schooling. In response to this lack, the first Algerian normal school opened its doors in Mustapha in January 1866 with seven European students and three indigenous ones. Although there was a need to train French teachers who could speak Arabic, the program followed was that of a French normal school; out of a weekly course load of thirty-four hours, only three were spent learning Arabic. In practice, then, this school focused on training French teachers for European schools. Nor did the few Muslim students present graduate to become French-speaking schoolteachers in these years. Only five indigenous students graduated between 1866 and 1869; three returned to their families, and one joined the cavalry school in Saumur.[19] The development of a bilingual teaching corps occurred only after 1883 when a decree extended to Algeria the French Ferry Laws concerning obligatory, free, and lay primary education.[20]

As the program in the normal school testified, by the mid-1860s many colonial administrators had become less sanguine about cultural assimilation occurring within the sort of hybrid structure represented by the Arab-French school even though the number of such schools grew and a second Collège arabe-français was opened in Constantine in 1867. Support for such schools waned as civil authorities gained ascendancy and a strong Arabophobe movement contributed to the discrediting of Arab-French schools.

This was the context that produced yet another measure intended to promote better relations among the different populations in Algeria. In 1867 Governor General Patrice de MacMahon passed a circular reflecting the emperor's concern to create schools that mingled Catholic, Jewish, and Muslim students. Rather than the creation of new institutions, the circular encouraged the development of "mixed" public communal schools whose task was to effect "the fusion of populations of diverse origins and races who inhabit the country."[21] The new municipal organization of 1868 reinforced the influence of civil versus military authorities, who were responsible in municipal councils for the financing of schools. On the ground, however, most municipalities saw no reason to maintain both municipal "French schools" and Arab-French schools, and so the latter progressively disappeared or were transformed into municipal schools. By the early 1870s the expression "Arab-French" had all but disappeared from administrative vocabulary. The numbers of Muslim students attending these schools also declined, as a consequence of racial tensions. In 1870 a mere thirteen hundred indigenous students (out of a population of more than 2.1 million) attended schools or *collèges* established by the Bureaux Arabes, and of this number only a handful were girls attending Madame Parent's school in Constantine.[22]

The triumph of civilian rule after 1870 and the hardening of racial lines that resulted in the creation of a Code de l'indigénat in 1881 meant the end of these early efforts to promote assimilation through Arab-French schooling.[23] In 1882 Madame Luce died in France, after having spent thirty years of her life promoting first schooling for indigenous girls and then vocational training. Although this evolution in her emphasis was in part a pragmatic reorientation imposed by the shifting climate of opinion in Algeria, it also reflected on a small scale the very real hesitations in French colonial educational policy. Should education and schools seek to make the Algerians more like the French? Or should they accept differences and seek to train subjects who would aid in the effort to make the colony profitable? Should schools focus on book learning and the mastery of language skills? Or should they primarily emphasize practical skills? These questions applied, however, mainly to boys; debates about girls' schooling revealed even more doubts about the wisdom of providing schooling at all.

GENDER AND DISILLUSION:
ON THE DANGERS OF EDUCATING MUSLIM WOMEN

The political and administrative changes of this time had clear repercussions for the schooling of Muslim girls. In the general satisfaction about rising numbers of schools and pupils, it was easy to forget that virtually the entire female indigenous population had no access to either French or traditional Muslim institutions. This neglect was not, of course, unusual in French colonies. In the sub-Saharan colonies of French West Africa, girls consistently were underrepresented. As late as 1935 public primary education welcomed 8,795 girls compared with 53,269 boys.[24] The decision in 1850 to include girls' schools in the decree establishing Arab-French schools had seemed to herald, however, a more egalitarian vision of indigenous colonial schooling. A decade later this vision was clearly under attack.

Questioning the Uses of Female Literacy

Evidence of disillusion can be found in the French newspapers published in Algeria. The director of *L'Akhbar, Journal de l'Algérie,* A. Bourget, was among the first to strike a distinctly negative note with respect to the project of educating Muslim girls and even offering them manual training in sewing. *L'Akhbar* ("news" in Arabic) was among the most important colonial newspapers of the period. Published weekly in both French and Arabic, it sought to address issues of concern to both the European and indigenous populations.[25] The paper reproduced the decree that created Arab-French schools in 1850, reported on the dates when students were expected to enter schools in the fall, and even noted the names of both girl and boy students who received prizes. In 1852 the journalist L. Toulouze, who frequently covered school-related subjects, wrote a long laudatory article about the prize-giving ceremony at Madame Luce's school in which he described the French schoolteacher as the "Campan of French Africa," referring to the woman Napoleon Bonaparte had appointed as the first director of his famous schools of the Legion of Honor in 1807. In this article Toulouze waxed lyrical about Madame Luce's "intelligent courage, which had surmounted all obstacles, and the achievements of her creative will." As evidence of this success, he highlighted the presence in 1852 of 117 young women who were receiving the gift of an intellectual and professional education. This education managed, without violating their religious beliefs, to moralize them and encouraged them and their families to "respect and love France . . . France, which has drawn them from their lives of nonchalance and ignorance to make them into intelligent and useful women."[26]

By 1856, however, Madame Luce's efforts were no longer appreciated with the same enthusiasm, testimony to the changing political and cultural climates. This is apparent in the article that the paper's director, Bourget, published about the "situation of the Moorish population." Although Bourget wrote positively about a proposal to create an artisanal training school for the male indigenous population, he was frankly skeptical about the need to educate indigenous girls. In essence, he argued that the gender equality in evidence in the creation of Arab-French schools for both boys and girls was misplaced and that the early concern to educate Muslim girls had been premature: "The more we consider this delicate question, the more we conclude that generous intentions were misguided and that we began with what should have concluded our efforts. We were proud to use women to regenerate Muslim society and we lost sight of the fact that in Muslim families women are in an inferior position, they are the servants of their husbands and their male children. As a result, offering a certain level of instruction to young girls had the unfortunate effect of highlighting their difference from their ignorant fellow male Muslims." He went on to state that elementary education and professional training for boys should have been the primary objective in order to give men a livelihood and the means to support women and children. Only then would they be in a position to appreciate the benefits of education and to seek educated wives. The commitment to girls' schooling and training was an error unless Muslim women could use these talents within workshops and sell their products for gain.[27]

Doubts about the usefulness of teaching Muslim girls to read and write continued during the late 1850s and were reinforced by budgetary concerns to reduce the cost of the French investment in the Arab-French schools. Together these factors contributed to rendering Luce's position in the French colonial hierarchy increasingly tenuous. In 1857 the unofficial decision to pay students 2 francs a day to attend both the boys' and the girls' schools was revoked. At the same time concern about urban poverty led the French emperor to support the creation in Algiers of a Muslim Welfare Bureau, which shifted attention from education to welfare and work.[28] For Madame Luce, this meant that a nursery school for girls younger than seven and a workshop for those older than thirteen were opened, draining both pupils and student monitors from her school. In the space of a year, her school went from educating 125 to 76 girls; Mademoiselle Chevalier's school suffered a similar loss, declining from 110 to 63 students.

In 1858 the decision to have Eugénie Luce's school visited by a group of women inspectors was clearly a response to the official perception that perhaps it was time to reconsider support for the schooling of indigenous girls. The women who conducted this inspection were the wives of local French notables. The baronness de Céry signed the eleven-page report, which was sent to the prefect of Algiers on 7 December 1858. The authors offered a resounding defense of Luce's institution, rebutting point by point the criticisms that were in the air. Their specific concern was to reintegrate the students who had been siphoned off to the nursery school or the workshop and to establish the school as an *école-ouvroir* (school workshop). Here young girls would acquire some learning, but especially they would learn to work and would receive payment for their work. The inspectors argued that the creation of a nursery school was an uninformed decision to impose European traditions on a non-European culture. On the contrary, rather than encouraging Muslim women to send their young children to a nursery school, and indeed, paying them money to do so, it would be far more useful to encourage the development of maternal feelings among these women: "Do not seek to weaken these feelings, let Muslim women care for their young children, and do not seek to attract these children to our schools until they are old enough for our educational and moralizing goals to reach their minds and hearts." The inspectors also opposed the existence of the workshop because of the need to envision education and work as a coherent whole. Maintaining a separate workshop was not only costly for the administration, but it undermined the chances of success for the school. Work and morality were tightly intertwined in the inspectors' rhetoric as they argued, "It is our duty to seek to moralize them and it is by work alone that this will be achieved."[29]

The report recognized the accusations of immorality that surrounded Luce's school: "It has been stated without proof that the instruction given to these young girls has not promoted morality and that many have later acquired a reputation for their misbehavior. This reproach is unfounded!" A few girls may have strayed from the straight and narrow, but the same was true of students attending the best French lay and religious schools and so the blame could not be laid on the schoolteachers, who offered only good examples, the inspectors wrote. This argument about morality was then used to protest against the decision to fire the elderly women who had earned a few centimes accompanying students to and from the school every day: "Our responsibility ends at the family's threshold, but in the walk from home to school, if we do not accompany them who knows what influences they might experience." The report called for the closure of the nursery school, the union of the workshop with the school, the reestablishment of women *conductrices*, and the merger of Mademoiselle Chevalier's school with that of Madame Luce's, recognizing that student numbers were not sufficient to support two such schools in Algiers.

A note written by Luce appended to this report in the archives shows that the report was taken seriously. On 7 March 1859 Chevalier's school was joined with that of the older, more experienced woman, and the separate workshop and nursery school both disappeared. Nonetheless, Luce complained that her request to obtain authorization to combine work with instruction in her school had been refused. As a result, students who wanted to earn money for their work were transferred from the school register to that of the workshop. In this fashion twelve of her students earned a total of 1,407.15 francs in the space of six months, but at the cost of leaving the school. From this point, Madame Luce would devote her considerable energy to defending the principle of work study.

Questioning Female Morality

Teaching indigenous girls to speak French lost favor between 1858 and 1861 in the context of considerable administrative reorganization. In 1858 general councils were created within each province, representing a new step in the politics of as-similation; members were appointed by the emperor and included both civilian and military figures, Frenchmen and indigenous notables.[30] The new concern to listen, to some extent, to the voices of Arab men would have a direct effect on Madame Luce's fortunes. By this time, as well, initial enthusiasms had died down with respect to the schooling of indigenous girls. General Yusuf, a former military interpreter, for example, supported the idea of Arab-French schools for boys but not for girls, writing, "I have not yet been able to imagine the path that might lead us through the barriers that retain the imprisoned [indigenous] woman."[31]

In the debates about what institutions would best serve the French civiliz-ing mission in Algeria, moral issues quickly surfaced in the discussions about Luce's school between 1860 and 1861. These issues were not new, since, as we have seen, a climate of suspicion had surrounded Eugénie Luce from the out-set of her public persona after her extramarital affair with Louis Luce had been discovered in 1846. At the time, colonial authorities had decided to turn a blind eye, given the absence of other qualified Frenchwomen who could speak Arabic. Over the course of the 1850s, however, doubts about the combative schoolteacher lingered for some and influenced the perception that her students were not al-ways as virtuous as desired.

Criticism of her students emerged periodically, but in February 1853 Rector Delacroix had defended the reputation of the school and its students in a de-tailed report to the governor general. In this report he argued that French efforts on behalf of girls should focus on work and moral education: "teachers should focus primarily on inculcating habits of order, submission and work." Still, he thought Muslim women should also know the rudiments of religion, reading and writing in Arabic, and elementary mathematics. Lessons in French, on the other hand, seemed superfluous to Delacroix, as well as to the person who an-notated the report, adding "very true" at this point. The report ended with a response to the question, "Is it true that the school in Algiers welcomes young girls who are already corrupted and dishonored?" Delacroix's response was a tentative no. "I have heard such things," he wrote, "but I suspect such criticisms are exaggerated because Madame Luce exerts an active surveillance over her stu-dents even outside the school. Moreover, the eldest students are the most exact and the most laborious. These qualities do not go along with depraved hearts."[32] If the governor general continued to have doubts on this score, the rector urged him to have the police watch over the school.

The rumors surrounding the student body also explain why Governor General Randon supported Luce's request to open a school for wealthy indigenous girls in 1854, arguing that elite families naturally hesitated to send their daughters to a school that welcomed "not only poor children, but also children of parents with suspect morality and whose familial education leaves much to be desired."[33] This request was not honored, but it demonstrates that moral concerns plagued the schoolteacher's efforts to educate indigenous girls.

This tendency to assume the existence of immoral behavior in indigenous families was partly the result of urban conditions in Algiers, which preoccupied the French colonizers during the 1850s. In 1853 Édouard-Adolphe Duchesne published a detailed report about the state of prostitution in Algiers which argued that the French conquest had generated "deplorable" consequences for the morality of the indigenous population: "Misery, the influence of the climate, the extreme laxity of morals, the common instinctive abhorrence for manual work among women from the south, the complete absence of religious principles, and the great facility with which Moors are able to repudiate their wives, are the major causes, I believe, for this indigenous prostitution."[34] While the French could not be blamed for all of these causes, certainly their confiscation of land had increased economic misery. Duchesne linked indigenous prostitution with an absence of schooling and urged the creation of workshops for women so they could find other ways of earning a living.

Indigenous women were not alone in being the objects of suspicion during these years. Duchesne had used the 1851 municipal statistics for Algiers to show that 138 of the 336 known prostitutes (41 percent) were of European origin.[35] In these early years of French colonization, Algiers attracted both male and female adventurers of all sorts whose lifestyles did not necessarily respect traditional moral precepts. The demographic studies of these years all denounced the high rates of illegitimate births in Algeria compared with rates in France.[36] Illicit living arrangements and illegitimate births were not limited to the uneducated working poor, however, and Eugénie Luce was not alone among women schoolteachers in giving birth to children outside of wedlock. Madame Luce's sewing mistress, Marie Antoinette Dufraisne, was also an unwed mother. Her daughter Ernestine was born in Paris in 1839 and accompanied Dufraisne to Algiers, where Dufraisne presented herself as a widow. Her death certificate, however, belies this claim to respectability. It is impossible to know whether Luce was aware of Ernestine's status, but she took her in as a student in her school and actively supported the "widow" Dufraisne's efforts to get a secure salary and an official position within the school. Clearly, she succeeded in convincing the authorities, since an inspection report in 1855 described the sewing mistress as a "deserving and respectable person, the daughter of an ex-colonel."[37] At Ernestine Dufraisne's wedding in 1856 to a merchant clerk, Louis Napoléon Luce and a retired colonel acted as witnesses, a sign that social positions were more fluid during these years in Algeria than in France.

Manual Training: The Commission of 1860–1861

The more relaxed moral standards that governed French sociability during the early decades of colonization became less acceptable during the second half of the century, as the settler population sought both political and social respectability. This was particularly the case for women.[38] The decision to establish a commission to investigate Madame Luce's school is striking testimony to shifting cultural politics that increasingly called into question the place of both European and indigenous women in the civilizing mission.

In October 1860 the General Council of Algiers convened to approve, among other items, the budget of the Arab-French schools.[39] Under pressure from the Municipal Council of Algiers, which had called for the closure of the girls' school and refused to foot any part of the bill, the twenty members of the council raised the issue of its cost, while no mention was made of that of the boys' schools. In the discussion it became apparent that support for Luce's institution was increasingly tenuous. Not surprisingly, the debate began around this issue of finances before moving on to more general political considerations of what the French were hoping to achieve through Madame Luce's school.

The first member of the council to speak questioned the 11,800 francs spent annually to run the school, asking "whether the results obtained were sufficient to justify the sacrifices this entailed." He believed not, "since public opinion was not favorable to the school. . . . Most of the young girls who leave the school fail to live up to what one expects of them." He thought the school should be shut down, or at least considerably restructured. In the ensuing discussion both the French and indigenous members of the council expressed their views on the subject. Ahmed Boukandoura, one of the two indigenous members and one of the most visible Muslim elites in Algiers, claimed that "no self-respecting Muslim would send his daughter to her school or take his wife from amongst its students."[40] The second indigenous member was of the same opinion, although he admitted that his knowledge of the institution came only from hearsay. Certainly, boys' schools were useful because they provided Muslim boys with the means to find jobs in commerce, industry, the administration, and the army, "but the same cannot be true for girls, for the simple reason that the instruction one is seeking to give them, cannot be reconciled with the duties that Muslim morality imposes upon women."

The French members of the council tended to be more supportive, suggesting in their exchanges that these arguments smacked precisely of Muslim prejudices with respect to women: "The ideas expressed by the indigenous member appear very judicious; however, he is too close to contemporary conditions in Muslim society, and as a result, his opinion does not appear completely unbiased." This French councilor argued that it was in the immense interest of Muslim women to receive an education that would advance the long-term goal of fusion between the two races: "The absence of good morals comes from misery and will only disappear with work." For French members of the General Council, the education of indigenous women contributed to the desired assimilation between the races, but there was uncertainty about the appropriate form of this education. One noted that the school had deviated from its initial objectives and produced only a "bad veneer for Muslims who no longer wish to place their children there." Still, there were rumors of change, according to this same member. Increasingly, the school taught mainly needlework, and given the reigning misery in Algiers, one should not underestimate the significance for some families of the 15 centimes per day that each student received.[41] In the end, the members voted the budget for the following year but also the principle of a commission to investigate the school and workshop.

This five-member commission was appointed in August 1861. All five commissioners were well-established men in the community: Toustain Du Manoir, Roland de Bussy, the baron de Vialar, Ahmed Boukandoura, and Adolphe Michel. The latter two probably had the strongest opinions on the subject before the two visits to Madame Luce's institution. Boukandoura was resolutely opposed to the existence of a school but supported the idea of professional training for girls, and Michel had penned a report early in August 1861 that denounced in no uncertain terms the project of teaching indigenous girls French. His criticism emphasized Luce's "equivocal" reputation among the Europeans and indigenous populations alike. Only the most poverty-stricken families sent their daughters to her school, he wrote, concluding, "It is sheer illusion to think that teaching urban Muslim girls to read, write and calculate according to our methods is a way to reform society." He then raised the specter of interethnic sex, suggesting that such education prepared concubines for European men, not wives for native men.[42] Given the composition of this commission, it seemed unlikely that Luce's school would survive the investigation.

In any case, the decision to visit the school in August, when it was not in session, determined not only the nature of the debates, but also the result. Accompanied in their second visit by two women patronnesses, Mesdames Bransoulié and Cougot, the five men questioned Eugénie Luce primarily about the workshop.[43] The twenty-nine-page handwritten report began with questions about "results in terms of elementary and professional instruction," but the bulk of the questions were economic in nature.[44] In asking questions such as how prices were fixed, how the buying and selling of products were organized, and how students used their salaries, the commission showed its interest in ascertaining the viability of developing professional training for girls. Luce's answers were clearly calculated to reassure. The students in the workshop produced handiwork that Madame Luce then sold, using the benefits to aid in the operating expenses of the workshop, in addition to giving small sums to the students and depositing money in student savings accounts. Thus, her students acquired both a skill and a means for gaining their livelihoods. For Luce, such training was the key to the future. "The bitter fruits of laziness," she wrote, "were causing urban Muslim society to degenerate into misery and corruption." Vocational education was the only solution. Despite this conviction, the commission noted that the workshop occupied only 17 students, compared with 137 within the school.

Eugénie Luce produced the following information concerning the students who had attended her school since its creation in 1845. Of the 1,035 girls, 680 (66 percent) had learned to speak, read, and write French; 15 had married "advantageously"; 6 had become teacher's aides in Arab-French schools; 1 had obtained a teaching diploma (although she had died in 1861); and 2 were sent as interpreters to the family of Abd al-Qadir. In communicating these results, she also insisted that those students for whom she had no information had not attracted undue attention, and "she did not understand the bad reputation some have sought to give her institution, since nothing immoral had ever happened in its sixteen years of existence." She argued throughout the investigation that she ran both school and workshop as a "mother of a family," eager to ensure the future of her fold. The commission, however, disagreed. Public notoriety and the private opinion of the members of the commission concurred in believing that this education contributed to the future immorality of the girls: "Upon leaving our schools, girls find no place in Muslim families and are not yet welcomed in French families. From this results an equivocal situation which leaves them vulnerable to dangerous suggestions." The commission argued that the initial decision to create such schools for girls was misguided despite efforts to preserve morality and respect religious beliefs. In the place of book learning and the acquisition of French, they argued for "fighting misery at its source, that is to say in laziness: inspire the taste, the need and the habits of work in natives of both sexes and we will be on the true path for the social transformation that we are seeking." The civilizing mission had changed its tone.

The commission ultimately decided that book instruction for Muslim girls made little sense. Indeed, Ahmed Boukandoura requested that the final report take note of his "energetic refusal of any school being associated with workshops," as he was convinced that for his fellow Muslims such a school caused families to flee. In the end, however, the decree that transformed Luce's school into a workshop allowed Eugénie Luce to provide lessons in French and mathematics if parents requested them, but no financing was given to support such lessons.[45] After sixteen years, the idea that girls should have the opportunity to become literate, and indeed that indigenous families should learn to value feminine literacy, had ceased to be part of the French colonial project in Algeria.

The commission's investigation and final report illustrate how the intellectual climate had shifted by the early 1860s in Algiers. Early illusions had faded, and the new politics generated by Napoleon III's "Arab kingdom" undoubtedly contributed to paying closer heed to some Muslim voices. Urban policies toward the Casbah, for example, focused on preserving "traditional" lifestyles, rather than enacting the sort of French order that characterized the lower city.[46] Similarly, gender policies paid closer attention to the expression of Muslim differences. As a result, the authorities heeded the opinions of men such as Boukandoura, despite the tentative misgivings of some. In the years that followed, educational policies toward the indigenous population would vary considerably, but girls' elementary instruction vanished as an issue. In accepting the idea that girls could do without intellectual learning, the French contributed to the reinforcement of gendered divisions within Muslim families as well as to the division between European and indigenous women. In 1873 the department of Algiers educated more girls than boys in both public and private schools; of the 12,230 boys and 13,750 girls, a mere handful were Muslim: 356 boys and 79 girls.[47] This puts into perspective the relative success of Luce's school before its disappearance.

THE TRIUMPH OF NEEDLEWORK
OVER BOOK LEARNING FOR GIRLS

The refashioning of Madame Luce's institution as an *école-ouvroir* represented more than just the rejection of book learning for indigenous girls. For the French it was a clear statement that assimilation was simply unworkable in the Algerian context. Certainly the workshop transmitted a form of professional training and an ethic of work that were perceived as more European than North African, but the end of language training and lessons in the rudiments barred indigenous women from the assimilationist model.

In the transformed workshop girls received apprenticeship training in sewing, knitting, and embroidery, including oriental embroidery. This was not a way to cut financial corners, since the amount of money previously allocated from the provincial budget for the schools was simply transferred to the Muslim Welfare Bureau. Two hundred fellowships were created for the apprentices within Madame Luce's workshop and for those of Madame Rose Barroil, who had opened a workshop in the late 1850s.[48] The training within these workshops lasted two years, after which the young women could remain as workers, receiving a salary for their work. This emphasis on vocational training reflected evolutions in France and was not completely to the detriment of any instruction, as the decree authorized both women to open a primary school for seven- to ten-year-old girls. Given that these schools had to be self-financing, however, they were effectively ruled out of existence.

Eugénie Luce clearly understood that the tide had turned, as her answers to the commission had shown. Vocational training was the key to the future, she had argued, the means of regenerating urban Muslim society. By promoting apprenticeship training, as well as lessons in thrift and economy, she hoped to produce young women who could earn their livelihoods as well as be decent mothers in indigenous families; at the same time, however, she strove for something more. During the fifteen years following the closure of her school, her workshop carved out a specific niche in the colonial economy, as she oriented production toward a luxury market in indigenous embroidery rather than more quotidian needlework. Ultimately, this legacy marked historical memory far more than the earlier school. Gone was the illusion that girls' education in French would produce a "fusion of the races."

Embroidery and the Revival of Native Arts

It was one thing to teach girls to sew and mend, and quite another to imagine these lessons to be an aesthetic project deserving the support of the colonial hierarchy. This orientation was already apparent, however, in the ways that Madame Luce showcased her students' handicraft in prize-giving ceremonies and exhibitions. Following the failure of her effort to establish a school for wealthy girls in 1854, she had marshaled support for the creation of a workshop for the production of luxury embroideries made with gold and silk that she set up in the neighboring house of the Omar Hassan Pacha family. In 1858 her workshop received brief official recognition, and a ruling placed her Muslim workshop under the responsibility of the prefect and the surveillance of the Muslim Welfare Bureau. The ruling's precision concerning the cost of objects to be made and the details about the running of the workshop highlight the economic role it was expected to play.[49] However, it was shut down a year later, along with the nursery school, a victim of the uncertainties of colonial policies with respect to women.[50] Nonetheless, Luce did not abandon her ambition to establish needlework as a trade with a period of apprenticeship, and by 1861 she had developed arguments for this training that positioned the workshop within a grander scheme. Vocational training was not just a remedy for urban poverty, but the first step in the revival of the indigenous arts.

The colonial archives contain little mention of Luce's activities once she stopped teaching French in favor of teaching embroidery, and so there are few traces of her voice justifying this orientation. One must search elsewhere to understand why, in the end, this proved a savvy move in the 1860s, one that brought her both recognition and material comfort in the final two decades of her life although not the same status as during those heady years in the 1850s when colonial dignitaries attended her prize-giving ceremonies.

The General Council presented the new focus on embroidery as a means of regenerating indigenous women through work but also as an economic decision: "The embroidery industry *created* by Madame Luce is destined to develop and become a true Algerian specialty," argued the committee of women benefactors in 1862.[51] By supporting apprenticeship training in this trade, the colonial authorities were responding to a reality of their own creation. The traditional handicraft sectors, as well as agriculture, were hit hard by the effects of the first four decades of French colonial rule. In Algeria, embroidery, unlike lace, was an exclusively female trade, and there existed an urban tradition of luxury embroidery for girls of the bourgeois class. During the early nineteenth century, women known as *mu'allimat*, or embroidery mistresses, taught bourgeois girls the techniques of lamé embroidery using gold or silver thread. By mid-century, however, signs of such training ceased with the disruptions caused by the French presence. The woman inspector who labored to resurrect "traditional" feminine Algerian handiwork in the interwar period, Marguerite Bel, argued that base commercial practices among both European and indigenous salesmen had resulted in the promotion of cheap and poorly designed products known as "Algerian embroidery."[52] In the process, the women who had made a living promoting fine artisanry had vanished.[53]

Bel saw Luce and her granddaughter, Henriette Benaben (known as Henriette Luce Benaben by the end of the century), as the first to recognize the value of this skill and the resulting handiwork because, in addition to promoting embroidery within her school, Luce also began a collection of fine embroidery. Interestingly, however, she relied on a fellow Frenchwoman to teach the necessary skills, a sign no doubt of the economic dislocations wrought by French colonialism. Still, it seems likely that Luce's knowledge of the tradition of teaching luxury embroidery came from her friendships with the wealthy indigenous families who opened their homes to her workshop in the 1850s. When forced to choose between teaching French or embroidery, she did not hesitate in 1861 to choose the latter, while also orienting this teaching toward a burgeoning luxury market rather than focusing on providing basic skills.

Madame Barroil made a different choice when her workshop received support from the General Council in 1861. The former Rose Jolly was born in Algiers in 1817, the daughter of a Spanish landowner. She married the merchant Anselme Barroil in 1837, but it seems likely that their marriage was not harmonious. By the mid-1860s when their daughter married they were not living together, which partly explains Madame Barroil's decision to open a workshop for girls in the late 1850s.[54] Her workshop, however, was not focused on the luxury trade, but rather on lingerie.[55] Her students earned less money from the sale of individual articles than those in Madame Luce's workshop, but the skills taught initially sparked more interest among local families. Annual reports from the General Council confirm the ways that the two establishments occupied different niches in the colonial economy. Madame Barroil trained students in more practical and housewifely skills, whereas Madame Luce produced workers for a market in luxury goods.

The Muslim Welfare Bureau that oversaw the two workshops allocated in principle two hundred scholarships of 6 francs per month for this training in needlework. The budget did not include a salary for sewing mistresses; Luce and Barroil were expected to pay their mistresses from the profits of their workshops. As a gesture toward her efforts over the years, the council allowed Madame Luce to retain her teaching salary of 1,500 francs per year; the attempts made by some council members to grant a similar salary to Madame Barroil were rejected, since her investment in improving the lot of indigenous women was far more recent. Initially, Barroil was more successful in attracting students to her workshop. In 1862 she already had one hundred apprentices, whereas Luce had only fifty-seven; by 1865, however, both institutions had their lot of one hundred apprentices, and each also welcomed workers over the age of sixteen, for a total of sixty-one women.[56]

The reports of the General Council emphasized the "advantageous marriages" of former apprentices, firmly anchoring this training in a moralizing project distinct from the dubious advantages of learning French. As one indigenous member of the council put it, the creation of these workshops "are the best means to pull the indigent classes from their misery and to moralize them, in addition to placing these young women in a position to contract advantageous marriages, which constitutes our only desire and only goal."[57] This same member also noted the presence of twenty Kabyle apprentices in Madame Luce's workshop, applauding how her establishment contributed to the well-being of both urban and rural women. By the late 1860s, however, in the context of intense economic crisis, the reports on the workshops increasingly noted the ways that they enabled women to earn a living. The unmarried women workers present in the workshop earned between 1 franc and 1.50 francs per day in 1868, and more than sixty married women working at home also earned money, thus contributing to household economies in dire need of extra funds.

The concern to provide native women with vocational training was not, however, a burning priority for the colonial administration during these years dominated by the Napoleonic dream of creating an Arab kingdom. As various measures sought to determine property and naturalization rights, massive revolts testified to the fragile control exerted by the French. Vocational training for boys did develop at this time, but information about such training for girls is scarce in the colonial archives.[58] In 1868 the administration of indigenous welfare was transferred in civil territories to the municipal budget. The tumultuous end of the military government after 1870 was not favorable for the indigenous populations, and certainly the plight of poor women and the nature of their embroidery skills seems to have vanished as a concern for the following three decades.[59] Although the funding continued, the regime that came to power in 1870 ceased to imbue such training with a higher objective, notwithstanding last-ditch efforts on the part of some deputies to argue that Luce's workshop constituted the "principal instrument of progress that a fertile initiative had laid at our disposal."[60] These deputies went further, however, recognizing how girls' education played a role in the gendered politics of citizenship: "All of the issues that cause problems for us are tied up in the relations of men with women: marriage age, polygamy, re-pudiation . . . paternal and marital power, uncles' authority over orphans who have lost their fathers, inheritance provisions; in a word, all that separates the personal status of natives from ours can only be modified through education."[61] These arguments failed to persuade.

A general reorganization of the Muslim Welfare Bureau in March 1874 high-lighted the more conservative reading of women's role in colonial Algeria. Luce's and Barroil's workshops were treated henceforth as private businesses. The bureau continued to recognize their contributions in offering work for the poor, but the workshops no longer received funding for scholarships.[62] For the settler govern-ment, which opposed the civilizing mission, workshops offered work, not the re-generation of indigenous womanhood through training in traditional art forms.

Madame Luce's virtual disappearance from the colonial archives in the 1860s signals the end of a moment in the French presence in Algeria when native girls' education seemed an important and worthwhile goal in the effort to win indig-enous hearts and minds. Training fingers was another sort of ambition that was far more conciliatory in colonial Algiers. Indigenous notables supported the al-leviation of poverty and the transmission of a marketable skill—both laudable goals—but they opposed efforts to teach their daughters French. In the 1870s the civilian authorities accepted this state of affairs, revealing their own priorities. In the French hierarchy of cultural goods, embroidery played a distant second to learning language.[63]

While in France politicians such as Jules Ferry and Jules Simon increasingly defended the importance of universal schooling for rich and poor, boys and girls, the concern for such schooling among the indigenous populations of Algeria declined. From the late 1860s on, the authorities promoted "mixed" schooling for both indigenous and European students, which meant integrating Muslim students into existing municipal schools. These measures hastened the demise of the experiments in Arab-French schools, and the numbers of both male and female indigenous students declined overall. The General Council in Algiers lamented this state of affairs year after year. In 1876 it drew on figures from the Ligue de l'enseignement (Teaching League), which sought to spread secular and free education for all. The Ligue reported that in Cairo 445 Muslim girls attended schools, whereas in all of Algeria fewer than 200 did so.[64] This was quite a change from the mid-1850s when Madame Luce had 160 students in her single school. In effect, "mixed" schooling eliminated all but the Jewish indigenous population from the colonial schools.

After 1860 the two figures who had most marked this effort to spread French education among the indigenous poor in Algiers, Auguste Depeille and Eugénie Luce, no longer generated the sort of attention they had at mid-century, but their colonial careers were not yet finished. Depeille returned to running a school for boys in 1871 after the failure of the Collège impérial arabe-français.[65] Luce ran her embroidery workshop for another fifteen years before moving back to France. While French colonial officials took little interest in her activities as an embroidery mistress, her students' handiwork increasingly attracted travelers and tourists who came in search of sunshine and exotica on the North African shores. The British in particular were fascinated by Madame Luce's *école-ouvroir* and framed her activities within a feminist narrative. The stories they told about her shed a rather different light on the changes in Madame Luce's fortunes and suggest the importance of moving beyond the French colonial perception of her school and workshop to understand her trajectory and its influence on imperial representations of education and work for indigenous girls.

PART III
Historical and Cultural Legacies

Previous page: Henriette Benaben (touching the young girl's head) in her embroidery school (the label on the image makes the name appear Arabic: "Ben-Aben"), ca. 1899. The veiled woman on the right would not have appeared in photographs of Madame Luce's school at mid-century because Madame Luce made a point of not allowing her students and teachers to wear veils. The cover illustration for this book, this image, and the illustration on page 189 were all photographed at the "school workshop" in a building known as the Palais Oriental on rue Marengo, just above the Casbah on the southwest edge of the city. Benaben also sold embroideries here. Photochrom print. Library of Congress Prints and Photographs Division, Washington, DC. LC-DIG-ppmsc-05551.

6 IMPERIAL NARRATIVES
Feminists and Travelers Tell Their Tales
(1857–1900)

French colonial sources tell a tale of demotion between 1858 and 1861 when Madame Luce's school lost official support and was transformed into an embroidery workshop. Although she remained in Algeria until the mid-1870s, the archives contain little information about her activities after the decree of 1861. In May 1864 she was granted three months of convalescence in France in order to take the waters at Vichy. Five years later she wrote to the prefect of the department of Algiers to protest the new measures under examination concerning vocational training for young "Moorish" women. Finally, in the fall of 1869, documents about her pension show that she was being encouraged to stop her professional activity at age sixty-five.[1] One might conclude from the relative dearth of archival sources that having turned sixty Eugénie Luce slowed down, became quieter, and ceased her battles to improve both her own situation and that of indigenous women.

Biographical information appears to concur with this reading, as both marriages and deaths wrought changes in her family. Her granddaughter Henriette, whom she had raised since infancy, married in 1869 and briefly left home. Then three years later Louis Luce, Eugénie's, companion and husband of thirty-five years, suddenly died. The following year her only daughter died, worn out from her conjugal sorrows, as her granddaughter suggested. All these events inevitably left their marks. On the face of things, familial matters and apparent poor health easily explain why Luce spent less time penning reports to the municipal or departmental authorities and why she appears to have attracted less attention.

In fact, however, age and family worry did little to stop Luce's activism; rather, she continued to seek and garner attention, but not from within the French colonial hierarchy. Instead, she used her workshop and the embroideries it produced to attract foreign visitors and to seek foreign sales. In particular, she sought out the company of British feminists wintering in Algiers and gave them the material necessary to construct a heroic and feminist portrait of herself. Through these cosmopolitan encounters, she established another narrative of her colonial activities that challenges the story told so far. Although Luce did not leave an autobiography, she took care during her final years in Algeria to spread her own version of her life by sharing reports and helping to translate for an English-speaking public all she had done to promote indigenous women's education and handicraft. In the process, she seems to have understood, more presciently than male French colonialists, that "oriental goods," be they little girls or native embroidery, had a certain market value within an imperial economy that extended well beyond France.

CONSTRUCTING A FEMINIST HEROINE WITH BRITISH ACCENTS

Numbers of British visitors in Algeria grew significantly after 1870, encouraged by the energetic consul general Robert Lambert Playfair. An ex-officer of the Indian Army, Playfair was an intellectual who spoke Arabic. During his years as consul general in Algiers (1867–1896) he did much to promote life in North Africa, including writing a guidebook to Algeria and Tunis.[2] British interest in imperial Algeria antedated his arrival, however, as Franco-British relations improved during the 1850s and word spread about the climate and welcoming urban infrastructures. Doctors, pastors, and middle-class women published numerous travel narratives and travel guides that vaunted the charms of life in the French colony.[3]

Women and Work: The Feminist Version

Among the best known of these winter visitors was the British feminist Barbara Leigh Smith (1827–1891), who first discovered Algiers in 1856 with her sisters and brother. Suffering from a nervous breakdown, she came seeking respite from the pressures of promoting women's rights in Britain. She behaved as a tourist in colonial Algiers, visiting the city and its environs, sketching the countryside and the people, collecting pottery, and socializing. Here she met and fell in love with Eugène Bodichon, an eccentric French army surgeon, a republican with social-ist friends such as Louis Blanc and Alexandre Auguste Ledru-Rollin, and a firm believer in France's civilizing mission in Algiers.[4] Although Leigh Smith's French was somewhat hesitant and Bodichon's English far from fluent, their romance flowered and in July 1857 they married. But because he refused to leave Algeria and she remained committed to her London activities on behalf of women, their married life was spent frequently apart; she wintered in Algiers, returning in the milder season to London and the feminist gathering spot at Langham Place.[5]

Barbara Leigh Smith Bodichon's salon in Algiers quickly became a meeting place for the cosmopolitan elites who lived there or visited. Although she devoted much of her winter months to socializing, painting, and sketching, she did not abandon her long-term interest in women's work. She was largely responsible for "discovering" Madame Luce and laying the grounds for a feminist reconstruction of Luce's life and activities that soon spread beyond her circle of close friends.[6] In a guidebook to Algeria, a place "Considered as a Winter Residence for the English," as the subtitle tells us, Bodichon contributed to making Eugénie Luce a heroine. Drawing on both the medical writings of her husband and her own observations, she provided chapters not only about the history and climate of the French colony, but also about "Native Manners and Customs" and "Life in Algeria." These latter two chapters devoted several pages to Madame Luce, whom she described as "the originator and energetic teacher and conductor of the Moorish school for girls, the first Christian woman who has made a breach into the prison life of the Eastern women. All honour to her name and success to her endeavour, the difficulty of which no one who has not examined her schools, can be aware." Bodichon presented Luce in this text and others as heroically overcoming French administrative difficulties in order to teach the language and "somewhat of the civilisation of the conquering race" to young Moorish girls.[7] Although Bodichon presented the feminist spin on Luce's activities, it was Luce herself who provided the material necessary to construct this story that brought her and her workshop enduring recognition in British circles.

The initial encounter between Barbara Leigh Smith and the older Madame Luce occurred over the winter of 1856–1857. Clearly, Madame Luce made an impression on the British feminist as a woman who had single-mindedly pursued a vision against considerable odds. Leigh Smith first positioned her as a woman worthy in the 1857 essay "Women and Work," written in Algeria, in which she advocated the need for gainful employment among middle-class women. Rhetorically, she used the tale of individual Western women's achievements to illustrate their qualifications for undertaking a wide variety of activities. Alongside Madame Luce, she highlighted such women as Florence Nightingale, the social reformer Mary Carpenter, the American prison reformer Dorothea Dix, the American doctor Elizabeth Blackwell, and the French infant school reformer Marie Pape-Carpantier. One year later, Barbara Bodichon published her guidebook, which devoted three pages to Madame Luce's school.[8] In 1861 the *English Woman's Journal*, the first feminist newspaper run only by women, featured three long stories about "Madame Luce, of Algiers," who had appeared briefly in articles of the journal since 1859. The extensive 1861 report was then combined and published a year later as a thirty-two-page brochure, *Memoir of Madame Luce, of Algiers*.[9] By then, Eugénie Luce had become a friend of the British feminist and her circle of friends.

In all probability, Bessie Rayner Parkes (1829–1925) was the person who actually wrote most of the prose about Madame Luce. Parkes, a longstanding friend of Bodichon, as well as a fellow feminist at Langham Place in London, first met Luce on a visit to Algiers in 1857.[10] During this first trip she wrote an initial article about Luce for the *Waverley Journal*.[11] Four years later she signed the articles in the *English Woman's Journal*, which are an expanded version of the story first presented in "Women and Work." Unlike Bodichon, she was fluent in French (also marrying a Frenchman, Louis Belloc), and in all likelihood she was the person who translated Luce's personal documents to add color to her portraits. Parkes clearly viewed the older woman as a friend; in 1859 she wrote to Bodichon saying, "Give my love to Madame Luce, & thank her warmly for that beautiful handkerchief."[12]

Eugénie Luce's story appeared in various forms in six different places between 1857 and 1866: the Scottish *Waverley Journal* (1857), Bodichon's "Women and Work" (1857) and her *Guide Book* (1858), the *English Woman's Journal* (1861), the *Memoir of Madame Luce, of Algiers* (1862), and finally in a book, *Vignettes: Twelve Biographical Sketches* (1866), which added information about Luce's workshop after 1861. These venues provided material that frequently found its way into other publications during the following decades. As a result, the French schoolteacher acquired a reputation in English-speaking circles that led travelers to her doorstep.

Despite their differences, each publication presented the same basic plot of Madame Luce's life to the British reading public: a dramatic story of a single woman's dream to bring the fruits of French civilization to Moorish women through the founding of a school for Muslim girls in Algiers. Using translated copies of official reports and letters, Parkes portrayed Madame Luce engaged in a struggle against tremendous odds—a victorious struggle, however, since she not only persuaded the colonial administration to sponsor her school, but was able to attract more than one thousand students between 1845 and 1861. Her students acquired a knowledge of the French language as well as professional instruction in needlework, thus contributing, in Eugénie Luce's words, to the moral civilization of the Arab woman. The final article in the *English Woman's Journal* concludes: "We think that this sketch of a long and noble struggle will not be read without interest even in this far distant England, while it may meet the eye of some who intend next winter to visit the bright and beautiful shores where the scene of our narrative lies, and cause them to feel that they have made something like a friendly acquaintance with the life and character of Madame Luce, of Algiers."[13]

This "friendly acquaintance" was very much a romanticized and individualized story that reveals the ways these British feminists constructed a form of European sisterhood in which the realities of Muslim womanhood largely disappeared. The correspondence between Parkes and her close friend Mary Merryweather provides insight into how Luce's life was progressively put into English words. As we have seen, Luce told her British friend stories about her childhood, her unhappy marriage, and her initial labors in Algeria (see Chapter 1). These confidences are the only story that exists of these early years, and they bear the selective mark of the autobiographer. Parkes wrote to Merryweather about Luce's decision to leave her husband and escape to Algeria and emphasized the lot of the poor working woman: "She left her little girl with her own family; coming to Algiers, she struggled on, giving lessons and when she had finished going to the Military hospital to wash and mend the soldiers linen for a franc a day."[14] Not surprisingly, Parkes did not mention the man or men who helped Luce during these difficult years between 1832 and 1845. Nor were there any revelations about the two illegitimate children who died. In her conversation, Luce struck the right note with her new British friends, focusing on her initial poverty, her mistreatment at the hands of her husband, her hard work, and then the happy ending, despite aspects of the story that deviated from traditional morality. Although Parkes noted that it looked a "little queer" for Eugénie to marry "Mister Luce" so swiftly after her husband's death, that aspect of her story seems to have been accepted as adding an interesting "French" touch to this portrait.

The published versions of Luce's life focused more specifically on her activities once in Algiers, particularly her struggle to gain administrative and financial support for the school she opened in 1845. The story emphasized the multiple difficulties of her enterprise: uncomprehending French officials, "tyrannical" Muslim men, and a local society where "Moorish women were valued by weight!"—"such was the human material which Madame Allix dared to conceive of as capable of being raised to something approaching the condition of her European sisterhood," Parkes noted.[15] Ultimately, however, Luce triumphed, thanks to her perseverance, which Parkes conveyed largely through the translation of official reports her friend gave to her. Although she regretted the quality of her translation, she emphasized: "In the hands of Madame Luce the polite and elegant French language acquires a decisive ring which is quite extraordinary. . . . The art of writing dispatches is one of the qualifications of a great general."[16] General or not, Madame Luce clearly knew how to maneuver not only with French officialdom, but also with her British friends. With the latter she sought to cultivate a sense of the community of oppressed sisterhood when recounting the obstacles put in her way, and she made clear that this sisterhood, as "civilized" European women, shared a common goal in their concern to educate girls and to offer them a means of gaining a livelihood once they left her school.

It is also clear that Luce read carefully what her friends wrote about her, with an eye to ensuring the accuracy of their reports. In December 1862 Barbara Bodichon wrote to the feminist Emily Davies, who was in charge of publication at the *English Woman's Journal* at the time, asking her to correct a mistake about Madame Luce's school. Davies promised to print such a corrective in the section "Answers to Correspondents," although there is no evidence that she actually did so.[17]

Parkes added a final chapter to Luce's tale in her 1866 *Vignettes*, which constitutes the longest of the twelve biographical sketches in the book. Here she described the French colonial government's shift in policy with respect to the education of girls that led to the school's closure in 1861: "Once this policy said, give the 'jeunes musulmanes' a good deal of instruction, and a very little needlework; then it said, give them nothing but instruction, and do not let them do needlework at all; and *now* it says, give them no instruction at all and let them do nothing but needlework!" Although Parkes regretted the passing of intellectual instruction, she wholeheartedly supported Luce's workshop because "knowledge of a trade may save them [the Moorish girls] from much misery."[18]

Both Bodichon's and Parkes's portraits gave ample treatment to the figure of Madame Luce and the embroidery work her workshop produced, leaving her students very much in the background. Like other British visitors, they perceived Muslim women as suffering from "utter debased ignorance" due to Moorish customs. In one of their first descriptions, they presented Muslim women as completely inadequate housewives, given their slothful existence and their lack of the most elementary knowledge of hygiene.[19] The girl students themselves were described as marginally more "civilized," having learned, thanks to Eugénie Luce, to "conceive of their own sex as of rational and responsible beings [*sic*], to think that they can earn money and support themselves," but they remained "rough and savage, and distress the looker-on by the coarse expression of face, which two generations of training cannot remove." Bodichon ended by noting: "The present Moorish teacher is a young woman, who in all ways looks like a French woman. She has passed a regular examination, and taken out her diploma; indeed, I was astonished to find that she was a Moresque and a Mussulman."[20] This affirmation of how civilization could overcome religious and racial differences helps to explain why the British visitors felt more at ease describing the far more legible Madame Luce.

But Parkes and Bodichon remained very aware of the national and, to an extent, religious differences between themselves and their heroine, who was in a sense anchored in her Frenchness, as revealed in her elegant writing and somewhat untraditional lifestyle. Interestingly, Parkes admired Luce for qualities she perceived to be more English than French—her sense of initiative and her energy: "In truth the history of Madame Luce's school is just a fair history of Algeria. The Government trying to do everything, and, of course, in the end breaking down. The people in England would set up a private subscription, and try all manner of eccentric experiments; but here no one has either money or individual energy enough to do it. Madame Luce has been the only one to try, and has not succeeded; at least, for this present administration she is in eclipse."[21]

But she was not in eclipse for British tourists, whose numbers steadily increased during the 1860s and 1870s.[22] British women's travel narratives reveal the interest Madame Luce's school and workshop held for British woman visitors, who seldom failed to recount their impressions of the founder. These impressions bear the distinct imprint of Bodichon's and Parkes's readings of her activities, presenting Madame Luce as a modern-day heroine, while the Moorish girls become an attractive oriental backdrop. Naturally, the brevity of their visits as well as difficulties of communication (either in French or in Arabic) militated against other readings; still, it is striking to see the influence of the feminist story in all those that followed. And lurking behind that story lies the imprint of Madame Luce's voice, captured nicely in this extract from the *English Women's Journal*: "That which the administration did not dare attempt, with all the means at its disposal, I accomplished upon my private resources only, with faith and will that overcame all obstacles. To-day, this 12th of June 1854, nine years after my foundation, the Government which profits by the fruit of my labors, appropriates even my ideas and my very phrases, which they print in the *Moniteur* as their own! And that without any compensation, nay, even while diminishing my salary and restricting the sphere of my action. Oh, justice of men!"[23] Luce was determined, thanks to her feminist friends, to establish a form of feminine "justice" that spoke in her favor.

British Lady Travelers: Feminism and Orientalism

Between the "discovery" of Madame Luce in 1857 and her death in 1882, at least six British women published travel narratives that included descriptions of their visits to Luce's school or workshop.[24] These British visitors brought to Algeria a number of prejudices concerning both French and Arab society, as well as the oriental fantasies that so fashioned the thinking and expectations of Western European travelers.[25] They were often critical of French colonization, and many, like this anonymous woman traveler in 1847, expressed disappointment not to discover a more "exotic" environment: "Viewed from the sea, Algiers looks like a huge sugar-loaf, embedded in an amphitheatre of hills. One naturally expects to see an Oriental city but how is that expectation disappointed!"[26]

By the 1860s, French urbanization, with its attendant comfort, explained why visitors sought the shores of Algeria, even if their descriptions often criticized the French colonization effort compared with British imperial expertise: "There is certainly much to interest the visitor in Algiers, and it promises to become in time a flourishing and valuable colony, though even the French themselves cannot deny that in the hands of the English its prosperity would have increased in a tenfold ratio."[27] A few years later the *Penny Illustrated Paper* offered harsher criticism of French results: "The French are not good civilisers—their profligacy, rapacity, cruelty, and faithlessness roused hate and horror both of their creed and their civilization."[28]

For British lady travelers, indigenous women were an object of fascination, but mostly from afar. Few of these women entered indigenous homes and so their commentaries repeated well-rehearsed stereotypes. The most common trope concerned the Moorish woman's "hopeless degradation," as Mabel Crawford wrote.[29] The Arab woman's seclusion, her presence in the streets as "a shapeless bundle of white muslin," her covered face—all rendered her illegible to these English visitors.[30] Barbara Bodichon argued that Moorish women were "mysterious and poetical when we can see nothing or but little of them," whereas a Madame Prus saw them more starkly, as "slaves of rather superior degree" to their husbands.[31] Ellen Rogers was even more direct, writing: "Few positions in life, not even excepting American slavery, can be so utterly wretched as that of the very poor Arab woman. Amongst the richer Moslems the degradation of the women is mental and moral."[32] Religion, the Quran, and social customs were all blamed for women's status in Algerian society, but few did more than mention these factors.

Travelers had little opportunity to discover the realities of urban indigenous women's lives even when they ventured into homes for special occasions. As a result, they failed to see evidence of the economic underpinnings of urban households and the role some women played as workers in the home. Nor were most travelers able to decode the forms of feminine sociability that existed, for example, in bathhouses or on roof terraces. Without speaking Arabic and without understanding the complexity of social arrangements in the city, it is not surprising that lady travelers resorted to stereotypes.[33]

In British women's narratives, Madame Luce was a far more interesting character than Muslim women. Her project was one British women could understand and describe because it mirrored to some degree their own metropolitan investment in feminist or philanthropic efforts. Moreover, available descriptions were at hand if inspiration failed the travel writer. This is particularly evident in the long chapter that Ellen Rogers devoted to her visit to Madame Luce's workshop in April 1863. Although she does mention learning a new and very pretty stitch from a "beautiful little Moorish child, who was edging a handkerchief in silk," most of her text is an abridged version of the article that appeared in the *English Woman's Journal*. Since her narrative also informs us of her socializing with Barbara Bodichon, it is clear that she was given the text, which she then copied to convey her admiration of Madame Luce's "indomitable energy."[34]

The prolific author Matilda Betham Edwards (cousin to the famous Egyptologist Amelia Edwards) offered perhaps the most literary description of Luce's workshop, which she visited in 1867. She was also the traveler who developed at greatest length a description of the girls whom Madame Luce sought to raise to "something approaching the condition of her European sisterhood," to borrow Parkes's expression. Also a friend of Barbara Bodichon, Edwards began her book with a sketch of Algiers by Bodichon, as well as a poem in her honor. Unlike Rogers, however, Edwards devoted several paragraphs to "the little Moorish girls at their embroidery frames"—one of the chapter subtitles—and offered a verbal painting of the setting:

Seated round the gallery, in rows, were about a hundred little Moorish girls, busy over embroidery-frames, their little brown legs tucked under them; their dark faces all life and merriment; their bright clothing making them look like beds of tulips in May. A pleasant young French lady, one of the directresses of the school or workshop, came up and showed us some really superb work; soft white curtains covered with lilies and roses, cloaks of real cashmere from Tunis, worked with arabesques in white floss, scarfs fit for the Queen of Sheba, linen to please Cleopatra. How one longed to be rich and to take home such spoils for one's sober English home!

These children are alike of rich and poor parentage, and a few little Negresses may be seen among them. The only thought to spoil the enjoyment of this bright and busy scene is that, excepting in needlework, they are mostly as ignorant as it is possible to be.[35]

The luxuriousness of Edwards's descriptions mimicked that of oriental paintings, but the girls appear far more as objects than subjects. Following this passage, Edwards wrote of Madame Luce and her efforts to teach the girls more than embroidery, pulling them from the ignorance that marred the charm of her portrait: "She began teaching her pupils to read and write, and was succeeding admirably when the veto of the government was put upon such innovations. It seems that the Moors do not like their wives and daughters to be more learned than themselves."[36] While the Orientalist interest in the visual pleasures of the exotic clearly influenced Edwards in her writing, she also expressed measured judgments about Algerian society and a sensitivity to ethnographic details that were not common in British women's writings about the Orient.[37] In particular, despite Bodichon's criticism of Muslim men's treatment of Muslim women, she argued that without being an Arabophile, she felt sympathy for the native man's inferiority within the colonial system: "It is undoubtedly true that his theory regarding women militates against any great advance in social and intellectual elevation; but in what way do his religious or social theories hinder him from becoming a useful member of society and a participator in government?"[38]

Most British women travelers were less open, however, and tended to follow the script offered by the writing of Bodichon and Parkes. This meant that they focused on Madame Luce and her struggles; her students were of interest through the exotic touch they added and the beauty of their handiwork. Thanks to Bodichon's salon, members of the British circles, who intermingled relatively little with other communities in Algeria, were introduced to an aspect of French colonization that might easily have gone unnoticed, especially once the French stopped supporting indigenous girls' schooling. The feminist portrait, however, was not the only reading at this time.

RELIGION AND COMMERCE IN THE
FOREIGN READINGS OF MADAME LUCE

For the British, whose empire by the 1860s extended across the globe, social life in Algeria was perceived as distinctly provincial, encouraging a tendency among them to socialize principally among their fellows.[39] Indeed, *Cornhill Magazine* described this "Society" in 1865 with an undeniable note of condescension: "Society here is probably much the same as in the provincial capitals of France; consisting chiefly of civil and military officials and their families, with a thin sprinkling of the commercial class, and on public occasion a dash of the native element."[40] Bodichon, however, like the wife of Governor General MacMahon, sought to promote a more cosmopolitan environment, bringing together people who might otherwise not have met. When Matilda Betham Edwards first arrived in Algiers in December 1866, she was told, "But you will, of course, receive invitation for all Madame de MacMahon's receptions and at Madame Bodichon's you will meet all the best people, French and English in the place."[41] According to Edwards, Bodichon was a "zealous pioneer in . . . the promotion of Anglo-French intercourse, the uprooting of international antipathies—antipathies from which she herself was wholly free."[42] In addition, however, she had a reputation for being genuinely interested in the indigenous population: "Her Catholic and sovereign nature recognized no barriers either of race, nationality or religion. Just as during her American tour some years before her heart had gone out to what Walt Whitman calls 'You dim-descended, black, divine-souled African,' then in bondage, so here, alike in Jew, Moor, Kabyle, Bedouin and the Negro, she saw no aliens, but as yet little understood brothers and sisters."[43]

If Parkes's writings put Madame Luce on the feminist map, Bodichon's salon ensured that her fame would spread more widely, notably among English-speaking visitors whose opportunities and interest in penetrating French homes were often limited. Thanks to Bodichon's initial efforts, Luce's school and then workshop attracted the attention of travelers with less feminist readings. Two distinct strands emerge in the different writings that touch on Madame Luce, her school, or her workshop. One sought to understand her work with respect to the British missionary activities elsewhere; the other, ultimately more successful, promoted the workshop for its commercial products.

Morality and Missionizing

One of the few male authors to describe Madame Luce was the Reverend Edward William Lewis Davies, who was active as a pastor in Algiers and published a guidebook to the city in 1858. One reviewer described the book in this fashion: "Written in easy, narrative style, by an English clergyman, in the fruitless search of health for his consumptive wife. A keen sportsman, a tolerable botanist, with some appreciation of good living, he has made his three months' stay in French Algiers a very inviting experience to those who are wearied of a monotonous life at home."[44] In his concern to indicate cultural resources for English invalids, he also included a good deal of information about the "quiet and rational amusement [available] to the English visitor at Algiers."[45] The chapter on the native population devoted three pages to Madame Luce, whose "extraordinary self-devotion" forced the French government to support her school "to extend, if possible, the benefits of a useful and liberal education to the future wives and mothers of the Moorish population." Davies then recounted her early efforts, focusing less on how she overcame the obstacles of male prejudice than on her "philanthropic views." Although colonial educational policy prohibited religious proselytism, Davies noted, "notwithstanding, she deems it her duty and no violation of her promise to inculcate moral practices such as a Christian would think it necessary to observe." He concluded his portrait by emphasizing the Christian nature of her task, one that fit well with the understanding British missionaries had about their role within the colonies: "Eventually, the result cannot fail to affect the social condition of the whole Moorish population, but especially that of the women, to whom instruction and occupation must prove a blessing. Truly Madame Luce has a mighty work in hand; but with her iron resolution, supported and encouraged by a firm trust in God, she is well fitted to the task: let any one look in her grand face and say if the combination of character which it indicates does not demonstrate a power equal to any emergency."[46]

Reviews of Davies's book in both the general and the religious press all echoed this admiration for Luce's initiative and spread news of her work well beyond feminist circles. In the *Dublin Review*, Madame Luce was described as having broken the ice among the upper classes concerning the education of women. Her example was a hopeful sign for the future of French colonization in Algeria.[47] More melodramatically, the *Christian Examiner* signaled Madame Luce's initiative as a sign of things to come within this "semi-Christian land": "She offers now the only promise for the future of that blood-bought soil, working in a noble spirit for the true elevation of a peculiarly capable, naturally religious, and generally self-denying race."[48] The cheap penny press was less sanguine about the future, given the "fanatical prejudices of the more bigoted natives," but nonetheless predicted "her excellent system must in time work a great change; and in all probability the children of her pupils will be brought up in a manner more calculated to enlarge the understanding and refine the mind than even those who were fortunate enough to be the first upon whom her social experiment was tried."[49]

Five years after Davies's trip to Algeria, Ellen Rogers and her husband, the Reverend Albert Rogers, wintered together in Algiers. The chapter of her book devoted to Madame Luce mostly recopied Parkes's article published in the *English Women's Journal*, but her personal perspective was not as resolutely feminist as that of her source. Instead, she saw herself as a missionary following in the footsteps of Mary Louisa Whately, whose work in Cairo founding and running a network of girls' schools had garnered her a wide following among the British faithful.[50] Whately's spirit accompanied Rogers throughout her visits, as she distributed tracts and scriptures and meditated on the means of spreading the Christian message to Muslims. When she saw Arab women in the Jardin Marengo, she lamented: "These poor veiled creatures—veiled in mind and body—bound in shackles which none but their own sex can loose, how one mourns over them, and longs to be able to reach them! But without a knowledge of Arabic, the hope is futile. The sight of them at almost every step, recalls Miss Whately's, 'Ragged life in Egypt,' with such added interest. I would we could employ an Arabic-speaking Bible-Woman amongst them."[51] Given Rogers's interest in the plight of indigenous women, she applauded Madame Luce's efforts to raise their status through book learning and industrial skills. Still, she concluded her description by noting, "One cannot feel quite the same interest in this work as in that carried on in Cairo by Miss Whately: the training in one case being for time, the other for eternity."[52]

Despite the absence of a missionary dimension in Madame Luce's establishment, British missionaries clearly saw similarities with institutions of their creation and drew attention to it as a result. When Bessie Rayner Parkes published her twelve vignettes in 1866, the reviewer Alexander Strahan regretted that

Madame Luce had no concern for conversion but nonetheless concluded that "the cultivation of Moorish female talent and originality in works of the needle, enables her to know her workingwomen, and be a real directress."[53] The same reviewer published a brief description of Parkes's book in the *Eclectic Review*, a high-brow monthly whose profits were donated to the British and Foreign Bible Society. He drew particular attention to the portrait of Madame Luce, whose name was "new to us."[54]

In reality, the readers of the *Eclectic* had already encountered Madame Luce in 1860 when the journal published a long article about Algiers that described in considerable detail the initiatives of this "stout, sunny-faced French woman." The article described three visits that Reverend William Hendry Stowell made to her institution, belying the oft-stated prohibition against male visitors to the school or workshop. The author depicted the French efforts to colonize in dire missionary terms as "the hand-to-hand struggle between nature and civiliza-tion—the Moor and the Catholic, between barbaric and Christian law." Despite the impossibility of religious proselytism within the school, Stowell approved of the language training and especially the "industrial education" that enabled the "Mahometan woman" to gain a "respectable livelihood." Unlike the rather prim Ellen Rogers, however, he devoted far more time to the appearance of the students, revealing how Orientalist fantasies could structure missionary tales: "She got together four little girls—such little girls, if they were like the present scholars whom I saw—dressed in full trousers and jackets, their hair twisted into long pigtails behind, and tightly bound with green ribbon, a-top of which were little caps of velvet, embroidered with gold thread. The nails of their little hands were tinged with henna, and their legs, perfectly bare from the knee to the ankle, were finished off with anklets and slippers—stockings being apparently unknown."[55] One cannot help noticing that Bessie Rayner Parkes's description of the students published a year later echoed almost word for word Stowell's prose, minus the moralizing overtones, such as the comment about the absence of stock-ings.[56] Parkes, like Rogers, borrowed from existing narratives, but she left out the more critical notes of the British clergyman, who continued in this fashion:

Imagine four young objects thus attired, densely ignorant, and choked up with preju-dices, brought to her swaddled up in veils by their mothers or an old servant, either of which would be equally invisible, save for a slit under the brow, permitting two black eyes to pick their way up and down the labyrinthine streets. Upon these four she set to work without delay; and by degrees, as a rumour of the school spread from household to household, by means doubtless of the morning calls which the Moorish ladies make from house to house, by stepping, like cats, from roof to roof, the school increased to thirty or forty pupils.[57]

This article was republished in the *Journal of Education for Upper Canada*, thus spreading to North America this particular representation of agile, catlike girls and women, swathed in prejudice but nonetheless attaining a greater degree of humanity, thanks to the efforts of Madame Luce.[58] Indeed, the article ended with a description of the objects sent to the 1855 Exposition Universelle in Paris, including a set of dolls dressed in native costume, "many of which were executed by a poor deaf and dumb girl, whose lot, but for Madame Luce, would have been deplorable."[59] For Stowell, Madame Luce's efforts to combat ignorance and degradation, combined with what he described as the "romantic" and "remarkable" nature of her life story, compensated for the lack of Christian education.

Lady Mary Elizabeth Herbert, née A'Court, adopted a very similar tone more than a decade later in her description of Madame Luce's workshop. A convert to Roman Catholicism, Herbert was known for her various travel writings, including the 1867 *Cradle Lands*, which documented her trip to Jerusalem. In her later explorations of the Casbah, she had visited first Madame Barroil's workshop and then that of Madame Luce: "No attempt is made in either of these institutions to give the girls any religious instruction. They are solely intended to raise their moral tone, and enable them to earn their own living respectably."[60] By 1870, when elementary instruction had been eliminated from Luce's institution, visitors such as Herbert increasingly associated work and morality: "Madame Luce and the Sisters of Charity are striving to raise these poor little things from [their] miserable position, and by teaching them needlework and embroidery to enable them to get situations in better-class houses."[61] Interestingly, despite the British interest in religion, or its absence, only Matilda Betham Edwards noted the presence of Islamic religious symbols within Madame Luce's institution: "The religious exercises of her little scholars are attended to, and you are reminded of their orthodoxy by the constant occurrence of a little hand, either cut in paper lying on their embroidery frame, or words in the form of an amulet round the neck. This symbol of a hand is supposed to have reference to the five principal duties [of Islam] before mentioned, the fore-finger signifying prayer, the second almsgiving, and so on."[62]

Given British anti-Catholicism, it is perhaps not surprising that missionary travelers simply noted how Madame Luce's school and workshop helped to improve indigenous morality. In a sense, Algeria was more of a playground for the British than a mission territory. And in this playground, the sort of rational recreation that increasingly prevailed involved monetary expenditures, notably the purchase of oriental embroideries. By the final quarter of the century, travelers who described Madame Luce focused overwhelmingly on the objects her students crafted, contributing in their way to the purchase and circulation of native Algerian women's embroidered goods.

Promoting Oriental Goods

From the outset, Bodichon and Parkes presented Madame Luce as a heroine for indigenous womankind, in part because of the vocational skills she helped girls develop. Their admiration, however, went beyond reasoning about feminine independence and autonomy as increasingly they actively promoted the "exquisite embroideries" associated with her students. Although Bodichon's guidebook in 1858 said nothing about textiles being for sale, by the early 1860s virtually all visitors commented on the possibilities for such purchases. The interest in these embroideries was part of a broader British fascination with things òriental, but it is important to keep in mind the way Madame Luce cultivated and responded to this fascination. Once her school had ceased to attract French dignitaries, she turned her attention to this admiring new public. In lieu of prize-giving ceremonies, she set up spaces to exhibit her students' goods, lent her embroideries to people like Bodichon and Parkes, and sent her objects to London for exhibition.

Evidence for this activism comes almost solely through the voices of British travelers and guidebooks. In 1860 Henry E. Pope devoted several pages to Madame Luce, "a lady whose name, in connection with reform, ought to be as immortal in French history as that of Sir Robert Peel in our own annals." This reference to the defender of British free trade was not fortuitous, because Pope then went on to laud the "cleverness of finger" that allowed Luce's students to earn a "very tolerable living. The ostrich Feather fans are principally the work of their hands. In these respects they are a thousand times better off than hundreds of our own poor milliners, whose strength ebbs daily away at the needle's point." He was the only visitor to note that the school/workshop sold not only fans and embroidered goods, but also busts of Madame Luce herself: "Personally, Madame Luce has a fine open face, and a rather commanding presence. Several busts and likenesses of her have been taken and may be obtained in the European shops."[63]

In July 1862 B.R.P., or Bessie Rayner Parkes, in the *English Woman's Journal* drew attention to the commercial aspects of Luce's work in a brief paragraph titled "Madame Luce and the Great Exhibition," referring to the universal exhibition in London:

Our readers who may remember the biographical account of Madame Luce, published in this journal in June 1861, are informed that a large case of Algeria embroidery, executed in ouvroirs musulmans under her supervision are to be found in the Algerine Department of the French court. The articles are for sale, and are chiefly adapted for expensive and beautiful toilettes: embroidered jackets, handkerchiefs, etc. Dolls dresses in Algerine costume, and a pair of rich curtains, are also to be found in the case, which adequately represents Madame Luce's extraordinary energy, and the exquisite manufacture of female handicraft in Algiers.[64]

Parkes encouraged her fellow citizens to discover and buy these objects crafted by Madame Luce's students. Indeed, the French catalogue for the Algerian exhibit makes clear that Luce saw the exhibit not only as a way of achieving international recognition—she won both medals and honorable mentions in the section "Ethnography, Indigenous Industries"—but also of selling a wide range of products. In the catalogue for the exhibition, the list of goods for sale in Madame Luce's exhibit is far lengthier than for other exhibitors: more than fifty objects are detailed, ranging in price from 800 francs for a shawl or a gold embroidered rug to a mere 5 francs for a doily.[65] The inclusion of a great number of doll dresses representing Moorish, Kabyle, and Jewish winter and summer clothing testifies to the ways Madame Luce exploited the British taste for ethnographic exotica to earn money for her workshop.

In 1866 when she published her vignette of Madame Luce, Parkes described in some detail the variety of goods produced within the workshop, emphasizing the quality of material and its cost: "There were curtains worked on Arab thread muslin which are certainly the most lovely specimens of embroidery in the world, and from the quantity of gold thread, cannot be worth less than £150 the pair." The cheapest objects were cloth Zouave jackets embroidered with real gold, which sold for about £6. According to Parkes, "the girls looked brighter and happier than is usually seen in Moorish bowers, and there is no doubt it is healthier to be there and working, than in their houses doing nothing. In the future, the knowledge of a trade may save them from much misery." This familiar argument was followed, however, by a new aesthetic argument: "In another point of view this ouvroir was most interesting—namely that of art; for these wonderful Arab embroideries were going out of the world, the very stitches forgotten, until the taste of the English visitors made a great demand for them." In this fashion Parkes positioned Madame Luce alongside British tourists, such as herself, together working to save a precolonial heritage: "If Madame Luce respects this beautiful instinct in the Arab women, and allows them to develop it untainted by false French taste, she will do good service to art."[66]

Ellen Rogers similarly perceived the British to be playing a key role in the development of native embroidery: "It seems that the revival of this branch of Arab art, is partly due to the taste and patronage of British visitors." During her stay in Algiers in the winter of 1863–1864, she described the existence of an exhibition room where men could admire the pieces for sale, while women were able to see the young workers at their looms. She admired, in particular, the white work—"exquisite cashmere burnouses, and mantels for ladies, worked in white floss silk or the beautiful muslin curtains embroidered in white and gold"—while also noting that the costliest objects require a "well-stocked purse": "150*l*. [pounds] the pair for Arab thread gold-embroidered curtains. Beautiful Zouave jackets are 6*l*. each." Fortunately, Madame Luce also sold objects "for every purse." Rogers concluded with a reminder that all these things had been exhibited in the Great Exhibition at Kensington and "will doubtless be remembered by some of my readers."[67]

Not all British visitors were as smitten by Madame Luce's workshop, however. Following a four-month stay in Algeria, Mrs. Lloyd Evans published a description of the colony ending with an appendix "with practical hints for visitors." Generally critical of the French, whom she described "as a body not good colonizers" (in contrast to the Scotch or the Germans), her praise came seldom without critical asides:

Supplies: The meat of course is not so good as in England, but much better than in most foreign places.
Shops: Dearer than in France but tolerably good. . . . Embroidery, as I have mentioned, is not first-rate as compared with Oriental work generally, but still effective enough, especially for furniture. It is dear for the quality. The best places for it are Madame Luce's and the "Ouvroir arabe," the latter cheaper, but the work less carefully executed.[68]

Most visitors, however, were more appreciative, including pious Lady Herbert, who mentioned, after describing the "quite beautiful white work" she admired at the workshops of Madame Luce and Madame Barroil, that she then purchased dresses from the former: "I ordered two ball dresses of Madame Luce, which were executed by these children with wonderful beauty and rapidity. They also embroider every kind of handkerchief and scarf, and that in the greatest perfection, there being no wrong side to their work, which therefore can be worn in any way."[69]

Even male visitors, whom one might imagine somewhat less entranced by visits of this sort, described the embroideries with some admiration. The British physician James Henry Bennet, who regularly wintered in Algeria between 1859 and 1874, noted after visiting a boys' school that he had the opportunity "to see a very interesting assemblage of little Arab girls from six to twelve years of age in the embroidery workshop of Madame Luce, a French lady. Partly from philanthropic motives she teaches young Jewish and Arab girls the art of embroidery, and under her auspices they become apt scholars, as was evident from the numerous and lovely embroidered objects of ladies' toilette that were shown us." He was, however, less interested in the material and their cost than in the exotic little embroiderers: "Many of the little girls were perfect little houris [the beautiful maidens who lived with the blessed in Allah's paradise]".[70]

The American politician Samuel Sullivan Cox similarly admired the "interesting juvenile group" that he found upon visiting Madame Luce's "House":

Some thirty beautiful Moorish girls, as fair as any such group in New York (save one of glossiest ebony), were all at work, sitting on the floor over their frames, and finishing the inwoven elegance of those fabrics which so astonish the Occidental lady by their perfection of needlework. I saw new meaning in Shakespeare's lines:—

"The hand of *little* employment hath the daintier sense."

These girls—nearly all—even the smallest, of four years, had the tiny nails of their pliant fingers stained dark with henna, and their hair coloured into a reddish wine-colour. This colour of the hair they retain till they marry. Then it is stained black. When the hair becomes grey, in their old age, they stain it red again.[71]

This description makes clear that whereas fabrics were ladies' concern, his attention was directed toward the "beautiful Moorish girls."

More commonly, Madame Luce's workshop was described by lady travelers, and by the 1870s British guidebooks steered the curious toward her door. The first Murray guidebook in 1873 mentioned her school, and the second edition referred to two quasi-educational establishments for Moorish girls, adding, "That of Madame Luce is well worthy of visit."[72] Lisbeth Gooch Strahan acknowledged using this guide and insisted that a visit to Luce's workshop "should on no account be omitted." Although she placed her description of Madame Luce in a chapter titled "Arrival at Algiers Dull and Useful Information," she clearly found the place both intriguing and worth the visit, since the prices were not excessive and "gentlemen are not excluded from the purchasing room."[73]

Strahan was probably one of the last British travel writers to visit the workshop during the reign of Madame Luce. After Luce returned to France in 1875, her granddaughter, Henriette Benaben, took over the establishment and continued actively to attract English-speaking visitors. In 1889 she paid for an advertisement in the local British newspaper, the *Algerian Advertiser*, which published the workshop's location at 7 rue Bruce and listed it as a "Highly recommended house."[74] In 1891 the British consul's guidebook to the city included a description of the workshop in a section on "shops and bazaars":

Of the many establishments devoted to the sale or manufacture of what are called *objets arabes*, none is more worthy of a visit than that of Madame Benaben, grand-daughter and successor of Madame Luce, in the Rue Bruce, nearly opposite the Cathedral. The latter lady devoted her whole life to two most laudable objects—the perpetuation of the exquisite embroidery for which Algiers has always been famous, and which, but for her, would now have become an extinct art; and the endeavor to teach Arab women to gain their livelihood in an honest matter. In their youth they are taught to work at the establishment, and when they marry and settle in life they continue to work at home, and bring the produce of their industry there for sale. Such thoroughly good "woman's work" is worthy of the highest praise and encouragement.[75]

This description closely echoes Parkes's earlier description, but by the 1890s all mention of girls' schooling had vanished in favor of promoting the goods that the girls produced.

An Irish visitor in the early 1890s, Ermengarda Greville Nugent, was more fanciful and less accurate in her description of the "Moorish embroideresses" gathered around Henriette Benaben. Adopting Orientalist tropes, she wrote that the girls turned out "fairy fabrics covered with delicate stitches worked by their henna-tinted fingers; an art which once formed the chief occupation in the harems, but which is now principally kept alive owing to her efforts." As the title of her book suggests, *A Land of Mosques and Marabouts*, she was in search more of the exotic than of evidence of work well-done.[76]

Joseph C. Hyam's *Illustrated Guide to Algiers* provided the most lengthy description of the establishment, recounting Madame Luce's early achievements in perpetuating a "magnificent art—embroidery" and then her granddaughter's efforts to develop and expand Luce's work:

The present directrice has since found it necessary to remove to more extensive premiss, and her school is now carried on in an entire Arab house—where visitors may see the little Moorish girls at their interesting work, in the square courtyard—in the Kasba, N.21 Rue du Rempart Médée. Indeed, during the last few years this industry has been obliged to create a second establishment, which is situated on the Mustapha Superior roads, almost adjoining the Scotch Church. It is a fine house of Oriental style, and serves admirably as show-rooms for the innumerable dainty objects of this exquisite embroidery, a native art, which, had it not been for Madame Luce, the founder, would have assuredly become extinct. There is also a philanthropic side in connection with these institutions, for Madame Ben-Aben continues to support several of the poorer Moorish women, who, for some reason or other, are unable to continue their work.

At the school in the Rue du Rempart Médée there are now about 30 Moorish girls, of ages from 5 to 15, and it is truly a picturesque and interesting sight to watch these little Mohameddan girls, in charge of their mistress, manufacturing Algerian embroidery.

No Visitor to Algiers should leave without paying a visit to Madame Ben-Aben's interesting ouvroir, where the public is always received and shown over the establishment in a most hospitable manner, which is legendary at this embroidery school.[77]

Across from this description, Hyam included a photo of the Moorish girls at Madame Ben-Aben's school of embroidery taken from a London lady's newspaper, *The Queen.*

Hyam's description reflected the new interest in Algeria at the turn of the twentieth century in exalting and preserving a mythic precolonial past; it also contained traces of the early feminist interest in how this act of preservation served the female working poor.[78] By the beginning of the new century, such interest in women's work had become far more widespread across the Western world, fuelled by international feminist congresses, in addition to universal exhibitions. As a result, women travelers increasingly described the Luce Benaben workshop in terms that emphasized how philanthropy contributed to the preservation of art forms in which girls and women played a central role.

Following a five-month stay in Algiers, the American visitor Mary Elizabeth Crouse recounted this story in a chapter titled "Hidden Ways":

In one Moorish house little girls are learning the embroidery stitch which their great-grandmothers knew. Early in the French occupation, a French woman, realizing that the art of Algerian embroidery was dying, founded this school which her granddaughter carries on. From the beginning they collected the rare old pieces, once so lavishly done; napkins long enough to encircle the table and to cover the laps of ten; fine indoor head coverings of the women; even exquisite caps for drying the hair. For a time these little girls will continue the beautiful work of the Moorish past, with all its suggestion of poetry. Attempts have been made in this school to teach the children reading, but the parents object, for it injured their chances of marriage. They leave their benefactress soon after their work becomes valuable; but she still cares for those who have grown old since her grandmother's time.[79]

Less focused on the personality of Luce or Benaben, this description shows how interest in oriental embroideries now conditioned travelers' interpretations. Artisanal work had acquired pride of place rather than the civilizing mission.

By 1900 such interest in how the workshop was preserving a vanished art form was also very present among the French (see Chapter 7), but in the years between 1861 and Madame Luce's departure from Algiers in the mid-1870s, this was not the case. Madame Luce's fame was far less apparent among her fellow countrymen and countrywomen, testimony to the influence of a French colonial script that read and translated her activities with mixed feelings.

THE FRENCH TRAVELERS' PERSPECTIVE

Both French guidebooks and French travel narratives paint a rather different portrait of Madame Luce and her work compared with the British descriptions. To begin with, French travelers to Algeria did not have the same curiosity about their fellow citizens. Nor was French tourism to Algeria as developed as British tourism in the 1860s and 1870s, particularly for women. Not surprisingly, French travelers were far more interested in describing exotic landscapes and indigenous dress or practices than in recounting a visit to a Frenchwoman's workshop. As the author Théophile Gautier noted in a letter home to his family in 1845, "Algeria is a magnificent country where only the French are too numerous."[80] Twenty years later, most visitors were more circumspect but rarely more interested in describing either the French or the other Europeans, nor do they appear as interested as the British in cataloguing the results of French colonization.[81]

Anonymity and Distance in French Guidebooks

French guidebooks reflect this lesser interest and offer a strong contrast to the Murray guide's enthusiasm about the woman Madame Luce and her activities.

Although in the early 1830s guidebooks to Algeria were directed to leisure travelers, the French concern to promote a settler colony quickly generated another sort of guidebook—one more oriented toward the prospective or newly arrived settler.[82] These guidebooks, or *annuaires*, might indicate the address of Madame Luce's Arab-French school, alongside that of Auguste Depeille's school for boys, but in neither case were the directors mentioned by name. Rather, they were included in lists of institutional categories. For example, the *Petite bibliothèque du voyageur en Algérie* (The Traveler's Little Library for Algeria) included the following addresses in a section titled "Diverse Administrations or Public Institutions":

École arabe-française [Arab-French school], rue Porte Neuve 39

École communale des arts-et-métiers [arts and crafts school], rue Bab-el-Oued, 10

Ouvroirs musulmans [Muslim workshops], rue de Toulon, 5 and rue Abderhame[83]

Readers had no clue that the first school was for boys and that the *ouvroirs* welcomed girls. Nor was there any indication in this guide that visitors might purchase embroidered goods at the latter, even though this section of the guidebook was full of promotional advertisements.

The guidebooks more directly aimed at travelers, rather than settlers, were more attentive to Madame Luce's activities although I have not found one that actually mentioned her by name. The first Joanne guide for Algeria was published in 1862 by the prolific travel guide writer Louis Piesse. This famous collection of erudite French guidebooks quickly acquired a reputation for the quality of the cultural information provided and the qualifications of its authors.[84] In this case Piesse established his authority in his preface, mentioning not only that he had lived for ten years in Algeria, but also that he worked in the civil administration and once back in Paris had helped with the publication of statistical information about the French institutions in Algeria. Who better to guide the visitor throughout the colony? Although he knew of Madame Luce's workshop, his portrait bears little resemblance to that of the romantic heroine that British writers portrayed.

In a series of paragraphs about the condition of the Moorish woman, Piesse described, without naming her, a Frenchwoman who opened a school for Moorish girls. He had heard tell that they were as capable as young Europeans in answering questions about grammar, arithmetic, geography, and history; in addition, they were talented seamstresses and embroiderers. All this proved, according to Piesse, that the Moorish woman was capable of learning. But Muslim prejudices against learning for daughters meant that only the poor attended the school, and for these girls schooling brought social problems, "because these children, whose intelligence is only partly formed, return home in the evening to their families, and sadly compare their own miserable condition, from which they cannot escape, with an unattainable well-being. Too superior for the men of modest condition whom they might hope to marry, they are scorned by the wealthier; and so, these poor unfortunate and learned creatures, contemptuous of the former and rejected by the latter, are reduced to doing what they would have done had they remained poor and ignorant." It is not clear whether Piesse is suggesting that these young women resorted to prostitution, as members of the General Council had argued, but when defending the decision to close the school, he certainly presents here a negative portrayal of the results of Madame Luce's efforts. Nor did he make any attempt to promote the embroidered goods of the workshop, arguing on the contrary that indigenous industries were generally in a bad way.[85]

A few years later Achille Fillias thought fit to remedy this neglect in his *Nouveau guide général du voyageur en Algérie* (New General Guide for the Traveler in Algeria). A geographer who knew Algeria well, having lived there during the 1840s and again beginning in 1859, Fillias wrote a guidebook filled with a wealth of very specific information more useful to the professional than to the traveler. In a chapter on "indigenous public instruction" he gave precise information about the number of students being educated in 1863: 298 boys and 35 girls. He explained that this very low number of girls was due to the decision to convert the girls' school into a workshop that offered girls apprenticeship training in all manner of handiwork. He then mentioned the existence of a second workshop, erroneously noting that it opened in 1863. Although he did not mention Madame Luce by name, Fillias clearly felt that her institution merited recognition, and in a section on "European and indigenous industry" he highlighted the presence of oriental or luxury embroideries on show at the Palais de l'industrie in Paris, objects that were the product of the workshops for girls in Algiers and Constantine.[86]

French Women Travelers of Two Minds

French travelers interested in embroideries or the products of indigenous industry undoubtedly found their way to Madame Luce's workshop in the Casbah, but there were fewer signposts to help those travelers reach her than in the English-speaking world once her school no longer attracted attention. Given the publicity around her school in the 1850s, it is striking to see how her name is not even mentioned in the guidebooks. The same "discretion" is apparent in the travel narratives of Frenchwomen, which are less numerous and less effusive than those of their British counterparts. In the absence of a French Barbara Bodichon, only three female travel narratives describe Madame Luce's school or workshop, and only two mention her by name. Moreover, the three texts that refer to her offer no coherent portrait; rather, they reflect the diversity of opinions concerning her action that was so prevalent in the colonial administration that had decided to close her school.[87]

The most favorable reading of Luce's activities emerges in Anaïs Dutertre's narrative describing a visit with her daughter in 1853. In this lengthy text (written at the request of friends, she noted in the preface) she portrayed herself following in the footsteps of French Orientalists, notably the painter Horace Vernet, whom she quoted while visiting Constantine. She visited Algiers toward the end of her travels, greeting the city with these relatively trite remarks: "Algiers! Here now is Algiers, the princess, the sultan, the favorite of governors and travelling princes." She saw the city as both oriental and African while getting in her own little dig at the British when she described a journalist who greeted the boat in order to note down the passengers' names: "This invention, which seems to us an absurd impropriety, must be a British import; it certainly reflects British interest in gossip." In Algiers she swung into a very social life that took her to Madame Luce's door. Although her narrative was not published until 1866, her travels occurred during the heyday of the Arab-French school in Algiers. Dutertre's portrait focused, like those of British visitors, on the director of the school herself, describing her as "*tout bonnement* [quite frankly] a simple and generous French woman who knows a great deal about progress, real, useful, charitable progress."[88]

In Dutertre's three-page presentation, Luce appeared as a woman seeking to improve women's inferior status in order that they participate more fully in the French civilizing project by acting on their families and husbands: "She thought that in Algeria one must seek to pull women . . . from the total ignorance which degrades them, from the deplorable laziness in which they vegetate and which renders them unfortunately incapable of achieving their own happiness." Madame Luce understood, according to Dutertre, that only the "regenerated Arab woman" would be able to "modify and render more pliant the men of this nation."[89] While her tone was somewhat less feminist and more moralizing than that of Parkes, Dutertre similarly presented Luce's accomplishment in heroic terms, describing the way Luce conquered obstacles placed before her by the French authorities. She insisted as well on the ways that Christian morality was intertwined with messages in the Quran without offending the students' families. Time would eventually produce results, she argued.

Dutetre positioned Luce at the center of a very oriental portrait; her school opened in the most Arabic section of Algiers in that "white beehive where streets are open corridors climbing upwards." Her students, while learning French, also executed beautiful silken and gold embroideries, "their admirable eyes sparkling with an alert and ardent intelligence." These students are presented not only as suitable subjects for passing painters but also as France's secret weapon within Arab families: "One sees at Madame Luce's the sorts of physiognomies which constitute a treasure for the painter; colorists would delight in the variety of costumes. . . . One will come to seek the students of Madame Luce to become the wives of the most honorable and most distinguished men of the nation."[90] Such statements echo Madame Luce's official reports, revealing the ways that she actively shaped visitors' understandings of her school. By the 1860s, however, she no longer controlled French opinion, as is amply clear in the description of Louise Vallory.

Vallory's narrative of Algeria in the early 1860s, À l'aventure en Algérie (Off for Adventures in Algeria), made no explicit mention of Madame Luce but described her institution in a chapter about "Interior Life" in Algiers. Furthermore, her portrait of the indigenous groups she met did not transmit the picturesque. Rather, she resorted to an almost ethnographic description of what she characterized as "a dying race." Her vivid prose described the Moors of Algiers as a bastard race, "flabby, spineless, weakened, enervated, as if whitened by the city's atmosphere." Her portrayal of Moorish women was even more critical, describing their languid futility coupled with an absence of morality and modesty. It is in this context that she mentioned Madame Luce's school, using terms similar to those of the General Council, rather than to those of Luce's self-promotional prose:

The Moorish women who mumble a bit of French and allow the curious stranger's eye to plunge into their private lives have very cosmopolitan hearts and morals. Many of them have been raised in a semi-French, semi-Arab school, founded I have no doubt with philanthropic objectives; in a large workshop where young girls learn above all to embroider, they are constantly distracted by the visits of strangers and bothered by a thousand irritants. The family life to which they return in the evening is completely at odds with life at school, they cease to know what to believe, they fail to know what to do and they test freedom through debauchery.[91]

Although according to Vallory French colonization and European tourism were partly to blame for the unfortunate results of this institution, she made clear that the nature of Moorish women was such that one could expect little from them. Futile and attached to traditional beliefs and habits, "[the Moorish woman] has little of that gleam which illuminates her thought processes." This searing disdain for the intelligence of her colonial sisters was not exempt from feminist overtones, as she blamed Moorish men for women's absence of liberty. But this criticism of male domination over women extended to her view of France as well, where women were unable to divorce, unlike in Algeria: "France, the country of extreme civilization and exquisite refinement; here women must languish in perpetuity in an antagonistic and often unhealthy cohabitation."[92] In the end, Vallory's text offers interesting insights into gender relations in both France and Algeria, but unlike fellow English travelers, she was not in the business of seeking role models in the task of introducing civilization, since she had her doubts about French civilization to begin with.[93] As the title of her book indicated, she went to Algeria in the spirit of adventure, seeking to understand what she saw, and her gaze was little directed to Europeans, and particularly Frenchwomen, who were objects of only minor curiosity.

The final travel narrative to mention Madame Luce is that of Louis Régis, the pseudonym for an unknown woman, according to the book's introduction. Like Vallory, the author spent time with Moorish families, but her remarks were far more measured than those of her predecessor. Her descriptions throughout the book testify to the ways she researched her subject, using statistics to complement her ethnographic details. The Moorish women she described were not lazy and languid, but were verbally proficient and relatively dutiful seamstresses, albeit uneducated. Régis warned against the French instinct to provide education, arguing for the dangers of gender imbalance in a country where men were also so ignorant. She accepted fatalistically that this was the consequence of a "hot climate," since European women were in general poorly educated as well—an affirmation that colonial authorities surely would have disputed. But she heartily approved of the efforts made by several women, including Madame Luce, to open workshops for poor young girls: "In this fashion, they acquire the means to earn their living and at the same time learn to model their behavior on healthy and virtuous principles. That seems to me the most we can reasonably expect to accomplish in our effort to improve the existence of the Arab woman." In her description of Algiers, Régis noted, like her British counterparts, that travelers should visit Madame Luce's workshop, as "it is one of the numerous good works efficiently patronized by Madame la Maréchale de Mac-Mahon [wife of the governor general]."[94]

This gesture toward Madame MacMahon, rather than to Madame Luce, highlights the contrast between French and British visions of Madame Luce's activities in Algeria. By the 1860s Madame Luce was clearly more successful gaining an audience for her story and a market for her goods within the British colony of Algiers. Furthermore, British feminist networks worked effectively to celebrate her story and make it available to a wide range of readers, as the missionary versions make apparent. Even in the United States, Madame Luce's activities attracted attention; the feminist Caroline Wells Healey Dall lectured to audiences about women such as Luce "doing the work of saints and martyrs," . . . "planting new germs of moral power and thought in every family circle which they touch."[95]

French visitors had no similar scripts to follow, as the French feminist movement was in its infancy at this time and the first feminist journal, *Le Droit des Femmes* (Women's Rights), began publication only in 1869. As a result, the travelers who wandered the streets of Algiers had guidebooks or contacts who might or might not direct them toward the school or workshop, but not toward Madame Luce in particular. Their descriptions, then, varied considerably, depending on their perspectives. One must turn to the British imperial narrative to discover a larger-than-life woman battling the forces of both Muslim and French misogyny. Perhaps, not surprisingly, the only French reading to approach such an interpretation was that of the fiery feminist socialist Hubertine Auclert, but this happened only after Luce's death, at the end of the century, at a moment when colonial cultural and gender politics had changed considerably.

7

THE REMAINS OF THE DAY
(1875–1915)

On 11 June 1882 the French newspaper *Le Républicain de Loir-et-Cher* reported: "On the fourth of June, Madame Luce, the erstwhile director of the school for Muslim girls in Algeria, died in Montrichard in her 79th year." The obituary emphasized her tireless energy dedicated to "the regeneration of the Arab woman through work and instruction": "Madame Luce, with remarkable good sense, succeeded through her secular teaching enacted a half century earlier [than in France] in turning Arab girls into excellent mothers and model wives. Her successes, of course, did not attract the same attention as battles but they nonetheless represent a great triumph over superstition and ignorance." The author, Luce's friend of thirty years Nicolas Eugène Paute Laforie (1815–1894), concluded on a note that mingled the domestic and the political: "She ended her days modestly, with her family and her friends; her only desire was to see the Republic triumph over its enemies through work, justice and peace." This notice offers a few hints about the final years of Eugénie Luce's life after she left Algeria in 1875 and settled down to enjoy her family, the pleasures of provincial life, and the fruits of a life well-spent.

Family matters weighed in Luce's decision to return to France, and her example concretely suggests the interconnections that existed between Algeria and metropolitan France for many nineteenth-century families. Although Eugénie Luce chose to die in France, she left her workshop in the hands of her granddaughter, Henriette Benaben, and maintained contact with her relations in Algiers. Luce left a variety of legacies behind her, both in France and in Algeria, where memory of her school and workshop resurfaced at the turn of the twentieth century. She left behind material goods but also an oeuvre, as the obituary mentioned. The inventory established at her death not only reveals her possessions, but also the ways that her years in Algeria brought her a certain degree of wealth. One must turn elsewhere, however, to discern her legacy in material goods—the artisanal handicrafts that circulated between France, Great Britain, and North Africa. Henriette Benaben left a collection of "oriental embroideries" to the museum in Algiers before her death in 1915. These embroideries are arguably the most permanent, and highly gendered, legacy of Madame Luce's Algerian sojourn. Objects from this collection appeared in many exhibitions, from Chicago in 1893 to Marseille in 1906; they were also prominently displayed in the celebrations surrounding the centenary in 1930 of France's conquest of Algeria. Even today, although the Luce Benaben Room no longer exists, objects from the collection are still on show in the Islamic art section of the National Museum of Antiquities in Algiers.

THE FINAL YEARS

Madame Luce never completely vanished from the historical record, but by 1882 when she died in Montrichard, she was no longer the public figure she had been in Algiers during the 1850s. Although the republican departmental paper in France published an obituary, other papers did not, perhaps because her remaining family members were either too distracted or too young to think about that sort of thing. Perhaps more striking is the fact that Algerian papers did not record her passing. Even journals interested in education, such as the *Journal Scolaire de l'Algérie*, which regularly carried obituaries, failed to record her death. Of course, her school had been ruled out of existence twenty years earlier, and she was no longer living in the colony when she died.

What do we know about her final years that might explain this relative silence? Her great-granddaughter's lengthy memoirs offer the most detailed information about these years. Through the writing of Jeanne Crouzet-Benaben, we can watch Eugénie Luce as she got older, fatter, and more proper—although not more pious. During her final years in both Algeria and France, she seems to have avoided the limelight and focused on her family, devoting herself in particular to the young Jeanne. Several chapters of Jeanne's memoirs address in detail her memories of this beloved old woman. She often addresses Eugénie directly: "I can feel that on this earth I was your last and your greatest love." She continues: "For this love, may you be blessed dear grandmother; your tenderness protected my early years, it still illuminates my childhood. As I wearily allow myself to meditate upon the past, [your] memory offers a consoling refuge."[1] In Crouzet-Benaben's prose, Madame Luce appears as a family member: mother, grandmother, great-grandmother, wife, and great-aunt. This loving portrait reminds us that Eugénie Luce was not just an actor in Algerian colonial politics, but also a woman in a family, with a capacity to love and care that appears to have amply filled her old age.

Family Matters: Picking Up the Pieces

The cold reality of death certificates tells a relatively sad story of the years after 1870 and the establishment of a civilian government in Algeria. Louis Luce's sudden death in 1872 rocked the life of "Maman Luce," as Crouzet-Benaben recounts this incident in her memoirs more than seventy years later. The loss of this companion of Luce's adult life in Algeria left a gaping hole that widened further a year later with the premature death at the age of forty-six of her only surviving daughter, Marie. Luce's older siblings at this point were also dead, and I have found no trace of her younger sister Olimpe. Fortunately, however, Eugénie was not alone during these years. Alongside the dozens of girls who daily appeared for lessons in embroidery and weaving, her house was also the home to her granddaughter, Henriette, who had returned to Algiers in the early 1870s, bringing her baby Jeanne and her husband Paul Benaben with her. Jeanne's writing in particular allows us to gain some insight into the time and energy Luce devoted to caring for her daughter, granddaughter, and then great-granddaughter. In this fashion, she may have sought to atone for having abandoned five-year-old Marie when she fled to Algeria in 1832. By the early 1870s her family and her homeland were increasingly in her thoughts, but Jeanne's presence in Algeria caused her to hesitate to return to France.

The relationship between great-grandmother and great-granddaughter was unusually close, the product of family history and particularly the familial tendency to wed young and unwisely. Married to the unreliable Félix Belly, Luce's daughter Marie appears not to have been much of a mother herself. As a result, Marie's daughter, Henriette Belly, grew up with her grandmother, attending her school during the 1850s, learning Arabic as well as the embroidery trade in the workshop. For a brief period in the early 1860s, Henriette's eccentric and frequently absent father sent her off to Paris to acquire another sort of education. He placed his young daughter, born and bred in French Algeria, into a British boarding school in Paris run by Mrs. Grenfell. Surrounded by British girls whose parents wanted their daughters to acquire a veneer of French culture and manners through life in the capital, Henriette developed an abiding love for the English people, the English language, and English customs, which explains in part the success she had vaunting the workshop's embroideries to British visitors at the end of the century. Henriette described her two years in Second Empire Paris, enjoying the cultural life and acquiring a modicum of instruction, as the only really happy years of her life.[2] Her father, however, failed to pay her tuition regularly, and so she was sent back to Algiers, where she lived with her grandparents, working in Luce's workshop and playing music with her grandfather. During a visit in 1864, the novelist and playwright Alexandre Dumas (fils, 1824–1895) spent time with the Luce family and described the beautiful seventeen-year-old Henriette as "having a beam of sunlight in her brain."[3]

Back in Algiers, Henriette fell in love with Paul Benaben, a young baritone whose theatrical performance as Nélusko in Giacomo Meyerbeer's *L'Africaine* had made a big impression in the cultural circles in Algiers.[4] Benaben was from Toulouse and had studied medicine before beginning a theatrical career. At the end of May 1869 the two married in Algiers; Henriette's father was absent, and the marriage act specifies that it was the women of the family, Marie Belly and Madame Luce, who gave their authorization for the twenty-two-year-old bride to wed. The demands of Benaben's profession led him to uproot the family frequently, and once back in France he quickly shifted his affections from his wife to other women: "He became again the *méridional*, lover of women, which he had never ceased to be except to the bewitched eyes of his wife," according to his disillusioned daughter Jeanne.[5] From Toulouse, the couple moved to Brussels where Benaben performed at the Théâtre de la Monnaie. This is where Jeanne was born on 23 September 1870 and first encountered Nicolas Eugène Paute Laforie, Eugénie Luce's friend who would become Jeanne's tutor at Luce's death. From Brussels, Benaben took his young family back to Algiers in 1871 where Jeanne, as a baby, experienced her only years of true family life, surrounded by her parents, grandparents, and great-grandparents. Madame Luce taught her to read and write; in the afternoons she played alongside the Moorish girls who embroidered.

This image of familial harmony, three generations briefly living and working together—Maman Luce teaching, Papa Luce playing the violin, grandparents Belly adoring the new baby, father Paul directing the national theater in Algiers—is obviously a reconstruction of the past, but it is one that conveys a taste of Luce's final years in Algeria when her public fame had vanished. The new civilian government was not interested in her workshop, and she had her hands full with her family.

The Return to France

The deaths of Eugénie Luce's husband in 1872 and daughter in 1873, as well as the new political climate in Algeria, no doubt contributed to her decision to return to the country of her birth. Jeanne explains the move in this fashion:

Maman Luce felt weighted down by the fatigue of old age and the long struggles she had waged. Combined with the sorrow caused by the loss of her dear companion, she began to think of her native Berry that she had left almost forty years earlier. Even though she had spent most of her life in Algiers, she did not want to die there; far different in this respect from my mother, she was one of those unrepentant Frenchwomen who refused to adopt the Algerian soil above and beyond death; who, at the appropriate moment, returned to establish their tombstone in the part of France they considered their cradle.[6]

Jeanne notes, however, that two things held Luce back: the workshop and Jeanne herself. Although Luce had raised Jeanne's mother in her own household, she considered Henriette "too young, too fanciful, not sufficiently poised, not sufficiently 'bourgeoise'" either to run the workshop or to educate her young daughter.[7] Still, nostalgia overcame these doubts, the family historian writes, and Maman Luce went home, not to the Berry, but to Montrichard in the nearby Touraine.

Again, these are not Luce's explanations, but rather the story someone told Jeanne, probably Paute Laforie, who retrospectively sought to defend his position with respect to Jeanne by criticizing Henriette's flightiness. One cannot help wondering where the myth of Luce's origins in the Berry comes from, echoing as it does a story she told her British friends as well. Was it simply to associate herself geographically with George Sand, "*la bonne dame du Berry*"? A way of distancing herself from the provincialism of Montrichard? For whatever reason, her great-granddaughter accepted this poetic license and compared the two women in this way: "You [referring to Maman Luce] still have your lovely George Sand figure, although less dark, your noble nose, your delicate and benevolent lips. We could call you as well: 'la bonne dame de Montrichard.'"[8]

Luce's decision to return to her birthplace may well have been anchored in a very French commitment to place, even if it appears somewhat odd to us that she would leave what remained of her family and the advantages of the European lifestyle in Algiers to settle alone in a small town that she had left forty-four years earlier. Undoubtedly, this kind of decision lends weight to those who have argued for the importance of local identities and memories in nineteenth-century France.[9] Luce's yearning to go home highlights the ways that early settlers remained tied to their families and birthplaces despite distance and infrequent encounters. She had maintained contacts with her extended family in France, notably through her nephews and great-nephews. Indeed, her final years in Algiers had been very occupied not only by her immediate family, but also by the presence of more distant relatives who came to work or to recover their health in Algeria during the 1860s and 1870s.

As the government encouraged settler immigration, travel conditions between France and Algeria became easier, faster, and cheaper so that families on both sides

of the Mediterranean were able to keep in closer touch, nourishing a familial colonial imaginary. Luce's great-nephew, Sténio Leroy, for example, arrived in Algiers
in December 1864 as a young teacher (*aspirant répétiteur*) in the *Lycée d'Alger*.[10]
At age nineteen, he was welcomed into Eugénie Luce's extended family, and at the
death of Louis Luce in 1872, he was the one to declare the death at the town hall.
Another nephew, Albert Perdrier, spent time with her in Algiers in an effort to
mend his failing health. Luce actively maintained these contacts, and so when she
returned to Montrichard in 1875, she also reentered a family network, with cousins
settled nearby in Angé, Tours, and Châtillon-sur-Indre. At age seventy-two, she
was still in relatively good health and was determined to enjoy life to the end. But
she was also lonely after decades spent surrounded by family and students in the
crowded streets of the Casbah.

Jeanne Crouzet-Benaben recalls the months after her great-grandmother's
departure as difficult ones. Her mother was now the head of the workshop, but
she did not have Eugénie Luce's business sense and connections to the local
indigenous families. The government had ceased sponsoring apprenticeship
training in 1868, and Henriette Benaben's efforts to gain support fell on deaf
ears. Meanwhile, she also had a six-year-old daughter under foot and a husband
whose eyes wandered. While intransigent in his views about feminine morality,
he had no scruples maintaining liaisons with women he met in his very public
role as director of the theater in Algiers. In January 1876, after fewer than seven
years of marriage, Henriette initiated an official separation; she later obtained a
divorce when this became possible in France.[11] Perhaps it was the separation that
prompted Luce to offer to take Jeanne into her new home in France and raise
her as the daughter she had failed to raise. At any rate, Henriette accepted her
grandmother's offer, and by 1876 Jeanne was living with her great-grandmother
on 19 route de Tour in Montrichard, discovering the charms of childhood in
provincial France.[12]

Old Age in Montrichard

Jeanne's descriptions of her great-grandmother are the only source that convey
a sense of the private woman behind the imposing façade constructed in the
public archives and evident in the portraits left by the photographer Moulin.
The image that emerges is far more appealing than the one that colonial officials noted, although conceivably Luce softened with age and revealed a side
of herself that had little reason to emerge in official documents. For Jeanne,

Maman Luce was a jolly old woman, full of youthful spirit and love of life. The picture she paints is of an earthy and corpulent woman, with erstwhile golden hair and faded blue eyes, who enjoyed good food and witticisms: "witticisms without bitterness, honest and bourgeois, mixed with the touch of *gauloiserie* [crude jokes] that women of her period enjoyed, that is to say women whose best years were during the reign of Louis-Philippe [1830–1848]."[13] Luce liked to recite poems and compose stories, as she had composed dialogues earlier for her Arab students. Jeanne recalls as well the pleasure Maman Luce took in singing the songs of Béranger and reciting the poetry of Chateaubriand. The young royalist of Montrichard who outsung the Bonapartist boy in 1815 was a very different woman some sixty years later, but traces of that studious yet fun-loving girl remained. A devoted republican, she transmitted to Jeanne an interesting mixture of popular radicalism with Béranger's songs and classical romanticism with Chateaubriand's verse.

The two of them lived with a servant in a small four-room house along the main road in Montrichard; in the back of the house, a courtyard allowed Eugénie Luce to raise a few chickens, and a garden welcomed Jeanne for play and amateur botanizing. With Jeanne, Maman Luce continued a lifelong habit of teaching, rewarding her with volumes of the comtesse de Ségur published by Hachette in its famous collection of children's books, the Bibliothèque rose, that began in the 1850s. The comtesse de Ségur provided Jeanne with a family, she writes, that was comical, tragic, ridiculous, and odious but one that peopled her imagination, as she shared a bedroom with her elderly Maman Luce thousands of kilometers from her mother in Algiers. In addition to reading about Ségur's mischievous Sophie, Jeanne dreamed about the imaginary worlds in the fairy tales of Charles Perrault, which she also read in the collection of the Bibliothèque rose, illustrated by Gustave Doré: "Oh those fairy tales! Along with the garden they were my educators. If Madame de Ségur's stories spoke of everyday realities, the fairy tales allowed me to live as in a dream. And how superior the dream was to reality."[14]

Like many little French girls in these early years of the Third Republic, Jeanne Benaben received her early education from a maternal figure, in this case her great-grandmother. But when she reached the age of seven, Luce decided that Jeanne should experience a proper school and spend time with girls of her own age and from her own social background. She therefore placed Jeanne first as a day student and then as a boarder in a small boarding school close to their home.

This choice of a private school and not the public primary school suggests that Eugénie Luce's educational radicalism when it came to educating indigenous girls was far more conservative once back in France. Although she had raised her granddaughter alongside indigenous girls from mostly poor backgrounds, she did not want Jeanne to mingle with working-class French girls. She did not choose, however, the private school run by nuns in Montrichard; rather, Jeanne attended the Pension Valeriani, a modest institution run by two sisters and attended by the daughters of shopkeepers and neighboring landowners.[15] Here Jeanne studied history, grammar, literature, geography, and the sciences, as well as English and the piano, two very feminine accomplishments that, Jeanne writes, Maman Luce wanted her particularly to acquire.

Although Luce was far from pious, she still had Jeanne prepare her first communion in 1880, and she seems in these final years to have been actively thinking about Jeanne's future, as she recognized her own life was drawing to an end. While Jeanne studied during the school year and played with cousins during the vacation, her great-grandmother plotted to keep her in France, far from her mother. Henriette's visit in 1879, after an absence of four or five years, did not leave a good impression on Eugénie Luce, whose concern for propriety increased over the years. Henriette acted more like a playmate than a mother: mother and daughter built imaginary worlds, dressed extravagantly, and acted out lives far removed from the realities of provincial France. The mother introduced her daughter to her new companion, Charles Klary, a photographer who ran a shop in Algiers, with whom they then traveled to Spain. There the couple tried to live from the proceeds of Klary's art, an effort that ended in failure, although Klary went on to become a well-known and prolific photographer.[16]

Following this brief reunion of mother and daughter, Jeanne returned to Montrichard and Henriette to Algiers. Although Luce may not have condemned her granddaughter's private living situation—she herself had, after all, lived with Louis Luce well before her first husband's death—she clearly disapproved of what she considered her fanciful and artistic outlook on life and its potential consequences for Jeanne. Luce failed to understand her beautiful granddaughter, who "did not aspire for fortune, had little concern for comfort, no fear of outside opinion, who made indigenous women her friends not her servants, who was generous to excess." Writing her memoirs in 1944, more than sixty years later, Jeanne offered this judgment of Maman Luce's relationship to Henriette: "Maman Luce, a generous heart, but with a fundamentally bourgeois outlook.

She had none of the narrowness of mind and the meanness of character, nor did she have the need to slander or the absence of simplicity of the bourgeoisie of a little town, but she maintained a fear of originality, a taste for an orderly life, copious meals, and an absence of fantasy; she did not have an artist's soul and my mother, her granddaughter, so enthusiastic and vibrant, had always frightened her a bit."[17] Jeanne felt it was this fear of originality that led Eugénie Luce to ensure that Jeanne would not return with her mother to Algeria after her death and conspired with her old friend Paute Laforie to protect Jeanne from the insecurity of an artist's life.

Friendship Networks: Organizing beyond the Grave

Jeanne's reading of her grandmother's character hardly meshes with much of what we know of Madame Luce's life. It seems wildly inaccurate to describe this woman who left on her own for Algeria in 1832, bore two illegitimate children, and then harassed the colonial government for eighteen months to fund her Arab-French school for Muslim girls as someone who sought an orderly life and lacked originality. But, of course, the life she led with Jeanne in Montrichard *was* orderly, and she undoubtedly never confided in her great-granddaughter about the sexual adventures of her youth. What rings more true is the idea that she was not an artistic soul, even if she did a great deal to promote indigenous art forms. The "fundamentally bourgeois outlook" was reflected in a keen business sense that was completely absent in her granddaughter Henriette. Luce may have believed in the fusion of the races and the regeneration of native art, but she also expected her efforts to ensure a regular salary and a decent pension. She negotiated with the colonial authorities about the latter and before leaving Algiers invested savings in a small business that sold stamped paper.[18] Above all, as she saw the end approaching, she wanted to be sure that Jeanne would be provided for, and she was very convinced that Henriette was not the woman for the job.

So Eugénie Luce asked friends to watch over Jeanne once she was gone. In particular, she entrusted her upbringing to Paute Laforie.[19] His presence in Jeanne's life says a great deal about the sort of woman Luce was and sheds light on her political leanings. If Luce's political beliefs must be read mostly between the lines, the same was not true for Paute Laforie, an educator and a committed republican. Jeanne's future tutor spent his youthful years agitating in secret societies, publishing in radical papers, and languishing in prison when the authorities cracked down. Most likely the friendship between Luce and Paute Laforie developed in Algeria where the latter was banished after Louis Napoleon's coup d'état in December 1851. How and where their relationship began is, however, difficult to establish with certainty. Paute Laforie started his teaching career in the Loir-et-Cher, and between 1847 and 1848 he taught at the *collège* at Blois.[20] Forced out of teaching in August 1848 because of his radical ideas, he continued to write and support socialist candidates during the early tumultuous years of the Second Republic. Arrested in December 1851 in the wave of repression following the coup d'état, he was initially imprisoned in Blois before being shipped to Algeria.

Eugénie Luce possibly met Paute Laforie in the late 1840s during one of her trips back to her family in France. They would have shared a similar radicalism about education and its ability to create greater equality. According to Jeanne, their friendship flourished in Algeria where he was initially interned in the camp at Douéra in April 1852 and then placed in residential confinement with an official.[21] This is probably where Luce got to know him better and was able to make his life more comfortable. The two remained in contact after Paute Laforie returned to France in February 1853 and moved from teaching into business, selling wood in Blois. By the time Jeanne met him in 1882 he was sixty-seven years old and no longer much of a firebrand, at least in her opinion. She described him as being from a petit bourgeois background, "leading a perfectly orderly life, almost excessively so; he lived in Paris with his son, a civil servant, and his wife, as well as the unmarried sister-in-law."[22] She saw no trace of the "ardent and passionate character" that had led to his being fired from teaching. On the contrary, in Jeanne's opinion, this man represented all that was settled and dull, a stark contrast to her extravagant and imaginative mother. However, he shared Luce's commitment to education and the belief that teaching represented the ideal future for Jeanne.

Luce persuaded Paute Laforie to accept the role of tutor for her great-granddaughter, a role he took seriously to the end of his life. After Luce's death, he and Henriette struggled over who would raise Jeanne since Jeanne's father abdicated his interest in her future at the moment of the divorce in 1887.[23] Henriette had legal authority over her daughter, but she ultimately bowed to her grandmother's desire, allowing Jeanne to remain in France and enter the Collège Sévigné, a new and highly respected private secondary institution. Paute Laforie paid the fees for this education and acted in loco parentis until his death. Over the following years, Jeanne would see little of her mother and a great deal of her tutor, whom she never particularly warmed to. In her memoirs, she describes the contrast between her mother, who would have liked Jeanne to become an artist, and Paute Laforie, who ensured that she would become a teacher; Henriette described Paute Laforie as the sort of man "who given an orchid would transform it into a potato."[24]

Paute Laforie was responsible, then, for Jeanne's move into secondary school teaching. A year before his death in 1894 he continued to intervene on her behalf, writing to Inspector General Eugène Manuel requesting that Jeanne Benaben obtain a teaching position in Paris: "As you probably know from Monsieur Dumas, neither ambition nor some frivolous taste justifies my request that my ward reside in Paris, rather my paternal feelings toward this charming child that my family and I have raised for the past twelve years. A position in Paris would allow me to maintain for a few more years the familial protection that her youth, her poverty and her charms require and that nothing can replace."[25] He obtained her transfer, although it is hard to know whether it was his influence or that of the writer Alexandre Dumas that did the trick.

Alexandre Dumas (fils) also played a role in Jeanne's life and suggests the position that the Luce Benaben family held in educated circles in Algeria. The author of *La dame aux camélias* visited Algiers in 1864, at the height of his literary fame, and met Eugénie Luce. He was clearly devoted to all of the women in this family and acted as a friend and mentor to young Jeanne. In her memoirs she wrote frequently about the famous writer, who was also a friend of George Sand. As a schoolgirl she described visits to his apartment on the avenue de Villiers in the seventeenth arrondissement in Paris. He lent her books and encouraged her scholarly aspirations, hoping she would become a *"femme forte de l'avenir"* (a strong woman of the future). More concretely, he also paid for half of her boarding costs and used his political and literary clout to ensure that her fellowship was renewed and to allow her to apply to the École normale supérieure de Sèvres, despite being underage. Thanks to Dumas, Jeanne met such figures as the historian Ernest Legouvé, whose book *Histoire morale des femmes* (1849) had revealed his feminist inclinations. She also vacationed with Dumas, meeting the famous surgeon Samuel Pozzi and his family. In later years Jeanne wrote about Dumas with far greater fondness than she did her tutor Paute Laforie. He represented the artistic legacy of her absent mother, in contrast with the bourgeois legacy represented by the elderly ex-schoolteacher.

MATERIAL LEGACIES

Eugénie Luce suffered a stroke during the night in early June 1882. Eleven-year-old Jeanne, who was sleeping beside her when the stroke first paralyzed her, alerted their maid and was promptly whisked away. She learned of Maman Luce's death a few days later: "Dead, Maman Luce? I greeted the news like a death sentence. (What had I done, innocent me, to be thus condemned?) Dead, Maman Luce? Impossible. Everything around me seemed to collapse. A selfish concern obsessed me, what would I become? Who would care for me?"[26] For the young Jeanne, Maman Luce and the comforting surroundings of her life in Montrichard were an anchor following her chaotic early years, first in Brussels and then in Algiers. After six years living in Montrichard, she barely knew her father, and her mother was far away. One can easily imagine her loneliness, shock, and fear. But her Maman Luce had taken pains to care for her, persuading Paute Laforie to watch over her and writing a will that ensured her material needs would be met. Luce was concerned to leave a legacy for Jeanne that she believed Henriette could not offer. As a result, in 1878 she rewrote her original will, leaving all of her possessions to Jeanne, not just half, as she initially intended. Henriette was an adult who could care for herself; Jeanne would need all she could get.[27]

In early June 1882, mourners accompanied Eugénie Luce's body to its final resting place in the cemetery of Nanteuil, a neighborhood of Montrichard. Within weeks a tombstone was erected that included a few words about the work she had accomplished in Algiers; the Arabic expression *"Inch'allah"* (if Allah wills), inscribed on the tombstone, offered a symbolic statement about Luce's sense of community with the Muslims with whom she had lived for more than forty years.[28] Given the time she had spent thinking about what would happen to Jeanne after her death, one suspects that Luce was also responsible for choosing the tombstone and the words that testified to her life and "beneficence in Algeria." By mid-August the necessary formalities had been taken care of, and an auction took place selling the contents of the house she had rented in Montrichard.

The information from the auction gives an intimate glimpse into the material realities of Eugénie Luce's life during its final years, as well as insight into her relationship with her family. Together with the papers dealing with the succession, these documents reveal that her years of labor in Algeria had left her relatively well off financially and certainly a far wealthier woman than when she had left Montrichard in 1832.[29] All told, she left a sum of 18,147.55 francs, which represented money from the sale of her material possessions (2,232.80 francs), the estimated value of unsold objects (270.05 francs), various small amounts that came from her retirement fund (141 francs), income from a stamped paper shop in Algiers (92.50 francs), a small sum of cash (20.75 francs), and especially the money from a loan and accumulated interest that she had contracted in 1875 (15,390 francs). She did not leave any property, however, since her housing had been paid for in Algiers and she had rented in Montrichard.

This sum of money positioned her firmly within the middle classes of the early Third Republic, as a comparison with a study done for the city of Lille in 1873 shows. Within the middle classes, the average sum left by those who wrote a will in Lille was 18,117 francs, although there were wide variations according to professions. Employees and civil servants left on average only 2,190 francs, and many left nothing at all.[30] Eugénie Luce's fortune was more representative of someone from the artisanal classes. The loan that formed the bulk of her estate may have been the result of savings over the years, but it seems more likely that it was the product of objects she sold just before leaving Algeria. In accord with French inheritance law, she ultimately left her granddaughter and great-granddaughter just over 9,000 francs each, which offered them a little cushion for the uncertain future.[31]

The objects sold in the auction show that Luce had a taste for collecting, although she had not had time to accumulate a great deal since moving back to France. A total of 205 lots were dispersed at an average price of a little over 10 francs. Only five lots sold for more than 100 francs: a Louis XIV armchair covered in silk and embroidery (an unusual choice that reflected "oriental" taste), a mirrored wardrobe, a regular wardrobe, and—the most expensive lot—the contents of her wine cellar: eighty bottles of red and white wine, as well as three hundred empty bottles and assorted objects related to wine. It seems that in her old age Eugénie Luce transferred her interest from embroidery to wine, the latter offering perhaps more immediate pleasure. In addition to the usual quantities of plates, glasses, linen, and the like, there were some traces of her life in Algiers, objects described as "Arabic" or "in Arab style": two bamboo footstools, two silver cups, and a tray. Probably, however, much of the linen and some of the rugs and chairs were also from Algiers. There was not much to show for a lifetime of teaching, although books represented a small percentage of the total value sold: 75.50 francs. The collection of books from the Bibliothèque rose appears to have been sold for a mere 6 francs; a few books received far higher prices, no doubt thanks to the existence of engravings: Milton's *Paradise Lost* (in translation),

La Fontaine's *Fables*, and a collection of illustrated songs by Béranger that Henriette Benaben purchased for 12 francs.

Luce's material belongings conjure up the image of a woman who liked fine wine and enjoyed her comfort. She possessed vases, wall hangings, and curtains to make her home cozy, but no jewelry aside from a gold watch. There is no sign that she had a library, as such, although the expensive edition of *Paradise Lost* shows she had literary interests, or perhaps just literary friends. In many ways the objects she left at her death confirm Jeanne's youthful impressions. By her late seventies, Eugénie Luce had become a bourgeois woman, accustomed to a certain lifestyle and the comfort associated with that lifestyle. She also gave evidence of her bourgeois mentality in her concern about planning for the future and saving, rather than spending, in order to provide for Jeanne.

The auction also reveals a bit about the place she held within the Berlau extended family and particularly with her granddaughter, Henriette Benaben. Some thirty people bid on the objects for sale. Strikingly, the person who spent the most was Henriette, who paid 286.55 francs and returned to Algiers with twenty lots from the sale. She bought linen, clothing, furniture (chairs and tables), and a rug, in addition to the songs of Béranger, whose lyrics inspired leftists throughout the century. Clearly, she wanted to keep traces of Luce's existence, and not just keepsakes. Given what we know of her in her later years, she probably chose the finer objects. Other family members were also present at the sale: Albert Perdrier came from Paris and bought linen and cutlery; Georges Perdrier from neighboring Angé bought pocket handkerchiefs and a cuckoo clock; Madame Jacques Perdrier bought various objects for the kitchen, including a coffee pot and aprons; and a cousin Berlau came from Buzançais in the adjacent department of Indre and bought two teapots. Paute Laforie was also present and spent a little less than 20 francs picking up a rug, twenty-four stockings, dessert cutlery, and a bedside carpet. Jeanne describes her unhappiness seeing all that was familiar vanish in a few days, although an unknown friend set aside for her three armchairs in old point tapestry that she kept "religiously" her entire life.[32]

The objects sold at the auction constitute a relatively ordinary legacy, but the presence of Henriette and other family members, eager to keep objects within the family, speaks to the nature of the bonds Luce had created. Besides this small legacy of material goods that represented something to her immediate family, Luce's more enduring legacy remained in Algiers, thanks to the extravagant and fanciful Henriette. The decision to return to Algiers without her daughter in October 1882 set Henriette Benaben on a distinctively unconventional path. After several years of uncertainty, she picked up the pieces of Madame Luce's workshop and then spent the rest of her life promoting "native art," as well as the professional training of "native" women. In the process she brought retrospective attention to Eugénie Luce, as the woman who revived the female "indigenous arts" in Algeria.[33]

HENRIETTE LUCE BENABEN: PROMOTING FEMALE HANDIWORK IN TURN-OF-THE-CENTURY ALGIERS

After the auction and the dispersal of Luce's material goods, Jeanne headed to Paris and a new life as a boarder at the Collège Sévigné, while her mother, Henriette, returned to the place she considered home. Born and bred in Algiers, she grew up speaking Arabic and learning to embroider with the little girls of her grandmother's school and workshop. Following her separation from Paul Benaben, and particularly the death of Madame Luce, she went back to the *ouvroir* in order to make it her living.

A *"Figure in Algiers"*

Henriette Benaben developed a very different relationship to the workshop, the girls she supervised, and the products they produced from that of her grandmother. She had not begun life as a teacher and considered the profession both uninteresting and petit bourgeois. She loved the arts in general—theater, music, literature, and poetry. Oriental embroideries ensured her livelihood, but her interest in them was as an art form and as a profession for indigenous women, not as a means for accumulating savings. Her heart belonged to North Africa, and she never aspired to "retire" to France, a country she knew only cursorily, although she loved Paris for its cultural life. At her death in 1915 she was buried in Algiers in the European cemetery Saint-Eugène, with Muslim-style headstones. On one side were inscribed the words:

Madame Luce Benaben, née Henriette Belly
She devoted her life to Muslim art
And to the welfare of the indigenous woman

On the other side, Arabic script says: "Here lies Madame Luce Benaben, the head of the ex-bureau of Arab art. May God welcome her in his vast paradise" (see the photo in the introduction).

Once "liberated" from the responsibility of caring for her daughter, Henriette devoted her life to the promotion of Arab embroideries and vocational training of indigenous women. In so doing she inscribed her activities as a form of legacy to her grandmother's lifework. In 1911 she was asked to inspect the handiwork being done in girls' schools in Oran and Montaganem. She began her report to the governor general writing, "Before all else, allow me to thank you for the emotions I experienced in witnessing the realization of my grandmother Madame Luce's dream: the spread of a methodical and general organization of handiwork in schools and the development of familial industry."[34] Rather than speaking of her own efforts in this direction, she praised Madame Luce. This accounts no doubt for her decision to associate her grandmother's married name—not her maiden name Belly—with her own. "Luce Benaben" is inscribed on her tombstone and appears frequently in the sources; as a result, tales of her workshop very often recalled its origins and Eugénie Luce's initial efforts.

Henriette Benaben was something of a celebrity in fin-de-siècle Algiers, like Eugénie Luce in her time. She was part of a cultivated French community who positioned themselves as indigenophiles. At her death in 1915 Charles Lutaud, the governor general of Algeria, and Charles de Galland, the mayor of Algiers, were among the officials who attended the ceremony. Family memory claims that she was also a friend of Hubert Lyautey, the military and then resident governor of French Morocco, who would visit her when he went to Algiers.[35] The publicist and journalist Victor Barrucand, who took over the newspaper L'Akhbar in 1902, was a close friend, as was the remarkable explorer Isabelle Eberhardt, known for her writing, her conversion to Islam, and her tragic death at age twenty-seven in a flash flood. During Eberhardt's stay in Algiers in the spring of 1902 she spent many hours with Henriette at her workshop, rue du Rempart Médée, and described the pleasure she had conversing with the group of intellectuals around her. Eberhardt's descriptions of Henriette confirm the judgment that Luce held of her granddaughter concerning her lack of pragmatic good sense: "Madame Ben Aben is the second woman I have met, after my mother, who is a fundamentally good woman, a visionary enamored of ideals. But in real life, how ignorant the two women are!"[36]

She may not have had her feet on the ground, but she nonetheless understood how to promote the causes dear to her heart. Like her grandmother, she welcomed photographers into her workshop over a span of many years. As early as 1880, photographer Alexandre Leroux, who directed the bimonthly L'Algérie Illustrée, took a series of photographs of her working space that later found their way into the collection of the Parisian Musée de l'homme.[37] French, British, and American visitors came to her workshop to buy embroideries, take pictures, and spread knowledge of her oeuvre. Local photographers in Algiers, Jean Geiser and Arnold Vollenweider, both took photographs of Henriette's workshop that were made into postcards.[38] These were then reworked using the Swiss polychrome method that converted black-and-white images into color. These images and the postcards were part of a growing mass-market curiosity about the exotic that fueled the demand for souvenirs of foreign climes.[39] Unlike the far better known images of scantily clad oriental beauties, these images translate another reality of cultural tourism at the turn of the twentieth century: the interest in the workers, the products of artisanal handicraft, and Moorish domestic spaces.[40] Not surprisingly, the artists who produced these images lived and worked in Algiers; their representations sought symbolically to highlight the way the French presence improved life within the colony.[41]

By the end of the century, Benaben's workshop and its handicraft products attracted not just visiting British and American lady tourists, but also the attention of visiting royalty. When Amélie of Orléans, the queen of Portugal, toured

"School of indigenous embroidery of Madame Ben-Aben." Postcard from the end of the nineteenth century. Note that in this "school" no older students or teachers are represented, and the French presence is attenuated by the absence of Henriette herself. Situated near the madrasa and the mosque just above the Casbah, this building offered easy access to visiting tourists. Photograph-editor, Arnold Vollenweider. Private collection, Michel Megnin.

Algeria in 1903, she took the time to visit the library, a rug-making school, and Benaben's workshop. Two years later, King Edward VII of England and Queen Alexandra visited an exhibition of Muslim art organized by the governor general in the newly built madrasa on the upper slopes of the city. The queen turned to Madame Benaben for information about embroidery techniques.[42]

Henriette Benaben's introduction to visiting royalty in the early twentieth century was a sign of new directions in cultural governance in Algeria.[43] Between 1900 and 1901 and again between 1903 and 1911 Governor General Célestin Jonnart in particular encouraged the rediscovery and promotion of indigenous art, architecture, and art forms, such as embroidery and rug making, in addition to improving social services for the indigenous populations. Benaben profited from this new interest but also actively participated in placing embroidery and the development of vocational skills for indigenous girls back on the colonial agenda.

Training Girl Embroiderers

Henriette Benaben annually trained between thirty and seventy girls within her workshop for twenty years between the mid-1880s and the early years of the twentieth century. There is little trace of this workshop in the colonial archives, however, and she received only episodic support from the Muslim Welfare Bureau. Guidebooks and visitors testify to the existence of the institution and offer some insight into its functioning. Between 1885 and 1895 Benaben ran the workshop in a Moorish villa on the rue Bruce. Advertisements in the British daily the *Algerian Advertiser* show how she cultivated a relationship with British tourists in addition to collaborating with her neighbors on the rue Bruce, the photographers Vollenweider.[44] As opportunities for professional training expanded for Muslim girls during the 1890s, her institution attracted more students, and by 1896 she had moved to a more spacious building on the rue du Rempart Médée. A few years later she opened a second establishment on the rue Marengo in the residential area known as Mustapha Superior where tourists wintered. This location included a space for exhibiting both embroideries and girls at work.[45] When her son-in-law, Paul Crouzet, visited the workshop in 1901, he published a description that shows how Madame Luce's legacy continued into the new century. Like her grandmother, Henriette had an older Muslim woman, known as a *conductrice*, bring the thirty-odd girls to the workshop. Aged between six and fourteen, the girls did not impress Crouzet by their diligence. On the contrary, he noted a strong propensity toward nonchalance, characteristic of the Moorish woman, in his opinion. In the presence of "Lelle Ben Aben," they set to work, however, showing an ability for delicate workmanship.[46]

The focus on embroidery rather than academic subjects continued at the turn of the century. By 1900 the opportunities for such professional training had spread considerably, and Benaben was only one among a number of Frenchwomen who ran institutions that offered indigenous girls the possibility of developing a skill and earning money for their futures. For the French authorities, the choice had gradually been made to privilege practical training for girls, rather than pursue the more assimilationist model of Arab-French schools created at mid-century.[47] In 1890 Clarisse Coignet, a feminist woman inspector, visited a number of indigenous schools and highlighted the difficulties inherent in teaching girls "in a country where the woman is reduced to the status of a domestic slave."[48] For her, schools that taught French and a veneer of French culture were doomed to failure; she urged vocational training instead but of a kind that would allow women to work at home.

The numerous reports that appeared in the early 1890s often nuanced or criticized Coignet's general findings, but the overall conclusions regarding girls' education followed the same reasoning: girls should receive practical training. In 1892 Émile Combes's detailed report on indigenous education highlighted the need to do something for girls, who were a small minority in schools with few opportunities to learn a trade.[49] Charles Jeanmaire, the rector of the Academy of Algiers from 1884 until 1908, was also of this opinion although he noted it was not enough to teach women to sew and embroider; the French also needed to develop a market for these indigenous goods. He directed his efforts toward the encouragement of indigenous education and particularly the place of art and artisanry in this education.[50]

A decree of 18 October 1892 that launched new efforts to develop indigenous schooling encouraged the creation of apprenticeship courses annexed to existing schools and specified with respect to girls' schools that sewing classes and home economics should occupy half of the school day. In 1898 the program for girls' vocational training was established; it was oriented toward the restoration of previously existing industries, notably "rug making and Arab embroideries as well as the making of bed-coverings and tapestries which had been so prosperous in the past."[51] Not coincidentally, this coincided with the objectives of Henriette

Benaben, who was consulted about the appropriate form of professional train-ing for girls and who carefully distinguished in her report the different needs of urban versus rural girls.[52]

By the end of the century Madame Luce's concern to preserve native embroi-deries while providing vocational skills to indigenous women had been written into educational law, and her granddaughter spearheaded the promotion of this twofold goal, even if she did not necessarily benefit from these measures. In 1899 Ahmed Brihmat, one of the more active indigenous members of the Algiers mu-nicipal council, recounted the familial story while noting that Henriette Benaben no longer received public support for her institution. His plea to the council was to provide her workshop with an annual sum of 2,500 francs for apprenticeship training. In the end the council voted (four votes for, three against) to allocate a sum of 600 francs.[53] Two years later the department of Algiers granted her 1,000 francs for her "professional school of Algerian embroideries."[54]

By the turn of the century, however, Benaben had shifted her priorities from teaching to promoting the indigenous arts and the place of women in these arts. A cultural climate favorable to the rediscovery of the indigenous past, as well as her connections to the people and institutions who, like her, were involved in the rediscovery of the precolonial past, undoubtedly contributed to her relative success in this area. In particular, she became a member of the Comité du vieil Alger (the Committee of Old Algiers), whose members sought to preserve and recognize the picturesque past of El Djezaïr. Toward this end she collected his-toric patterns for the embroideries, which she then had her students copy; she even persuaded Isabelle Eberhardt to collect such patterns and embroideries as she traveled around Algeria.[55]

At Henriette's funeral service in 1915, her friend Mayor Charles de Galland emphasized the artistic dimension of her work and traced this to the influence of her grandfather Luce, "a musician of taste who found philosophical meaning in artwork and in the sweet tones of his violoncello."[56] She seems to have stopped training girls in her home between 1906 and 1910, devoting her energy instead to the promotion of native art. Not only did she give her collection of embroideries to the new Museum of Algerian Antiquities, but at her death she was described as being an assistant in the museum.[57] Certainly, in these prewar years Benaben acquired a reputation as a woman with taste and feminist sensibilities concerned with promoting the well-being of indigenous women. For most observers, she was seen as pursuing her grandmother's vision as well.

Commemorating and Exhibiting

Both Eugénie Luce and Henriette Benaben left traces of their efforts to promote the feminine indigenous arts and in their lifetimes actively developed knowledge and appreciation of Algerian embroideries in particular. Luce focused on public events, prize-giving ceremonies, local exhibitions in Algiers, and the universal exhibitions of Paris (1855 and 1867) and London (1862) to make her school and workshop known (see Chapter 4). This concern to provoke interest in women's work and exhibit it across the sea was relatively pioneering at mid-century; when Henriette took over the business, she pursued this strategy but in a context that was increasingly marked by spectacle and commercialization. By the turn of the twentieth century the circulation of both people and goods between Algeria, Europe, and the Americas was far greater.

Henriette Benaben's efforts on behalf of indigenous women's handicrafts received support from the group of people who wished to encourage indigenous art in Algiers. More widely, however, her efforts coincided with a moment of cultural effervescence in the connection between Algeria and mainland France. This resulted in the increasing presence of colonial objects and goods at universal exhibitions, in the multiplication of colonial congresses that showcased Algerian products, and in the development of collections in the indigenous decorative arts. All of these factors meant that in colonial cultural circles Henriette Benaben's initiatives aroused the sort of interest that Luce's school for Muslim girls had initially attracted in the late 1840s. By 1900 visitors to Algiers were struck by representations of native girls weaving and embroidering, not learning French.

Discovering and Promoting Indigenous Art

The promotion of indigenous art and neo-Moorish architecture manifested itself in a variety of ways in turn-of-the-century Algiers. Institutions and associations were created both to preserve the past and to incorporate older traditions into the construction of a modern city that respected this past. Henriette Benaben's workshop usefully served to remind the new colonial authorities of women's roles in the social, cultural, and economic fabric of precolonial Algiers. As a result, the publications and surveys of these years inevitably addressed the place of embroidery, lacework, or rug making in their analyses of indigenous art forms.[58]

The universal exhibition of 1900 in Paris marked a distinct turning point in the public and political interest surrounding the native art industries, even

though a number of initiatives in the 1890s had begun to testify to this new interest. In 1893, for example, Georges Marye, who later would become responsible
for the Muslim section of the new Museum of Algerian Antiquities and Muslim
Art, had published an article in *Nouvelle Revue* concerning the artistic education
of the indigenous populations. He criticized the absence of such an education,
noting that the British were far in advance of the French in recognizing the quality of indigenous art. He argued for the need to study the history of industrial
arts with an eye to preserving tradition.[59] A few years later, in 1897, Governor
General Jules Cambon followed Marye's advice when he ordered a survey of the
existing indigenous art industries. Interrupted by the administrative shuffles at
the end of the century, the survey nonetheless produced initial reports that recommended the creation of pottery and ceramic schools.

   Individual European men and women also established artisanal schools at
this time. Alongside Henriette Benaben's workshop in Algiers, Madame Delfau
opened a rug-making school in 1898. The studies commissioned in these years
noted the proliferation of similar vocational schools outside of Algiers. Among
the figures who are frequently cited, one finds Madame Missier in Kalâa, Mademoiselle Quetteville in Oran, and Madame Saucerotte in Constantine. In 1900
in Tlemcen, the Alliance Française helped to found a weaving school run by the
Saëton sisters.[60] Occasionally these schools received financing from the Direction of Indigenous Affairs; this was the case for Madame Delfau in Algiers, for
example, until 1906.[61]

   A number of studies from the early twentieth century testify to the new interest surrounding the indigenous arts and artisanal handicraft. Given the role
of women in embroidery, lace making, and rug making, they received a fair
amount of attention in the various published reports. Stéphane Gsell, who would
do much to promote the Islamic decorative arts in the new museum, commissioned Marius Vachon, a member of the Superior Council on Technical Education, to give a series of conferences while surveying the situation in the spring
of 1901. Like most of these men, he deplored the contemporary decadence he
found in these various industries, while vaunting the heritage of the past. His
141-page report, which explored a wide variety of industries in Algeria and then
compared them with industries in Europe, lauded Madame Luce for her early
recognition of the importance of professional training. He described her as having founded a professional school for Arabic embroideries in 1845—no mention of French lessons here: "This institution has continued to this day under

the direction of the granddaughter of the founder, Madame Ben Aben, with a subsidy of 2000 francs from the Government General." He noted, however, that "given the absence of sufficient resources and more efficient encouragement, the school is on the verge of closure."[62]

The same year, Émile Violard published a brochure about the indigenous industrial arts that also positioned Madame Benaben as the heroic successor of Madame Luce, "a schoolteacher imbued with enlightened patriotism and a great heart." Her professional school had inculcated generations of indigenous workers with "the secrets of this marvelous art" (embroidery). However, after years of efforts, Henriette Benaben had exhausted her financial and physical resources and been forced to sell off her remaining art objects, which had served as models for her workers.[63] After World War I, in 1922, Violard wrote another brochure on the same subject that similarly extolled the Luce Benaben family for their initiative in the domain, while regretting that, on the whole, the French colonial authorities had been far less successful than these individual women in the development of the indigenous arts.[64]

Arsène Alexandre's thorough examination of the indigenous arts industry in 1905 reiterated his predecessor's recognition of the Luce family's role in promoting certain art forms and family industries. He focused in particular on the importance of encouraging training schools for both boys and girls, and he insisted, like Vachon and Violard, on the importance of Henriette Benaben's embroidery school: "In the superior interest of the applied arts which concern us here, we naturally support the continuation of this school. It is part of the history of Algeria and the workshop, which we so admire, must remain a sort of national school for indigenous embroidery."[65] This survey was published both separately and in several installments in *L'Akhbar*, ensuring that the results went beyond the relatively limited circle of cultural authorities.

Interest in this artistic education was also evident in metropolitan France, encouraged in part by Benaben's son-in-law, Paul Crouzet, who was beginning his upward climb within French educational circles.[66] In 1904 he accompanied Inspector General Félix Hémon to Algeria and took him to visit the Benaben workshop. Hémon then published an article in the *Revue Pédagogique* about indigenous art schools in Algeria that paid effusive tribute to both Eugénie Luce and Henriette "Ben-Aben" in developing professional skills among young indigenous girls. His article finished by noting that the renewal of indigenous art could also serve the cause of primary education.[67]

In 1908 Governor General Célestin Jonnart responded to the results of these various surveys by creating a Service of Indigenous Arts under the responsibility of the rector of the Academy of Algiers. The Arabist Prosper Ricard was placed in charge of this service and spent the next several decades promoting Muslim art in the Maghreb through his various appointments, first in Algeria and then in Morocco. He was appointed inspector of artistic and industrial education in indigenous schools in Algeria a year later and devoted a great deal of energy to surveying the state of this education and suggesting ways to improve it.[68] In particular, he defended traditional handiwork against the menace of European machine-made products. To this end in 1911 he opened a drawing cabinet to collect patterns that then served as models for a variety of indigenous arts.[69] The government purchased from Henriette Benaben items that contributed to this collection.[70] Although Ricard's detailed study of Algerian and Moroccan lacework does not mention her explicitly, his text took care to situate these artistic objects within a social context. Girls and women produced lace and made a living from it, he explained. For these women workers to survive economically, they required the sort of training provided in workshops, such as the ones already existing in Algiers, Miliana, and Bougie.[71] Lacework was also, of course, an art form that merited public exposure through exhibition. Henriette Benaben could not have agreed more wholeheartedly.

Her efforts to promote vocational training and to showcase the products of this training were part of a broader movement that she influenced, thanks to her lifelong experience living and working with indigenous girls and women. As a result, it is not surprising to find frequent references to her in the sources describing the renewal of indigenous arts, nor is it surprising to find her name associated with the various colonial or universal exhibitions that increasingly attracted attention to the cultural heritage of Algeria.

Exhibiting Embroideries, Exhibiting Girls

In the 1850s Eugénie Luce had regularly exhibited the handiwork produced within her school with the goal of selling scarves, handkerchiefs, curtains, and dresses in order to pay the girl workers and to purchase materials. Henriette Benaben's efforts at the end of the century were rather less mercantile and more artistic and patrimonial. She collaborated actively with museum directors and the proponents of industrial education to collect traditional patterns and then to exhibit handiwork produced using age-old techniques. These exhibitions contributed to the new interest in "oriental" embroideries, not just in Algiers, but also in France, England, and even far-off Chicago.[72] The embroideries were always situated in a context, however, and acquired a social meaning beyond their quality, thanks to the stories and images that circulated around them. Visitors were encouraged to envision the delicate art as flowing from the nimble fingers of young indigenous girls, grouped together under the wise supervision of a Frenchwoman. This celebration of the "positive" aspects of French colonization was then woven into a story that almost always went back to Madame Luce and her initial efforts in the mid-1840s, testimony to the ways her influence continued well beyond the grave.

Jeanne Crouzet-Benaben reported that her mother attended universal exhibitions in both Paris and London. Certainly in 1878 the products of the workshop were on display at the Parisian exhibition in the section devoted to lacework and clothing. The exhibitor is listed as Madame Luce, head of the Muslim workshop in Algiers, which trained forty young girls. By 1878, however, Eugénie Luce was living in Montrichard with Jeanne and so it is far more likely that Henriette Benaben was responsible for sending the clothing, dolls, and embroideries to the Parisian exhibition. Her lover at the time, Charles Klary, also exhibited photographs at the exhibition.[73]

In the following years Benaben continued to participate in both universal and more local exhibitions, thus drawing attention to her workshop. Its products received prizes at the French colonial fairs of Rouen in 1884 and Lyon in 1894.[74] Although less financially savvy than her grandmother, she understood that exhibitions garnered international attention and ensured a regular stream of visitors to her door. She sent both embroidered wall hangings and girl workers to the World's Columbian Exhibition in Chicago in 1893, insisting to the organizers that she wanted them to be exhibited in the Woman's Building. As a result, they received attention in the various reports about the fair published in both English and French. Indeed, Maud Elliott's description of the Woman's Building included two photos of "Madame Luce Ben-Aben's school," where both the embroideries and girls workers were presented for admiration.[75] Consistently in the exhibitions, the presentation of embroideries was associated with schooling and training, as the figures suggest. One photo depicts a young girl working at a handloom surrounded by the products of her industry: wall hangings, curtains, bathing caps, and scarves. Beside her an embroidered nameplate advertises Madame Luce Benaben's Arab embroideries in Algiers. Another image focuses only on the embroideries.

Moorish girl embroidering at the World's Fair of Chicago in 1893. The embroidered sign for the workshop is now preserved at the Musée du quai Branly (see the image in the Conclusion). Image reproduced in Maud Howe Elliot, *Arts and Handicraft in the Woman's Building of the World's Columbian Exposition* (Chicago, 1893).

Hangings embroidered in the school of "Mme Luce Ben-Aben." Image reproduced in Maud Howe Elliot, *Arts and Handicraft in the Woman's Building of the World's Columbian Exposition* (Chicago, 1893).

Benaben once again sent girl workers to the Franco-British exhibition in London in 1908, which was probably the final exhibition of her career. One report described the "little Moorish girls, sweet students of Madame Benaben," handing a superb bouquet of French roses to Queen Alexandra when she visited their exhibit.[76] This interest in displaying North African girl workers continued until the late 1930s as a way of highlighting the French success in giving women a trade.[77]

The exotic interest in little girls seems to have been less on display at the universal exhibition in Paris in 1900 where Benaben exhibited embroideries alongside other Frenchwomen who, like her, were increasingly recognized for their professional schools and their contribution to the revival of indigenous arts. Press reports reveal the effect of Jonnart's efforts to promote these arts. On 8 December 1900, for example, *L'Algérie à l'Exposition Universelle de 1900*, the weekly newspaper that reported on Algeria's presence at the universal exhibition in Paris, had this to say about these women's efforts: "These arts had almost completely disappeared when a few people of taste set about restoring them. Private initiative has had excellent results. This is evident in the Algerian section of the universal exhibition. Mesdames Delfau and Benaben from Algiers, Saucerotte from Constantine, Missier from Kalâa, have shown what intelligence and initiative can produce."

By the turn of the twentieth century, Henriette Benaben's efforts were clearly directed toward promoting indigenous artwork and encouraging the new interest this sparked among colonial cultural authorities, notably such men as Georges Marçais and Stéphane Gsell, who were active in the museum world. These men were responsible for encouraging exhibitions of Muslim art, both in France and in Algeria, and in accumulating the first collections of this art. In Algiers, Gsell organized an official exhibition of Muslim art in 1905 in the madrasa of Algiers in conjunction with a meeting of the International Congress of Orientalists. Henriette Benaben was part of the organizing committee and lent objects from her collection to the exhibit. The press widely covered the event, which was meant not only to draw attention to the hidden treasures of the past, but also to earn money for the new Museum of Algerian Antiquities and Muslim Art. Here, as elsewhere, the promoters of Islamic artwork associated its rediscovery with the work of certain Frenchmen and Frenchwomen. Typical of this positioning was the article by C. Bayet in *Revue de l'Art Ancien et Moderne* that devoted a paragraph to "Madame Luce Ben-Aben," her workshop, her art collection, and her contribution to the exhibit.

Well-known in the Casbah, she has assuaged many miseries and she recruits children, young girls, who learn embroidery. Over the years she has accumulated an admirable collection of embroideries, which includes pieces from Algeria, Morocco, Turkey, as well as Asia Minor. Many pieces were lent to the exhibit. She has even found pieces that allow apprentice workers to learn the variety of motifs and stitches. She is able in this way to provide her students with the most beautiful models. The results are very encouraging and the influence of Madame Ben-Aben all the more meritorious in that she has a real sense of Arabic art, she is penetrated by it, her enterprise is an artist's work without commercial considerations.[78]

This praise both of indigenous artwork and of the Frenchwoman who was capable of appreciating it was also apparent in the long description that Georges Marçais devoted to indigenous art in Algeria in 1906. He noted, however, that it was private not public initiative that was at the origin of these "industrial indigenous arts." And, in his description, he paid his dues to Madame Luce, who created, he wrote, the "first workshop for the confection of indigenous embroideries" in 1845: "This work was too humanitarian for the French State not to support it." Conscious that this handmade production could not compete commercially with European mechanical procedures, Marçais pled for the necessary rehabilitation of traditions and "old models," so well exemplified by Henriette Benaben's workshop.[79]

Collections

In a series of portraits titled "Figures d'Alger," Victor Barrucand, the director of *L'Akhbar*, devoted a lyrical article in 1906 to Madame Luce Benaben, educator and muse. He described her working a miracle of sorts on the Barbary Coast thanks to her efforts to preserve the art of embroidery. Her concern, however, was always for the girls, with "agile fingers, squatting before looms, pulling the colored threads of patterns that came from a cruel and splendid past." His prose depicts a charming and vivacious teacher of the arts, who welcomed queens and women travelers in the city of Algiers. Barrucand republished this elegy to Benaben, friend and fellow indigenophile, at her death in 1915, noting at the end of the article that her art collection had been donated to the museum in Mustapha (that is, the Museum of Algerian Antiquities). There, on the heights of Algiers, visitors could discover a unique collection, although it was no longer possible to see the young artisans at work.

The Museum of Algerian Antiquities and Muslim Art was first established in 1892 from what remained of the collection of the permanent exhibition of Algerian products. A new building was inaugurated in the Parc Galland in April 1897 under the directorship of Georges Marye. The initial collection did not include embroidery, as the first catalogue testifies.[80] But embroideries were added as the "industrial arts" gradually earned pride of place in the art world. Henriette Benaben actively contributed to this process, donating her collection a few years before her death. In 1931 historian and archeologist Georges Marçais argued that the best collections of Algerian embroideries were in this museum in Mustapha, the Victoria and Albert Museum in London, and the Museum of Chicago (presumably the Field Museum).[81] A few years later Marguerite Bel, inspector of artistic and professional teaching in indigenous girls' schools, described the Museum of Algerian Antiquities collection of Algerian embroidery as the most perfect manifestation of Algerian art of the eighteenth century, and she lauded "Madame Luce-Ben Abben" for having saved these art forms from dispersion and destruction.[82]

There is little evidence that Henriette Benaben gained much financially from her years spent teaching and collecting embroidery in Algeria. One might legitimately wonder whether she, like Eugénie Luce, as some of her critics charged, took advantage of young girls, exploiting their workforce for her own profit or that of the colonial authorities. Certainly, Benaben gained notoriety and a form of symbolic recognition through the workshop and its products. And she made her living from this activity, as her grandmother had earlier. Still, the overriding impression left from the accumulated sources is that both women were genuinely concerned to equip girls with the tools of a trade, enabling them to earn a living and acquire higher status within their society. Henriette Benaben clearly combined this proto-feminist concern with a passion for embroidery as an art form that brought recognition and appreciation to women and the country she ultimately adopted so completely. To this extent her activities paralleled those of Frenchmen such as Charles de Galland, the mayor of Algiers, who sponsored the Muslim-run Rashidiya association to allow the native elite "to reach the highest level of culture."[83] Her Islamic-style headstones symbolize in many ways her life-work, and the collections she left testify to her efforts to render visible the ways indigenous women contributed to the cultural patrimony of Algeria. At her death, the Museum of Algerian Antiquities baptized room E the "Salle Luce Ben Aben" in recognition of her efforts, displaying, among other objects, a collection of bonnets, scarves, and curtains.[84] In 1922 the municipal council honored her name by granting her burial plot in perpetuity, and in 1934 a small street was named the rue Luce Benaben in her honor not far from Mustapha Superior, where her British admirers had wintered over the years.[85] Tellingly, after Algerian independence in 1962, the street was not renamed like most that bore the imprint of French colonial domination. Henriette Benaben's struggles to promote the welfare of indigenous women, as the gravestone reads, were not reinterpreted and rejected.

The same cannot be said about her grandmother, Eugénie Allix Luce, who started the family's involvement in Algeria. From the outset, her motives were questioned and her good faith challenged. British visitors proclaimed her a heroine, but French administrators saw her as opportunistic and avaricious, a perception that emerges strongly in historian Yvonne Turin's 1971 analysis.[86] In the end, it is important to keep in mind how subjective our readings of past lives remain, as we sift, interpret, and translate what others have left behind.

CONCLUSION

19 September 2011, Montrichard

The end is in sight. This weekend I went to Montrichard. I wanted to see the land-scapes Eugénie grew up with, the place she returned to die, and I wanted to make sure there really was no sign of her in the cemetery. The sun shone brightly although the temperature was cold for the season. Montrichard was hillier and more picturesque than I imagined; outside people buying baguettes and Sunday pastries, inside men watching a rugby game on big screens in the cafés. I took pictures of her house at n° 19 route de Tours, which is a nondescript two-story building. And I visited the cemetery. No sign of Eugénie, as the municipal secretary had informed me earlier on the phone. For lack of space, her remains were moved in 1979. Still, I took pictures here as well of the plot where her body used to lie. Visiting her home highlights for me the difficul-ties of the biographical project. I don't really see her traipsing down the main street, or teaching girls to read in a makeshift classroom. I wonder why she never spoke of the Cher river when describing her home. But as I paddle a canoe down the Cher from Monthou-sur-Cher, where her mother died, to Montrichard, where Eugénie was born and died, I feel a sense of closure. I can let her go and think about moving on.

This return to my research diary suggests what should be clear after following Madame Luce's adventures from Montrichard to Algiers and back: biography, like all forms of history, is about interpretation. In the process of researching and writing, I have formed the sort of "friendly acquaintance" with Madame Luce that her British friends sought to encourage in their prose; this inevitably colors the portrait I have painted.

I have enjoyed the companionship of Eugénie Luce, in part no doubt be-cause she remains enigmatic, despite my efforts to get to know her. I admire the courage she demonstrated in leaving France for Algeria in the early 1830s and the energy she spent setting up her school and then embroidery workshop for indigenous girls. I clearly share certain of her convictions, especially the impor-tance of teaching girls to read and write as well as to acquire marketable skills. I also share with her the experience of living in a land where I was not born, interacting in a language that is not my native tongue. I was struck to discover over my years of research that despite pulling up roots in her late twenties and spending more than forty years in Algeria, Eugénie Luce never broke her ties with her family and felt the need to return to France to die. I understand these instincts in the same visceral way.

Fortunately, my sense of identification with her is far from complete. Madame Luce was a woman of her times who believed in the French civilizing mission in Algeria and embraced the idea that teaching French to Arab girls would serve the "fusion of the races." I recognize the weight of beliefs in cultural and racial superiority that guided her actions, which today appear repugnant. Yet her interest in Arab culture, her willingness to learn the language, and the relationships she developed with local families speak to an openness and curiosity that many of her fellow settlers did not share. I hope in the end to have conveyed some sense of who she was, while recognizing that I have not resorted to psychological analysis and have little probed her more intimate attitudes toward sexuality, love, and motherhood.

I have shied away from the intimate Eugénie Luce partly because of the absence of source material. I did not find journals, personal writings, or memoirs that would have allowed me to explore the private person in more detail and shed light on the passions that inspired her to flee France, bear illegitimate children, and pursue a vision against considerable odds. For the most part, I have allowed her actions and the reactions she inspired to guide the portrait I have painted, without much speculation about the Eugénie who loved men, good food, and her great-granddaughter. That private woman was important to her friends and family, but if there had been only that, I would not have written this biography.

In the course of my research I did find four "private" letters and the rather enigmatic poem she sent to Enfantin in the 1840s. Retrospectively, I realize that this discovery in September 2004 pushed my "project" into becoming a biography. In these writings we get a glimpse of the woman she imagined herself to be: "an enfranchised and independent woman," she wrote in November 1840, claiming an autonomy and a political self that Frenchwomen would only legally acquire more than one hundred years later. The letters speak as well of feelings of affection and romantic love that allowed her to escape the "slavery" that characterized her status as a woman. These letters may indeed offer insight into the psychological underpinnings of Luce's life, but for me, the historian, they speak above all about the politics of women's lives. She was seeking to write herself into history, and she succeeded. Whether one sees her as the "originator and energetic teacher and conductor of the Moorish school for girls" or the "Grandmother of Algerian Art," I hope to have shown my readers that her life story merits telling.[1]

PORTRAITS AND INTERPRETATIONS

Who was Eugénie Luce? Was she a utopian dreamer who honestly believed girls' education could change the nature of French colonization? Was she an adventurer in search of new horizons? Was she a calculating colonial woman pushing language instruction and then embroidery according to the tides of colonial politics? Was she a proto-feminist seeking to promote female independence and autonomy? Or was she a complex mixture of all these types?

The basic outline of her life may not appear to offer the stuff of biography. She was born into the lower middle classes; grew up at home; married a schoolteacher; had four children, three of whom died in infancy; migrated to Algeria; opened a school; became a widow; married a man who was a musician; ran a sewing workshop; raised a great-granddaughter; and died. This outline omits, however, the reasons I first was drawn to her story: her eloquent plea to include indigenous girls and women in the French civilizing mission. It also omits the aspects of her character that emerged only through closer study: her opportunism and shrewd business sense, her sense of family, and her commitment to education. Above all, the biographical outline offers no inkling about her robust enthusiasm for life.

Friends and family all described her as a forceful and energetic woman. Her British feminist friends admired her prose and her determination to succeed against overwhelming odds. Although at times critical, they nonetheless approved of her commitment to providing schooling and training for Arab girls; they saw her as a feminist sister. In the obituary he wrote after her death, her close friend Nicolas Eugène Paute Laforie emphasized her lifelong commitment to girls' education, her heartfelt republican values, and her dedication to family and friends.[2] Jeanne Crouzet-Benaben, her great-granddaughter, added yet another touch to this composite portrait and conjured up a more bodily presence. In her writing we see a corpulent, tender, and at times bawdy elderly woman. She emerges from the shadows of Jeanne's memories as "a beloved wrinkled figure waving to me and smiling."[3]

These descriptions offer insights into both the private and public woman, but they remain portraits of an individual who is not yet inscribed in the pages

of history. Certainly, the British newspaper articles were a step in that direction. Both Barbara Bodichon and Bessie Rayner Parkes strove to create a pantheon of woman worthies who had added their marks to their times, and they
included Madame Luce in this group. But, as we have seen, there was little echo
of these British feminist efforts on the other side of the English Channel. Why
did French feminists not identify Luce as a kindred spirit? And why, after forty
years of women's history, do so few historians know the name of Madame Luce?

The heyday of Eugénie Luce's fame in the 1850s and early 1860s was not a pro-
pitious moment for French feminist activists. The repression that followed the
Revolution of 1848 dashed the hopes of the most vocal leaders despite the existence of a transnational feminist movement.[4] Eugénie Niboyet, a Saint-Simonian
activist who had published *La voix des femmes* (The Voice of Women) calling
for women's rights, turned her attention to workers' associations and badgered
the French government for financial support. Both Jeanne Deroin and Pauline
Roland, who had spoken out with passion during the revolutionary years, were
sentenced to prison in 1850. Once released, Deroin left France permanently for
England, where she published an *Almanach des femmes* in 1852 and 1853 that described women's achievements throughout the world. She did not include Madame
Luce in her almanac, however; she probably knew nothing of her endeavors.[5] Her
fellow combatant Roland was sent off to exile in Algeria and died in 1852. One
cannot help wondering whether Roland and Luce met in Algeria and recognized
that they shared similar convictions. No trace of such an encounter exists.

References in the historical record show that George Sand wrote at least
two letters to Luce in 1864, but these letters have disappeared.[6] Most likely Luce
initiated the correspondence, seeking to draw the illustrious woman novelist's
attention to her activities in Algiers. She may have been encouraged to do this
by Alexandre Dumas (fils), who was in Algeria at the time, as well as Solange
Clésinger, Sand's daughter. But she clearly failed to make much of an impression.
As historian Michelle Perrot has argued, Sand's politics during the Second Empire were not directed toward the collective struggle of women, and her refusal
to support the feminist claim to vote in 1848 is well-known.[7] Unlike Bodichon
and Parkes, Sand did nothing to spread knowledge of Luce's effort on behalf of
indigenous women. This is far from surprising, considering the embryonic nature of the feminist movement in France during these years.

By the time French feminists began organizing in the final years of the Second Empire, Eugénie Luce was at the end of her professional life and no longer a

news item in either Algeria or France. The newspaper *Le Droit des Femmes* (The Rights of Women) (1869–1870, 1879–1891), which registered feminist aspirations in France, spoke a great deal about girls' education and women's work but very little about the colonies, unlike the British *English Woman's Journal* (1858–1864). As a result, when Hubertine Auclert moved to Algeria in 1889, she had no knowledge of Madame Luce's efforts on behalf of Arab girls. As a socialist and France's first self-proclaimed feminist, Auclert held far more radical political views than Luce. Her primary struggle in France was for women to achieve the vote, but in Algeria, she placed education high among her priorities.

Auclert followed her husband to Algeria in 1889 and lived there until his death in 1892. During these years she maintained an active political correspondence and undertook research on the situation of Arab women, which she published in 1900 as *Les femmes arabes en Algérie.*[8] In the course of this research, she encountered Henriette Benaben, who told her about her grandmother's school in the early years of French colonization. This inspired Auclert to write three separate petitions to the government, in 1892, 1900, and 1911, calling for the creation of schools for indigenous girls. The initial petition to Minister of Public Instruction Henri Bourgeois requested that the government allocate the same funding for the education of indigenous girls as it did for that of boys:

At the present moment, Algiers does not have a single school for Arab girls. We request, Sir, that you reestablish as quickly as possible the two Muslim-French girls' schools created by virtue of the decree of 14 July 1850 that specified Arab girls would have schools where they received elementary instruction.

Despite the success of these schools, assiduously attended by 226 students who promptly assimilated our ideas and morals, the General Council of Algiers eliminated them in 1861 in order to please a few despotic Muslim men who were vexed to see instruction opening a breach in the tyranny they exert on women and in their hatred of France.[9]

Auclert concluded her petition with the hope that in 1892 the government would not allow girls to wallow in ignorance, given the existence of schools between 1845 and 1861. She did not mention Luce by name in these petitions, but it is clear from the details she offered that she had heard the story of Luce's school and hoped that past example might inspire the future.

Once back in France Auclert continued to press the governor general about the inadequate provisions for girls' elementary and professional education in

Algeria,[10] and she wrote on the subject in her book about Arab women. Unlike the presentation Parkes offered in the *English Women's Journal* some thirty years earlier, Auclert was not interested in bringing Luce to life through a (romantic) presentation of her life story. Rather, her concern was to show that Arab girls had successfully learned French and acquired vocational skills, belying both French and Arab misogynist prejudices. Moreover, she saw the school's closure as a lost opportunity to have Arab women participate in the task of assimilation: "Quickly convinced of the validity of our civilization [women] could have helped us in powerful ways to win over the Arabs, to rally the Muslim world to our point of view."[11] She used Eugénie Luce's story for her political ends but made no effort in the process to inscribe her in a feminist pantheon.

It is probably more noteworthy that Luce's great-granddaughter, the moderate feminist Jeanne Crouzet-Benaben, also never made such an effort in her many writings about girls' and women's education. True, she wrote lovingly about Luce in her memoirs, but the figure she depicted was her "Maman Luce," not a proto-feminist model. And yet all of Crouzet-Benaben's life was marked by Luce's interest in girls' education, since Luce ensured that Jeanne would pursue her education and study to become a teacher. Crouzet-Benaben left her mark on girls' education not as a teacher, however, but as an educational activist, publishing quarterly bulletins between 1909 and 1939 about the status of girls' education in France and elsewhere. These bulletins, which appeared in the widely read *Revue Universitaire*, championed women's access to higher education and pressed for changes in educational laws that would allow girls to prepare for the baccalaureate in the public secondary school system.[12] Crouzet-Benaben was not a historian, however, and she seems to have had no desire to learn more about her great-grandmother's role in changing educational conditions for Arab girls. This is all the more striking in that she was married to Paul Crouzet, who in 1920 was given responsibility for education in the colonies, although not in North Africa.[13] The two wrote extensively about education throughout their lives, and Crouzet even published an article about Madame Luce in 1903, but his wife never did the same.[14] This tells us something about the degree to which Luce's school had faded from French historical memory in the interwar period.

In 1971 when Yvonne Turin published her important study of schools and medicine in colonial Algeria, Eugénie Luce reemerged as an historical actor. Turin looked carefully at the dossier concerning the Arab-French schools and devoted several pages to "Allix-Luce" and her school. Her portrait, however, is highly critical. In her eyes, based on the reports she found in the colonial archives, the woman was a greedy adventurer, seeking attention and a livelihood, with little genuine concern for Arab womanhood.[15] This viewpoint echoes Turin's strong anticolonial denunciation of the entire project of Arab-French schools and bears the marks of a specific moment in colonial historiography. Fifteen years later Yvonne Knibiehler and Régine Goutalier's portrayal of Madame Allix-Luce was not as damning in their book on women in the colonies. They used the material Turin presented to highlight the existence of indigenous girls' schools, but their interest was less in the schoolteacher than in the students.[16] Similarly, the study by literary historian Denise Brahimi of French women writing about their Arab "sisters" used Auclert's description of Luce's Arab-French school, but never mentions Luce by name.[17] None of these studies emphasizes Luce's notoriety in mid-nineteenth-century Algiers or how she cultivated British taste for her students' embroideries. As a result, these historical studies position Eugénie Luce, and particularly her school, within a historical context and suggest the way she took advantage of this context to obtain financing for her school, but they shed light on only one aspect of her public persona.

More recently, postcolonial literature and methods have renewed interest in Algeria and generated a number of important studies about colonial education, urbanism, demography, and aesthetics.[18] Not surprisingly, the postcolonial "rediscovery" of Madame Luce began in Britain with the writings of art historian Deborah Cherry on the British feminist interest in Algeria. Her focus, however, was not on Luce, but on the ways feminist subjectivities, discourses, and practices were constituted within an imperial context, including through the material circulation of objects, such as embroidery, between Britain and Algeria.[19] In 2003 the Australian art historian Roger Benjamin described how Luce and her granddaughter contributed to the advancement of the indigenous decorative arts and analyzed in particular the image of a young Arab girl weaving in Benaben's workshop. While recognizing how contemporaries focused on Benaben's philanthropic motives, he sees the issue as more complex: "Late-twentieth-century Westerners might equate the *ouvroir* with child labor, notwithstanding salubrious conditions or the widespread tradition in North Africa and the Middle East of employing female children for rug-making." Unquestionably, however, the Benaben workshop both inspired and was part of a broader cultural movement. "In the Algerian situation," Benjamin writes, "the revival—or 'reinvention'—of tradition in indigenous hands was the aim: the Luce family practices went on to become a key policy platform in the French Maghreb."[20] Although the Luce family is not the object of sustained analysis, its members are clearly presented as important actors in French colonial cultural politics, whose motivations, however, appear more mercantile than feminist or philanthropic.

Using the material that Yvonne Turin first explored forty years earlier, Claudine Robert-Guiard's book about European women in colonial Algeria presents a more feminist and sympathetic reading of Luce's school and workshop. She questions Turin's description of "Madame Allix" as being a "savvy and unscrupulous woman," arguing that while economic motivations undoubtedly underlay Luce's activism, she appears to have genuinely adhered to the French civilizing mission and to have contributed as well to the preservation of indigenous art forms.[21] Her interest in showing the role of European women in the French colonization of Algeria echoes my own and provides the necessary historical context for envisioning a more gendered reading of this process.

Dalila Morsly has recently argued for the importance of Eugénie Luce's school in teaching French to Arab girls. From Morsly's sociolinguistic perspective, "Madame Allix-Luce is a witness, an actress, a passer at this inaugural moment when the French language is introduced through colonization."[22] Unlike Robert-Guiard, who doubts whether Luce's school did more than welcome poor children and teach them manual skills, Morsly suggests that the teaching of French had an effect that has yet to be explored in any detail. Careful attention to the textbooks indicated in inspection reports, as well the results of such inspections, leads her to conclude that Luce's students successfully mastered the lessons they learned using the Peigné method for French and the Depeille method for Arabic. This interesting argument shows how closer attention to the history of both European and indigenous women in the history of Algerian colonization changes our understanding of the effect of the French presence.

Like Turin before him, Osama Abi-Mershed's *Apostles of Modernity* explores the early efforts at spreading schooling in Algeria. And also like his predecessor he devotes pages to Madame Allix-Luce's interactions with the colonial government, focusing on the rhetoric she employed to gain support and then the arguments used to discredit her school in 1861.[23] His analysis suggests, as I have, that her initiative represented a specific relatively egalitarian moment in French colonial cultural politics, but he does not pursue its implications for the future. To my eyes, the closure of Eugénie Luce's school merits far closer attention precisely because of the legacy the decision left for indigenous girls' education. This is where a biographical approach and a commitment to women's history offer an opportunity for reinterpreting the colonization of Algeria with the introduction of a more gendered perspective.

GENDERING THE COLONY

Scholarly interest in the colonization of nineteenth-century Algeria has flourished in recent years on both sides of the Atlantic. Unlike scholarship on the British empire, however, the role of women and the category of gender have not significantly inflected recent interpretations, with a few notable exceptions.[24] And yet, the interest in the social history of Algeria, as well as in exploring this history through the lens of cultural contacts, negotiations, and tensions, clearly calls for perspectives that systematically integrate the presence of both European and indigenous women. Gender, along with race and class, conditioned debates around such issues as family, sexuality, medicine, law, education, and work.[25] This book, which explores the "tensions of empire" around questions of girls' education and women's work, brings to light new actors, suggests perspectives for future work, and introduces more complexity into our understanding of the colonial encounter in Algeria.[26]

Madame Luce's activities, alongside those of other teachers, nurses, nuns, and small business women, shed light on the social history of women's work in early colonial Algeria, an area that until recently has received little historical attention.[27] Beyond that, however, this story highlights how European women's lives intersected with those of indigenous women. Historians have often argued that the arrival of European women exacerbated racial tensions and introduced boundaries between populations in colonial settings.[28] This may have occurred in early colonial Algeria, but regardless of whether such encounters contributed to tension, my research reveals an urban society in which they were frequent and where boundaries were relatively fluid.[29] Eugénie Luce lived surrounded by the indigenous populations of the upper Casbah; she visited Muslim families and used her connections to attract both students and her teaching mistresses. We know little about the effects of these encounters on her students. Nefissa Bent Ali is the only student who used her education to earn a French teaching degree, but five other students became assistant teachers, and far many more learned to sew. The story I have told reveals, in particular, the presence of Muslim girls and women within a market economy in Algiers producing goods that generated income for the school and for themselves, as well as clothing that helped to alleviate the poverty of the urban poor.

Although the "elusive girl students" I described rarely have names, their presence in the school and workshop are testimony to a form of cultural encounter that I hope will provoke further investigation.

In the imperial circulation of material goods among Algeria, France, Britain, and the United States, the artisanal handicrafts produced by indigenous girls were far more visible than the girls themselves. The final chapters of this book that speak of these cultural and material legacies suggest the need for more research on how women's work, and not just their bodies, contributed to an imperial commodity culture. Cultural historians interested in Orientalism and its avatars have made much of the eroticized female bodies that circulated via postcards, ethnographic travel guides, and colonial novels.[30] Christelle Taraud's work on prostitution has alerted us to the more sordid aspects of this exploitation of the female body.[31] I argue here for the importance of studying the material culture that testifies to the ways women contributed to the social, economic, and cultural changes in nineteenth-century Algeria. Both European and indigenous women were involved in the "rediscovery" of Algerian handiwork at the turn of the twentieth century, and yet the tale of their labors remains little known, outside the work of Julia Clancy-Smith.[32] In 1930 Augustin Berque regretted the shadows enveloping France's collaborators in Algeria—the women "whose agile fingers have woven the future."[33] He might have added that the shadows lengthen when the fingers are dyed with henna and the bodies wrapped in cloth.

What remains, however, are the objects that were produced, sold, and exhibited. And yet, we know so little about their significance and their uses because clothing and textiles rarely hold the same pride of place as art objects in the cultural hierarchy of goods. Observers criticized the Europeanization of artisanal handicraft, but Luce and Benaben sought to return to "traditional" methods, patterns, and cloth. How successful were they in transmitting skills and traditions, and what difference did their efforts make in the development of an imperial commodity culture? These questions exceed both the scope of this project and my competencies as historian, but I ask them in order to draw attention to the objects that remain.

Henriette Benaben sold pieces of her collection to the museum in Algiers; other pieces made their way to the Victoria and Albert Museum in London (shown in the introduction). In 1961, long after Henriette's death in 1915, her grandson, Jean-Philippe Crouzet, donated 195 objects from this collection to the Musée de l'homme in Paris. The donation included eighteenth-century Algerian embroideries, examples of elite urban clothing in Algiers between 1860 and 1900, and a variety of embroidered objects made within the Luce Benaben workshop.[34] In 1946 Jeanne Crouzet-Benaben had already sold an assortment of pants, handbags, belts, vests, bath caps, and jewelry to the Musée de la France d'Outre-Mer (now merged into the Musée du quai Branly).[35] In 1961 Jean-Philippe Crouzet was not interested in money for the collection but requested in exchange for his donation that his "magnificent collection of objects, jewelry and folkloric Arabic clothing" be exhibited and not just stored.[36] Sadly, in 2011 I found only two items on display, and not the most representative. Nonetheless, images from the collection at the Quai Branly conjure up this world of feminine artisanry. Even when unfinished or incomplete because of age, the delicate embroidery is an incitement to learn more and to fill in the picture.

Attention to the work that women and girls in colonial Algeria accomplished offers another way to read the history of the French civilizing mission between 1830 and 1914. Most studies emphasize the contrast between the years before 1870 and those that follow, particularly when one looks at educational policies.

Unfinished placemat in satin and silk from the Luce Benaben workshop, 1880. In the center the Arab inscription reads, "Politeness is a precious thing." Musée du quai Branly. Inv. 71.1961.74.132.

Embroidered ensign for the workshop of Madame Luce "Ben-Aben." The decorative theme is traditional but has been modernized with floral motifs. The silk that used to cover the beige cloth is almost completely gone. Musée du quai Branly. Inv. 71.1961.74.157.

Madame Luce's story dramatically highlights how indigenous girls' education vanished as a cultural goal a decade before the settler règime came to power in 1870. By 1882, when Eugénie Luce died in Montrichard, few inhabitants in Algeria supported the idea of indigenous girls' education. Ironically, her death occurred just as the Third Republic was promoting greater educational justice for girls and women in France: in 1879 normal schools for girls were created throughout the country, in 1880 a public system of secondary schools came into existence, in 1881 a superior normal school for girls was created, and by 1882 primary education had become free, obligatory, and secular for both girls and boys. Undoubtedly, Eugénie Luce viewed these changes with pleasure, since they ensured that her great-granddaughter would be able to pursue her studies in these new institutions for girls. But none of these measures applied to the indigenous girls of Algeria, and we will never know what she thought of that. Ten years after Luce's death Hubertine Auclert protested indignantly at this state of affairs to little effect. Instead, the Frenchwomen who continued to live and work in Algeria reoriented their efforts toward vocational training for girls, thus contributing to enduring inequalities in the educational opportunities for indigenous girls compared with indigenous boys, and especially compared with European girls. In 1907–1908 statistics reveal that a mere 8 percent of school-age native boys attended schools, and a mere 0.7 percent of girls.[37]

Recently, George Trumbull IV has pursued Clancy-Smith's arguments that after 1870 in Algeria "the moral arguments underpinning the civilizing mission arose out of the colonial ethnography of gender" and that the civilizing mission cast gender relations as a moral problem requiring political solutions.[38] His ethnographic sources conjure up naked female dancing bodies and prostitutes, not young girls learning to read or to embroider. Even Auclert defended the education of Moorish girls as a moral issue, arguing that it would lead them to refuse polygamous relationships, a position that secular French reformers defended as well.[39] The civilizing mission that Eugénie Luce promoted in the late 1840s did not place moral issues at its center. Instead, she saw girls' education as the solution to a political problem: that of achieving the "fusion of the races." The problem was not women's status in Algerian society, but France's efforts to make Algeria French. And the French could not afford to forget women in this process.

Her project changed over time, however. The details of this change, recounted in this book, shed light on the evolution of France's civilizing mission over the century. Still, girls' education did not disappear; instead, it became more professional, less political, and ultimately far less interesting to the travelers and ethnographers whose writings have inspired recent scholarship. The end-of-the-century travel writer Paul Eudel wrote evocatively in *Hivernage en Algérie* (Wintering in Algeria) (1909) about the spectacles of women dancing, but he barely mentioned the girls working at their embroidery after he visited Benaben's workshop. Nor did he have much to say about the results of religious missions in Kabylia despite clear evidence of their influence.[40] The task of civilizing had assumed new objectives at the end of the nineteenth century, or perhaps, as historians, we have been misled by our sources. More careful attention to the social practices that emerged from the interactions between the French and the indigenous populations may change our interpretations. The growth of professional schools, like the spread of religious missions, offers fruitful avenues for future work.[41]

QUESTIONING THE ARCHIVES AND HISTORICAL MEMORY

Madame Luce's colonial adventure offers an important lesson about archives, the preservation of the past, and the transformations and contingency of historical memory.[42] Her story appears very different depending on who does the telling and when. From the outset, colonial administrators did not agree among themselves about her motives, and when they retold her story for the centennial celebrations of the conquest, it read very differently from earlier versions. In 1930 Madame Luce was not forgotten, but she was presented as a woman who saved the dying art of embroidery, not as a schoolteacher who pursued the civilizing mission.[43]

French interpretations of Madame Luce differed notably from those of the British, but even the British perspective varied depending on the traveler's point of view. Pious Protestants did not see and report on the same things as independent feminists. Eugénie Luce produced the material for some of these tellings, but she had no way to control the different versions that developed over the years, particularly once she was dead. By shifting archival viewpoints, querying the silences, and doggedly pursuing an individual, I have highlighted the constructed nature of the archives and the need to question both what remains and what has disappeared. No matter what one's final judgment of Madame Luce is—adventurer, feminist, or businesswoman—she singularly failed to conform to dominant representations of middle-class womanhood in nineteenth-century France. And yet, her great-granddaughter perceived the elderly Maman Luce as "bourgeois" and fundamentally conservative.

Two very different cemeteries highlight the fragility of historical and even familial memory. In 2009 I found Henriette Benaben's tombstone in the Saint-Eugène cemetery in Algiers. Although fallen into disrepair, it was still standing as a testimony to the woman who "devoted her life to Muslim art and to the welfare of the indigenous woman." Although I doubt that many Algerians know of her existence, the National Museum of Antiquities in Algiers still honors her name, and curators are aware of what she accomplished.[44] In 1934 the municipal council of Algiers granted a concession in perpetuity as a sign of recognition of what she had done. Perhaps more significantly, she has entered the fictional world of the Franco-Algerian writer Leïla Sebbar as a woman who challenged contemporary conventions, who lived freely, and who introduced girls to handiwork but also to the cultural world of the French.[45]

Eugénie Luce's tombstone has vanished from the cemetery in Montrichard, and local historians are unaware of her existence. In 1979, in the absence of a familial response, her earthly remains were shifted to a communal plot, and a new tombstone was erected for the Maréchal family. Less poetic than her granddaughter, Eugénie Luce might well have accepted this pragmatic erasure of her final resting place with good grace. Would she also have accepted the descriptions of herself as the "Grandmother of Algerian Art"? I would like to think not. True, she encouraged the development of handiwork and made a tidy living in the process, but her goals had been more ambitious when she was writing to Enfantin and her faithful supporter the comte Guyot. "Grandmother of Algerian Art," I can hear her saying, "*pourquoi pas?*" But above all, her story shows that you cannot ignore women when attempting to pacify a country. You need them on your side. You need to listen to their stories. And you need to include them in your histories.

Reference Matter

NOTES

ABBREVIATIONS

AD   Archives départementeles
AN   Archives nationales
BHVP Bibliothèque historique de la ville de Paris
CAOM Centre des archives d'Outre Mer
GGA   Gouvernment général d'Algerie
GGPP Girton College Private Papers

INTRODUCTION

1. CAOM, GGA 22 S/2, letter from Mme Allix to members of the Conseil d'administration of Algiers, 31 January 1846.

2. *Le Républicain de Loir-et-Cher*, 11 June 1882.

3. CAOM, GGA 22 S/2, report to the Prefect of Algiers, 1 November 1850.

4. CAOM, GGA 22 S/2, letter of 14 July 1845 from Algiers, signed "ALLIX," language teacher, to Her Royal Highness the Queen of the French.

5. CAOM, GGA 22 S/2, explanatory note concerning Madame Allix's institution, 6 March 1846.

6. CAOM, GGA 22 S/2, letter from Adolphe Michel to the Director General, 8 August 1861.

7. Saint-Simonianism was a radical French social movement during the 1830s and 1840s. Madame Luce had Saint-Simonian friends in North Africa. See Chapters 1 and 2 for more detail.

8. Barthelémy Prosper Enfantin was the spiritual head of the Saint-Simonians (see Chapters 1 and 2).

9. Farge, *Le goût de l'archive*.

10. The scholarship on biography is immense, particularly since the late 1980s when it became more fashionable. For an overview of the challenges biography poses, see Dosse, *Le pari biographique*, although this book does not address at all the effect of women's history on biography. In English, see the very useful "Roundtable: Historians and Biography." The articles therein show how in the United States women's history has had a considerable epistemological influence on biographical writing.

11. See in particular Rogers, *From the Salon to the Schoolroom*.

12. For a recent biographical approach to Émilie de Vialar, see Curtis, *Civilizing Habits*.

13. For French women's history, see in particular Margadant, *The New Biography*. An extensive literature on feminist biography exists, with a useful introduction in Caine, *Biography and History*.

14. See Ernot, "L'histoire des femmes." Edith Thomas is an interesting exception to the tendency in France to explore the collective rather than the singular. Historian, novelist, and journalist, she published a number of biographies of women "worthies," including one on Pauline Roland in 1956 and one on Louise Michel in 1971.

15. Karen Offen's explorations of French feminist attitudes toward the French Revolution offer insights on the complicated relationship between women's history and the memory of this history; see "Women's Memory." Christiane Veauvy notes that the Saint-Simonian women did not hark back to revolutionary women in an effort to inscribe their actions in a political continuity; see Veauvy and Pisano, *Paroles oubliées*, 40.

16. Recent examples of French biographical writing on the modern period include Fraisse, *Clémence Royer*; Houbre, *Grandeur et décadence*; and Association les femmes et la ville, *Germaine Poinso-Chapuis*. In 2012 Françoise Thébaud is at work completing a biography of the feminist socialist Marguerite Thibert.

17. The British and American interest in biography is clearly visible not only in individual biographies, but in the publication of dictionaries highlighting the contributions of educationists. See Eisenmann, *Historical Dictionary*, and Aldrich and Gordon, *Biographical Dictionary*. In the United States, Kathryn Kish Sklar's biography of the educator Catherine Beecher (*Catherine Beecher*) had an enormous influence on the writing of women's history.

18. See my review of Jean Houssaye, ed., *Femmes pédagogues*, vol. 1, *De l'antiquité au 19ème siècle* (Paris: Éditions Fabert, 2008), in *Histoire de l'Éducation* 128 (2010): 93–95.

19. For a broad presentation of scholarship on French women's education, see Rogers, "L'éducation des filles" (pp. 77–78 for references to biography).

20. Smith, *The Gender of History*.

21. See the new final chapter in the second edition of Thébaud, *Écrire l'histoire des femmes et du genre*, 185–238, esp. 214–15.

22. The project of creating a biographical dictionary of French feminists has existed for years but has not yet reached fruition. However, the regional Association les femmes et la ville has produced *Marseillaises, vingt-six siècles d'histoire*, which includes a biographical dictionary. More recently, a number of biographical dictionaries on women reveal the new interest in individual lives. See Diebolt, ed., *Dictionnaire biographique*, and Cova and Dumons, *Destins de femmes*.

23. I am deeply indebted in my approach to the scholarship of Michelle Perrot; see in particular *Les femmes ou les silences de l'histoire*.

24. Recent work that suggests the existence of such an imaginary includes Salinas, "Colonies without Colonists," and Sessions, *By Sword and Plow*.

25. See Clancy-Smith, "Changing Perspectives."

26. Berque, *L'art antique*, 122–25.

27. Taraud, "La virilité en situation coloniale." Also see Berenson, *Heroes of Empire*.

28. B.R.P., "Madame Luce, of Algiers" (June 1861): 227.

CHAPTER 1

1. In French families in the nineteenth century, the second given name tended to be used on a daily basis; the first name was often that of a close family member. For simplicity, I use the name "Eugénie" in these early chapters, since her surname changes during these years.

2. Girton College Archives, GCPP Parkes 6/73, Bessie Rayner Parkes to Mary Merry-weather, n.d. [1857]. I have respected spelling and punctuation.

3. B.R.P., "Madame Luce, of Algiers" (May 1861): 158.

4. For Eugénie's early life, see ibid. (May 1861): 159–62. All following quotations are from this article.

5. In reality, 6 June 1804 was a Wednesday.

6. Education inspectors played an important role in making the French teaching corps more professional. They visited schools and reported to the prefect on teachers' qualifications and teaching methods, as well as on the characteristics of the student body. The organization of the inspection system for primary education developed after the Guizot Law of 1833.

7. Dupré, *Notice historique*, 31.

8. These records are available in the departmental archives of the Loir-et-Cher. The first name Sylvain is spelled at times "Silvain," and the last name at times "Berleau."

9. Regourd, "Allons à l'école," 9.

10. AD Loir-et-Cher, 300 Q 11, no. 36, 9 April 1810.

11. For maps that register the results of this survey, see Furet and Ozouf, *Lire et écrire*, 59.

12. AD Loir-et-Cher, L 423, Recensement de l'an 4 Montrichard; Eugénie's uncle Léonard Berlau is listed as a gendarme at that point.

13. B.R.P., "Madame Luce, of Algiers" (May 1861): 161.

14. Regourd, "Allons à l'école," 14.

15. For a list of the available schools, see *Annuaire du département de Loir-et-Cher*, which was published yearly from 1806 to 1850. For a discussion of educational resources in Blois, see Bergevin and Dupré, *Histoire de Blois*, 536–37. For a general discussion of middle-class girls' education in early-nineteenth-century France, see Rogers, *From the Salon to the Schoolroom*, 45–75.

16. AD Loir-et-Cher, Series T, Liasse 160, 1811–1835, letter to the Mayor of Montrichard, 30 October 1820. In 1824 Regourd notes that Rafarin is praised for offering girls a "brilliant and solid education"; "Allons à l'école," 14.

17. AD Loir-et-Cher, 3M 240, letter from Sylvain Berlau to the Prefect, 21 June 1816.

18. AN, F[17] 10181, Écoles primaires, académie d'Orléans.

19. See Regourd, "Allons à l'école," 91.

20. AD Loir-et-Cher, Series T, Liasse 380: 1735/2//1002, Instruction primaire, 1812–1828, letter of M. Berlau of Montrichard to the Prefect, 6 April 1824.

21. Demographic tables can be found in Dupâquier, *Histoire de la population française*, 427. At this time the average age at marriage was twenty-eight for men and twenty-seven for women.

22. AD Indre-et-Loire, 1 T 756, États des situations des écoles primaires, 1830–1834; extrait du registre des délibérations du comité d'instruction primaire du canton de Bléré, séance du 10 juin 1831.

23. See Mayeur, *Histoire de l'enseignement et de l'éducation en France*, 299–419.

24. Dupeux, *Aspects de l'histoire*, 160–66, quotation at 161.

25. See Ronsin, *Les divorciaires*.

26. For information on women and reading, see Lyons, "Les nouveaux lecteurs" and *Readers and Society*.

27. Dupeux, *Aspects de l'histoire*, 166–70.

28. See Picon, *Les Saint-Simoniens.*

29. See Moses, *French Feminism,* and Riot-Sarcey, *La démocratie.*

30. Jeanne Deroin, *Profession de foi,* quoted in Riot-Sarcey, ed., *De la liberté des femmes,* 135–36.

31. See Mainardi, *Husbands, Wives, and Lovers.*

32. See Walton, *Eve's Proud Descendants.*

33. Vidalenc, "Les techniques."

34. Dupeux, *Aspects de l'histoire,* 339–74.

35. See McBride, "Public Authority," and Fortescue, "Divorce Debated and Deferred."

36. For more on the violence of the French conquest of North Africa and the opposition it provoked, see Clancy-Smith, *Rebel and Saint;* Brouwer, *A Desert Named Peace.* For a study of domestic politics and the French conquest and settlement, see Sessions, *By Sword and Plow.*

37. For a quick overview of French travelers' reactions to Algeria, see the anthology of texts in Laurent, *Le voyage en Algérie.* For a focus on women travelers, see Champion, "Représentations des femmes." For a description of this movement among the English, see Melman, *Women's Orients.*

38. Emerit, *Les Saint-Simoniens,* 63.

CHAPTER 2

1. B.R.P., "Madame Luce, of Algiers" (May 1861): 162.

2. Crouzet-Benaben, *Souvenirs,* 31–32.

3. For the early measures concerning the settlement of Algeria and emigration procedures, see Sessions, *By Sword and Plow,* 267–81.

4. Cited in ibid., 269.

5. AD Loir-et-Cher, 1M 79, Rapports de police (propos séditieux, opinion publique), 1832.

6. Alexis de Tocqueville, "Notes on the Voyage to Algeria" (1841), cited in Clancy-Smith, "Exoticism," 34. For a discussion of the use of ethnic categories, see also Pouillon, "Simplification ethnique." Throughout this book I refer to "indigenous populations" rather than to "Algerians," since the latter term referred to the European settlers in Algeria throughout the nineteenth century.

7. Marmier, *Lettres sur l'Algérie,* 43. See also the anthology of travelers' texts in Laurent, *Le voyage en Algérie.*

8. For an analysis of the themes French writers developed in their descriptions of Algeria, see Tailliart, *L'Algérie dans la littérature française,* 323–438.

9. Robert-Guiard, *Des Européennes,* 20. I have used the figures in this useful book, but not the author's calculations, which are inaccurate. For a general presentation of these early years, see Boyer, *Évolution de l'Algérie médiane.*

10. *Annuaire de l'État d'Alger* (1833), 112.

11. Taraud, *La prostitution coloniale,* 73. Édouard Duchesne estimated that in the 1830s there were approximately 300 prostitutes for a population of 25,000 inhabitants (1.2 percent), compared with Paris, where there were 4,000 for a population of 900,000 (0.44 percent); *De la prostitution,* 28.

12. Kateb, *Européens, "indigenes" et juifs,* 72.

13. See Çelik, *Urban Forms*, 11–57.

14. Robert-Guiard, *Des Européennes*, 27.

15. On Émilie de Vialar, see Curtis, *Civilizing Habits*, 101–29. For religious schools in Algeria, see Rogers, *From the Salon to the Schoolroom*, 228–36. For clarity in English, I will use the expression "religious order" to refer to these communities of women although the proper term is "congregation."

16. *Annuaire de l'État d'Alger* (1832), 23–24.

17. Ibid. (1833), 117.

18. From the outset the French sought, in particular, to "civilize" Arab Jews; see Schreier, *Arabs of the Jewish Faith*.

19. B.R.P., "Madame Luce, of Algiers" (May 1861): 162.

20. See Cardoza, *Intrepid Women*, 103–26.

21. Birth, death, and marriage certificates for Algeria are available online at the Archives nationales d'outre mer website, http://anom.archivesnationales.culture.gouv.fr/cao mec2/recherche.php?territoire=ALGERIE.

22. Robert-Guiard, *Des Européennes*, 90–93.

23. Martin and Foley, *Histoire statistique*, 293.

24. Ibid., 324. See also Robert-Guiard, *Des Européennes*, 140–45. In 1840, for every 1,000 births, 630 children younger than the age of ten died.

25. In mid-September 1835, the administration reported 2,714 cases of cholera in the city, 1,534 of whom died; Curtis, *Civilizing Habits*, 109.

26. See Prochaska, *Making Algeria French*, 91.

27. Service Historique de l'Armée de Terre, 34 YC 1186, Registre du 26e régiment de ligne.

28. See Levallois and Moussa, eds., *L'orientalisme des Saint-Simoniens*; Abi-Mershed, *Apostles of Modernity*.

29. Cited in Emerit, *Les Saint-Simoniens*, 59.

30. Fakkar, "Le Saint-Simonisme," 161. See also Voilquin, *Souvenirs d'une fille du peuple*.

31. In 1835 the Saint-Simonian Clorinde Rogé sought to persuade the Bey to open a school for female "slaves." Her initiative, however, did not come to fruition; Régnier, *Les Saint-Simoniens en Égypte*, chap. 5. For the role of travel to the Orient among Saint-Simonian women, see Schlick, "Travel as Praxis."

32. For a history of these scientific expeditions to North Africa, see Bourguet, Lepetit, Nordman, and Maroula-Sinarellis, eds., *L'invention scientifique de la Méditerranée*.

33. See Emerit, *Les Saint-Simoniens en Algérie*, 57–106, quotation at 87. Enfantin left for France on 20 November 1841; he returned to Algeria between 2 December 1843 and 7 July 1846.

34. See Moses, *French Feminism*, 41–116, and Riot-Sarcey, *La démocratie à l'épreuve des femmes*.

35. See Emerit, *Les Saint-Simoniens*, 88–93.

36. Arsenal, Fonds Enfantin, 7679, folio 121, letter of Allix to Enfantin, 6 November 1840.

37. Voilquin, *Souvenirs d'une fille du people*, 329.

38. Arsenal, Fonds Enfantin, 7679, folio 122, letter of Allix to Enfantin, 15 June 1841.

39. Abi-Mershed, *Apostles of Modernity*, 73–74; Enfantin, *Colonisation de l'Algérie*, 125–28.

40. Arsenal, Fonds Enfantin, 7679, folio 123, letter of Allix to Enfantin, 10 December 1845.

41. Arsenal, Fonds Enfantin, 7679, folio 125, undated poem.

42. Arsenal, Fonds Enfantin, 7679, folio 124, letter of Allix to Enfantin, 30 May 1846.

43. Arsenal, Fonds Enfantin, 7679, folio 123, letter of Allix to Enfantin, 10 December 1845.

44. AD Loir-et-Cher, T, Liasse TV 375, 1832–1843.

45. AD Loir-et-Cher, T, Liasse TV 165.

46. AN, F¹⁷ Registre *2632.

47. AD Loir-et-Cher, 73 Q 20 Saint-Aignan, registered on 27 February 1837.

48. CAOM, GGA 22 S/2, decree of 10 July 1845.

49. CAOM, GGA 22 S/2, letter of 14 July 1845 from Algiers signed "ALLIX," a language teacher, addressed to Her Royal Highness the Queen; letter of comte Guyot to Allix on 6 November 1845.

50. AD Oise, 2E 60/253.

51. AD Oise, Recensement de la population de Compiègne (1841).

52. See Rogers, *From the Salon to the Schoolroom*, chap. 4.

53. Arsenal, Fonds Enfantin, 7679, folio 123, letter of Allix to Enfantin, 10 December 1845.

54. Henri Dru was Luce's contemporary, and the families remained close until the two men's deaths within a month of each other in 1872. At Dru's death on 14 February, members of Eugénie's family declared his death, and Dru's son Alfred signed Louis Luce's death certificate on March 23.

55. Allen, "Félix Belly"; Belly, *Les amazones*. See AN, F¹⁸ 267, for a dossier concerning press censorship of his writings.

56. Crouzet-Benaben, *Souvenirs*, 35.

57. Ibid., 37.

58. For Luce's stint in the military, see Service Historique de l'Armée de Terre, 34 YC 1186, Registre du 26e régiment de ligne.

59. Archives de Paris, marriage certificate between Eugénie *veuve* [widow] Allix and Napoléon Louis Luce, 19 May 1846.

60. Crouzet-Benaben, *Souvenirs*, 35.

61. CAOM, F⁸⁰ 515, first trimester 1854, inspection of M. Depeille's school.

62. His name is associated in particular with the societies La lyre algérienne and Les enfants d'Algérie.

63. For details about Luce's musical activities in Algiers, see Charles-Roux, *Nomade j'étais*, 422–27. Charles-Roux wrote me that she got this information from conversations that her father had with members of the conservatory in Algiers.

64. Rey-Goldzeiguer, *Le Royaume Arabe*, biographical index, "Luce, Mme, wife of a bandmaster, freemason."

65. Luce, *Abrégé théorique*.

66. Klein, *L'enseignement à Alger*, 33.

67. See Pasler, *Composing the Citizen*, 401–50.

68. Christianowitsch, *Esquisse historique de la musique arabe*, 9; Arnaudiès, *Histoire de l'Opéra d'Alger*, 121.

69. *L'Algérie Française. Journal de la Démocratie Algérienne*, 29 March 1872.

CHAPTER 3

1. For a succinct reading of the girls' school in relation to the boys' schools established at the same time, see Abi-Mershed, *Apostles of Modernity*, 139–43, and Turin, *Affrontements culturels*, 50–56.

2. Cited in Abi-Mershed, *Apostles of Modernity*, 34.

3. For a discussion of the debate, see ibid., 1–16. Abi-Mershed argues, like Turin before him, that educational policy shifted considerably during the years between 1830 and 1870; despite the presence of an assimilationist discourse, reform in these years did not seek to substitute indigenous schools with metropolitan institutions. On the contrary, he argues that Saint-Simonian officials promoted association as an ideal.

4. 9 December 1837, cited in ibid., 59 (translation slightly modified). In 1832 Lepescheux had the title of inspector general of public instruction. He had previously tutored the son of the duc de Rovigo, commander in chief in Algeria between December 1831 and March 1833; Turin, *Affrontements culturels*, 40.

5. See for example the article concerning the province of Algiers that defended the opening of schools in place of brothels as sites of contact: *L'Algérie. Courrier d'Afrique, d'Orient et de la Méditerranée* 111 (26 July 1845): 4.

6. See Turin, *Affrontements culturels*, 43–44. By 1838 the student population did include, however, a small percentage of Moors. See also Abi-Mershed, *Apostles of Modernity*, 61–63.

7. Perrot, *Alger*, 52.

8. Turin, *Affrontements culturels*, 43–51; Abi-Mershed, *Apostles of Modernity*, 68–69. Louis Charles Auguste Depeille (1813–1890) arrived in Algeria in 1839 and devoted his entire career to teaching Arab students. He is also the author of a textbook on the teaching of the Arab language; see the biographical note in Messaoudi, "Savants, conseillers, médiateurs," vol. 3.

9. Turin, *Affrontements culturels*, 63. Information about this school, the Demoyencourt pensionnat, can be found in Messaoudi, "Savants, conseillers, médiateurs."

10. *Tableau de la situation des établissements français dans l'Algérie* (1838), statistical tables at end of volume.

11. Archives of the Soeurs de la Doctrine Chrétienne de Nancy, Annales religieuses, 1852–1867, note concerning Mother Thècle Braulot, 500.

12. AN, F[17] 7677, report by General Inspector of Studies Artaud to the Minister of War and President of the Council on the teaching of Arabic to the French and of French to the indigenous populations in Algeria, Algiers, 30 November 1842, cited in Messaoudi, "Savants, conseillers, médiateurs," vol. 3, 283. This report contradicts the statement often made by contemporaries and repeated by historians that girls' schools did not exist before the French presence. Marnia Lazreg indicates, however, that in wealthier families girls attended school with boys until the age of nine or were tutored at home; see *The Eloquence of Silence*, 25.

13. "Voyage de M. Salvandy en Algérie," *L'Algérie. Courrier d'Afrique, d'Orient et de la Méditerranée* 176 (22 June 1846): 3.

14. Quotation from Lorcin, *Imperial Identities*, 80. For the organization and activities of the Bureaux Arabes, see Frémeaux, *Les bureaux arabes*. Abi-Mershed describes in detail the intellectual underpinning of the men active in the Bureaux Arabes; *Apostles of Modernity*, 71–95.

15. CAOM, GGA 22 S/2, letter from Mme Allix to members of the Conseil supérieur d'administration, 31 January 1846.

16. CAOM, GGA 22 S/2, letter from the Widow Allix to the Minister of War, 28 February 1846.

17. CAOM, GGA 22 S/2, letter from Allix to the Queen of France, 14 July 1845.

18. CAOM, GGA 22 S/2, letter from Count Guyot to the Governor General, 6 November 1845.

19. CAOM, GGA 22 S/2, manuscript letter to the Minister of War, 28 February 1846. This same text is available at the Bibliothèque nationale de France: Allix, *Requête de Mme Vve Allix*.

20. CAOM, GGA 22 S/2, letter of Mme Allix to the members of the Conseil supérieur d'administration, 31 January 1846.

21. CAOM, GGA 22 S/2 and F^{80} 1732, "Note explicative sur l'institution de Mme Allix" (Algiers: Imprimerie Besancenez, 5 March 1846), seven pages. This passage is cited in Abi-Mershed, *Apostles of Modernity*, 137–38. I have somewhat modified and completed his English translation.

22. CAOM, GGA 22 S/2, letter to Count Guyot, 29 December 1845; translated in B.R.P., "Madame Luce, of Algiers" (June 1861): 226.

23. CAOM, GGA 22 S/2, letter to the Minister, 28 February 1846; see Abi-Mershed, *Apostles of Modernity*, 140.

24. Turin, *Affrontements culturels*, 52.

25. B.R.P., "Madame Luce, of Algiers" (June 1861): 230.

26. CAOM, GGA 22 S/2 and F^{80} 1732, "Note explicative sur l'institution de Mme Allix."

27. *Journal d'Éducation Populaire*, vol. 5, 3rd series, no. 53 (May 1846): 132.

28. Arsenal, Fonds Enfantin, 7679, no. 124, letter from Allix to Enfantin, 30 May 1846. There is no sign that he came to her aide.

29. B.R.P., "Madame Luce of Algiers" (June 1861): 234.

30. The details of her search for funds are recounted in detail in B.R.P., "Madame Luce, of Algiers" (June 1861): 233–36.

31. The members of the Conseil superieur d'administration combined representatives of both civil and military authorities; it acquired more authority after measures taken in September 1847 that reorganized civil affairs and created a municipal regime in six cities, including Algiers; see Julien, *Histoire de l'Algérie contemporaine*, vol. 1, 267.

32. See Caron, *À l'école de la violence*, 226–30. His database of 114 individuals charged for sexual offenses between 1843 and 1865 includes no women.

33. CAOM, GGA 22 S/2, letter of the Inspector of Public Instruction [A. Lepescheux] to the Director of the Interior [Guyot], 22 January 1846.

34. CAOM, GGA 22 S/2, letter of Count Guyot to the Governor General, 8 January 1846.

35. CAOM, GGA 22 S/2, letter of the Governor General to the Minister of War, 25 October 1846.

36. CAOM, GGA 22 S/2, register of decisions of the Conseil supérieur d'administration, 7 October 1846.

37. CAOM, GGA 22 S/2, letter of Madame Luce to the Minister of War, 20 October 1846.

38. His irreverence extended to poetry mocking the Ministry of War; see Bibliothèque des archives d'Outre-Mer, Belly, "Au maréchal Bugeaud."

39. CAOM, GGA 22 S/2, letter of Madame Luce to the Minister of War, 9 December 1846.

40. CAOM, GGA 22 S/2, letter from the Director of the Interior [Guyot] to the Minister of War, 16 December 1846. This letter included the various letters of recommendation.

41. CAOM, GGA 22 S/2, letter written on behalf of the Governor General to the Minister of War, 22 December 1846.

42. Abi-Mershed, *Apostles of Modernity*, 123–33.

43. See Levasseur, *L'enseignement primaire*, 252, who draws on the figures published in the *Tableau de la situation des établissements français dans l'Algérie*, which was published annually from 1838. All of these figures should be used with caution.

44. Levallois shows the importance of Urbain's support for schooling in the decision to extend Arab-French schooling in 1850; *Ismaÿl Urbain*, chap. 15.

45. For details of the military hesitation about Muslim girls' education, see Abi-Mershed, *Apostles of Modernity*, 133–43. Many of the Arabists in the Bureaux Arabes had doubts about the wisdom of starting with girls' education.

46. *La France Algérienne*, 17 January 1846.

47. CAOM, F^{80} 1566, État de situation des écoles primaires de l'Algérie au 1 January 1847.

48. CAOM, F^{80} 1566, report by Lepescheux to M. the Director on the situation of public instruction as of 31 December 1846, 13 March 1847.

49. Boyer, *L'évolution de l'Algérie médiane*, 150.

50. Urbain, *Algérie*, 40.

51. CAOM, F^{80} 1566, report of the Rector of the Academy to the Minister, 25 April 1849.

52. Boyer, *L'évolution de l'Algérie médiane*, 147–51. For the general context during these years, see Boyer, *La vie politique*.

53. See Jeanmaire, "Algérie."

54. See Abi-Mershed, *Apostles of Modernity*, 119–22.

55. The decree is reproduced in ibid., appendix 6, 244–49.

56. See ibid., 134.

57. Turin, *Affrontement culturels*, 182. She notes that the municipalities were reluctant to finance these schools because of their expense, which explains why the prefect rather than city officers had authority to distribute funds to the Arab-French schools.

58. CAOM, GGA 22 S/2, letter of Madame Luce to the Prefect of Algiers, 1 September 1850.

CHAPTER 4

1. Bodichon, *Women and Work*, 50–51.

2. See Léon, *Colonisation, enseignement et éducation*, 118–19; Turin, *Affrontements culturels*, 182–85; Abi-Mershed, *Apostles of Modernity*, 143–46 (includes translations of these two decrees in the appendixes, 244–52).

3. See Grew and Harrigan, *Schools, State, and Society*. For a local study of the influence of religious schooling, see Curtis, *Educating the Faithful.*

4. For the years 1850–1873, see Table 6.4 in Abi-Mershed, *Apostles of Modernity*, 196.

5. CAOM, GGA 22 S/2, file titled "nomination," 17 January 1853.

6. CAOM, GGA 22 S/2, file titled "nomination." At the time of the school's opening, Robin de Montmain presented a list of twenty-two students seeking enrollment.

7. CAOM, GGA 22 S/2, letter from the Prefect to the Minister of War, 18 December 1851.

8. CAOM, GGA 22 S/2, letter from the Minister of War to the Prefect, 7 January 1852.

9. Abi-Mershed, *Apostles of Modernity*, 141, notes that in late 1855 an effort was made

to reduce the number of boarders at Luce's school; nonresident workers were prohibited from overnight stays in Algiers without military authorization.

10. CAOM, GGA Series E, liasse 230 (1), notes to the Minister, 16 November 1850 and 29 August 1851. Captain Boissonnet was in charge of the emir in Amboise and was responsible for his moral well-being; see Aire, *Abd-el-Kader*, 152.

11. Contrary to the French promise, Abd al-Qadir had been moved from his prison in Pau to that of Amboise on 8 November 1848, where he and his family remained until 11 December 1852.

12. B.R.P., "Madame Luce, of Algiers" (July 1861): 298–99.

13. Profound thanks to Michel Levallois for sending me his notes about this affair. Letters between Ismaÿl Urbain and Laurent-Estève Boissonnet about Luce's students were exchanged between August and October 1851. The originals are at the Bibliothèque nationale d'Alger. See the letter from Eugénie Luce on 20 December 1850 to the prefect. At the same time the French sent Si Mohammed Chadli al-Qusanti to keep the emir company. The quotations are from this correspondence.

14. B.R.P., "Madame Luce, of Algiers" (July 1861): 299.

15. See the analysis of this incident in Warnier, "École de jeunes filles musulmanes."

16. B.R.P., "Madame Luce, of Algiers" (July 1861): 307.

17. CAOM, GGA 22 S/2, report of Rector Delacroix to the Governor General, 15 February 1853.

18. In urban boys' schools simultaneous education had mostly replaced mutual education by the 1850s. In girls' schools, Chapoulie has shown that mutual education was still dominant; see his "L'organisation de l'enseignement primaire."

19. See Messaoudi, "Savants, conseillers, médiateurs," vol. 2, 709–10. For a description of the language training in Luce's school, see Morsly, "La classe de Madame Allix-Luce."

20. This program resembled that established in *salles d'asile* in France. In 1836 these preschools taught writing, reading, arithmetic, and natural history; in 1855 history, geography, and linear drawing were added to the curriculum. See Luc, *L'invention du jeune enfant*, 200–218.

21. See Huguet, *Les livres pour l'enfance et la jeunesse*, 404.

22. CAOM, F[80] 515, first trimester 1854, inspection of Luce's school.

23. CAOM, F[80] 516, fourth trimester 1855, inspection of Luce's school.

24. Peigné, *Méthode de lecture*. This immensely successful reading textbook was reedited countless times.

25. For the Depeille method, see Depeille, *Méthode de lecture*.

26. Messaoudi, "Savants, conseillers, médiateurs," vol. 1, 308–9.

27. CAOM, F[80] 516, fourth trimester 1855, inspection of Luce's school.

28. CAOM, F[80] 521, first trimester 1856, inspection of Luce's school. Dufraisne first started receiving this salary in April 1851 (GGA 22 S/2). In 1855 the position was eliminated for budgetary reasons, but by the following year, Luce had persuaded the administration to reinstate it. Dufraisne died in 1871 at the age of sixty-nine.

29. CAOM, F[80] 516, June 1855, inspection of Luce's school.

30. See Turin, "Une page de publicité scolaire." In 1852 students received both clothing and a number of books, including the following titles: *Voyage autour du monde* (Voyage around the World), *Conquête de l'Espagne par les arabes* (The Conquest of Spain by the

Arabs), and *Album de la jungle* (The Album of the Jungle). For a description of prize-giving ceremonies in mutual schools in Brittany, see Chalopin, *L'enseignement mutuel en Bretagne*, 125–35.

31. CAOM, GGA 22 S/2, description of the prize-giving ceremony by Governor General Randon, 15 June 1854.

32. CAOM, F⁸⁰ 515, first trimester 1853, inspection of Luce's school. This inspection lists a wide variety of objects produced by the students, from socks and shirts to decorative furniture coverings.

33. CAOM, F⁸⁰ 515, second trimester 1853, inspection of Luce's school.

34. CAOM, GGA 22 S/2, copie d'un report du Comité des dames inspectrices des écoles arabes-françaises de jeunes filles, sent to the Prefect of the department of Algiers, 7 December 1858, with "Note de Madame Luce" added afterward.

35. See the entry "caisses d'épargne scolaires" in Buisson, *Nouveau dictionnaire de pédagogie*, available at http://www.inrp.fr/edition-electronique/lodel/dictionnaire-ferdinand-buisson/.

36. CAOM, F⁸⁰ 521, first trimester 1856, inspection of Luce's school.

37. CAOM, GGA 22 S/2, report of Delacroix to Governor General, 15 February 1853.

38. See Parayre, *L'hygiène à l'école*.

39. CAOM, F⁸⁰ 515, first trimester 1853, inspection of Luce's school.

40. CAOM, F⁸⁰ 521, first trimester 1856, inspection of Luce's school.

41. CAOM, F⁸⁰ 521, second trimester 1856, inspection of Luce's school.

42. CAOM, F⁸⁰ 508, fourth trimester 1854, inspection of Parent's school in Constantine.

43. CAOM, F⁸⁰ 516, first trimester 1855, inspection of Chevalier's school in Algiers.

44. CAOM, F⁸⁰ 521, first trimester 1856, inspection of Luce's school; GGA 22 S/2, "Minute du Ministre de la Guerre au Préfet au sujet des difficultés qu'a Madame Luce à nourrir ses élèves pour le prix de 15 centimes par jour," 26 December 1855.

45. CAOM, F⁸⁰ 1572, 30 November 1851, letter to the Minister of War concerning the province of Constantine.

46. Cardinal Lavigerie set up orphanages for boys and girls in 1872 following the terrible drought of 1866–1867. For a discussion of the debate around this initiative, see Taithe, "Algerian Orphans."

47. CAOM, F⁸⁰ 521, second trimester 1856, inspection of Luce's school.

48. CAOM, F⁸⁰ 515, second trimester 1854, inspection of Luce's school.

49. Hémon, "Les écoles d'art," 309.

50. See Rogers, "Teaching morality and religion."

51. Félix Hémon describes this first ceremony in "Les écoles d'art indigène en Algérie."

52. CAOM, GGA 22 S/2, prize-giving speech by Eugénie Luce, 20 October 1852.

53. CAOM GGA 22 S/2, description of the prize-giving ceremony by the Bureau Arabe, 20 October 1852. Lazreg also offers a long description of this ceremony and quotes extensively from the dialogue recited; *The Eloquence of Silence*, 68–75.

54. CAOM, GGA 22 S/2, report of 15 June 1854 about the ceremony on 24 May 1854.

55. For a harsh condemnation of the hypocrisy of these events, see Turin, "Une page de publicité scolaire."

56. See "Les écoles musulmanes à Alger," *Journal d'Éducation Populaire* 3, 4th series (1855): 30–35; *Almanach de l'Algérie*, 169–71.

57. CAOM, GGA 22 S/2, report of 15 June 1854 about the ceremony on 24 May 1854.

58. See the documents in CAOM, F⁸⁰ 1573, on this subject.

59. CAOM, F⁸⁰ 515, second trimester 1854, inspection of Luce's school.

60. This introduction of a cash economy in the working of the school was relatively precocious. By the twentieth century, however, French colonial schools commonly resorted to the sale of products produced by students; see Deleigne, "Entre la plume et l'*angady*."

61. Klein, *L'enseignement à Alger*, 20.

62. *L'Illustration*, no. 1 (28 May 1853): 339–40; also see Klein, *L'enseignement à Alger*, 20.

63. In 1851 the only country aside from Great Britain to present the products from its colonies was France, with an exhibition dedicated to Algiers; see Greenhalgh, *Ephemeral Vistas*, 56. As early as 1849, the French organized a separate exhibition of Algerian products.

64. *Rapport sur l'exposition universelle*, 438. There were 10,003 exhibitors from France.

65. *Catalogue explicatif*, 202.

66. *Exposition universelle de 1855.*

67. Lacroix, "Algérie, ses produits à l'exposition universelle." Lacroix briefly served as director of civil affairs of Algiers in 1848 and then prefect of Algiers in 1849.

68. Hugonnet, "Écoles de garçons et écoles de filles."

69. Mondenard, "L'Algérie, terre oubliée des photographes en Orient."

70. B.R.P., "Madame Luce, of Algiers" (July 1861): 307.

71. CAOM, GGA 22 S /2, letter from Madame Luce to the Prefect of Algiers, 1 September 1850.

72. See Warnier, "École de jeunes filles musulmanes."

73. CAOM, F⁸⁰ 1572, minutes from the Service de l'Algérie of the Government General of Algeria to the Minister of War, 30 January 1851.

74. Kateb, *Européens, "indigènes" et juifs*, 70. See also Clancy-Smith "Exoticism, Erasures, and Absence."

75. Pope, *The Corsair and His Conqueror*, 88.

76. B.R.P., "Madame Luce, of Algiers" (July 1861): 297.

77. CAOM, GGA 22 S/2, letter from the Prefect to the Governor General concerning the doubling of the schools in Algiers, 5 February 1855. For more information on the education of orphans, see Taithe, "Algerian Orphans."

78. CAOM, F⁸⁰ 516, third trimester 1856, inspection of Luce's school.

79. Information about her comes from the inspection reports of the school, as well as from Parkes, who reported on her death; B.R.P., "Mustapha's House."

80. CAOM, F⁸⁰ 515, fourth trimester 1853 and first trimester 1854, inspections of Luce's school.

81. CAOM, F⁸⁰ 1573, letter from the Prefect of Algiers to the Governor General, 13 September 1853.

82. CAOM, F⁸⁰ 1573, letter from the Minister of War to the Governor General, 10 November 1853.

83. CAOM, F⁸⁰ 1573, letter from the Minister of War to the Governor General, 18 February 1854.

84. CAOM, GGA 22 S/2, letter from the Prefect to the Governor General on the subject of the doubling of girls' schools in Algiers, 5 February 1855.

85. CAOM, F⁸⁰ 508, first trimester 1854, inspection of Parent's school. For a discussion of official French attitudes toward *la femme arabe* (the Arab woman), see Clancy-

Smith's classic article "Islam, Gender, and Identities." She describes in particular General Daumas's extensive writing on the subject, noting how he anticipated later ethnographic studies. She also observes that most of his material came from pastoral-nomadic communities. Urban women both in the nineteenth century and today remain underresearched. For some insights into work traditions within the home, see Clancy-Smith, "A Woman without Her Distaff."

CHAPTER 5

1. Lorcin, *Imperial Identities*, 76.
2. See Surkis, "Propriété, polygamie et statut personnel," and Christelow, *Muslim Law Courts*.
3. See Clancy-Smith, "Islam, Gender, and Identities."
4. Rey-Goldzeiguer, *Le Royaume Arabe*.
5. Abi-Mershed, *Apostles of Modernity*, 171–72.
6. For a history of the Muslim elite's response to French colonization, see Clancy-Smith, *Rebel and Saint*, chap. 6. For the history of the French administration of Algeria during these years, see Rey-Goldzeiguer, *Le Royaume Arabe*.
7. Rogers, "Retrograde or Modern?"
8. *Tableau de la situation des établissements français dans l'Algérie, 1862*, 187–89.
9. Renson, "Les soeurs de la doctrine chrétienne en Algérie." For an analysis of the role of female missionary orders in promoting Muslim girls' education in Tunisia, see Clancy-Smith, "L'éducation des jeunes filles musulmanes," as well as her article "Muslim Princes, Female Missionaries, and Trans-Mediterranean Migrations: The Soeurs de Saint-Joseph de l'Apparition in Tunisia, c. 1840–1881," in White and Daughton, *In God's Empire*.
10. *Tableau de la situation des établissements français dans l'Algérie, 1864*, 117–18. For a general overview of European schooling, see Léon, *Colonisation, enseignement et éducation*, 146–51.
11. See Abi-Mershed, *Apostles of Modernity*, 194–97. Léon estimates that two thousand *zawiya*s were operating in Algeria between 1865 and 1880; *Colonisation, enseignement et éducation*, 120.
12. *Tableau de la situation des établissements français dans l'Algérie, 1864*, 241.
13. Abi-Mershed, *Apostles of Modernity*, 195–96.
14. For a particularly critical vision of French educational policies with respect to private indigenous education, see Turin, *Affrontements culturels*, 216–50.
15. The Collège impérial arabe-français adopted the same rulebook as those that Lambert had written up for the schools of Mehemet Ali in Egypt; Emerit, *Les Saint-Simoniens en Algérie*, 296. In 1863 Victor Duruy, the future minister of public instruction, toured Algeria in his capacity as inspector general. He visited and admired the Collège impérial.
16. See descriptions of the program in Emerit, *Les Saint-Simoniens en Algérie*, 295. The students did not learn Greek and Latin.
17. For more on Perron, see Lançon, "Le destin du lettré Nicolas Perron."
18. Rey-Goldzeiguer, *Le Royaume Arabe*, 433. Information on this school can also be found in Abi-Mershed, *Apostles of Modernity*, 190–91, and Turin, *Affrontements culturels*, 278–81.

19. Abi-Mershed, *Apostles of Modernity*, 192–94.

20. See Colonna, *Instituteurs algériens*.

21. Turin, *Affrontements culturels*, 214.

22. See Ageron, *Les Algériens musulmans*, 2:320.

23. See ibid., 2:317–23. For a critical analysis of the violence of the French indigénat system that focuses on New Caledonia, see Merle, "De la 'légalisation' de la violence."

24. See the table in Barthélémy, *Africaines et diplômées*, 40.

25. For more information on the press of this period, see Ihaddeden, *Histoire de la presse indigène*.

26. Toulouze, "Distribution des prix de l'école arabe-française dirigée par Madame Luce," *L'Akhbar*, 30 September 1852.

27. Bourget, "Situation de la population mauresque," *L'Akhbar*, 19 December 1856. An excerpt of this article is also in CAOM, F[80] 1573.

28. *Moniteur de la Colonisation*, 16 December 1857. A decree of 5 December 1857 created the Muslim Welfare Bureau in Algiers. See also Cherbonneau, "Notice sur les écoles arabes-françaises de filles."

29. CAOM, GGA 22 S/2, report of the women inspectors of the Arab-French schools to the Prefect of Algiers, 7 December 1858.

30. Julien, *Histoire de l'Algérie contemporaine*, 411–15. For a study of the General Council in Algiers, see Boyer, *L'évolution de l'Algérie médiane*, 218–31.

31. Cited in Turin, *Affrontements culturels*, 287.

32. CAOM, GGA 22 S/2, report of Rector Delacroix to the Governor General, 15 February 1853.

33. CAOM, F[80] 1573, letter from the Governor General to the Minister of War, 18 February 1854; underlining in the original.

34. Duchesne, *De la prostitution dans la ville d'Alger*, 70. For a study of prostitution in colonial Algiers, see Taraud, *La prostitution coloniale*.

35. Duchesne, *De la prostitution dans la ville d'Alger*, 58.

36. See Robert-Guiard, *Des Européennes*, 89–99.

37. CAOM, F[80] 516, first trimester 1855, inspection of Luce's school.

38. See Ann Stoler's classic essay, "Carnal Knowledge and Imperial Power."

39. Conseil général, 1860, *Procès-verbal*, 63–68. The quotations that follow come from this document, large extracts of which are also available in CAOM, GGA 22 S/2.

40. The documents do not name the members who speak, but it is easy to identify one of the two indigenous members: Boukandoura. He was an assistant judge in the appellate court and continued to play an important role in regional politics after the establishment of the civilian regime; see Christelow, *Muslim Law Courts*, 96.

41. This financial incentive to attend the school was supposedly stopped in 1857, but it appears to have continued, a sign, no doubt, of Luce's clout.

42. CAOM, GGA 22 S/2, letter of A. Michel to the General Director, 9 August 1861. Also cited in Turin, *Affrontements culturels*, 276.

43. It is difficult to identify the two women precisely, but it seems likely that Madame Bransoulié was the wife of Jean Maximin Bransoulié, director of the drawing school, and that Madame Cugnot was the wife of a banker.

44. Report transcribed in Conseil général, 1861, *Procès-verbal*, 270–76, and also in

CAOM, GGA 22 S/2. Turin describes this commission and its results; *Affrontements culturels*, 273–76. The figures and quotations that follow come from this report.

45. CAOM, GGA 22 S/2, decree of 19 September 1861.

46. See Çelik, *Urban Forms*, 37.

47. Boyer, *L'évolution de l'Algérie médiane*, 350.

48. She first requested authorization to run a workshop in February 1856.

49. CAOM, GGA 22 S/2, Règlement de l'ouvroir musulman, 20 May 1858.

50. CAOM, GGA 22 S/2; see Luce's "Note" following the report of women inspectors concerning her school, which was sent to the Prefect of Algiers on 7 December 1858.

51. Conseil général, 1862, *Procès verbal*, xxi–xxii; emphasis added.

52. Bel, *Les arts indigènes en Algérie*. The text is not paginated; see the pages under the heading "Broderies algéroises."

53. See Clancy-Smith, "A Woman without Her Distaff," esp. 33–36.

54. Information about Madame Barroil comes from the civil registers available online at the Archives nationales d'outre mer website, http://anom.archivesnationales.culture .gouv.fr/caomec2/recherche.php?territoire=ALGERIE. The reports of the General Council describe her workshop along with that of Luce's.

55. Information about both workshops can be found in Desprès, *Les ouvroirs musulmans*.

56. Conseil général, 1865, *Procès verbal*, xliii.

57. Conseil général, 1863, *Procès verbal*, 8.

58. The semiofficial newspaper *L'Akhbar* published a number of long articles about vocational training, describing its characteristics in both France and Algeria during these years. In 1866 the authorities created the École d'arts et métiers for Kabyle artisans; within the normal school that was founded in Algiers in 1865, agricultural lessons were emphasized as well. For information about vocational training at this time, see Boyer, *L'évolution de l'Algérie médiane*, 353–54, and Turin, *Affrontements culturels*, 267. Colonna discusses the republican arguments in favor of assimilationist educational policies in the 1880s and 1890s and their limited success on the ground until the 1920s; *Instituteurs algériens*, 15–63.

59. Julia Clancy-Smith has studied the tensions between artisanal and academic schools at the end of the century, noting the importance of local context in these developments; see in particular her "Envisioning Knowledge."

60. *Session législative de 1870*, 155.

61. Ibid., 156.

62. Cherbonneau, "Notice sur les écoles arabes-françaises de filles," 317.

63. See Rogers, "Language Learning versus Vocational Training."

64. Conseil général, 1876, *Procès verbal*, 557.

65. CAOM, GGA 22 S/3, inspection of 27 June 1871.

CHAPTER 6

An earlier version of this chapter appeared as Rebecca Rogers, "Telling Stories about the Colonies: British and French Women in Algeria in the Nineteenth Century," *Gender and History* 21 (April 2009): 39–59.

1. CAOM, GGA 22 S/2, Rapport au Gouverneur Général au sujet du traitement de Mme Luce, directrice de l'ouvroir de la rue de Toulon, 11 October 1869.

2. Playfair, *Handbook for Travelers*.

3. For information about the British presence in Algeria, see Redouane, "La présence anglaise en Algérie," as well as her dissertation "Les Anglais et l'Algérie." In 1867 the traveler Mrs. Lloyd Evans wrote that the winter colony of British visitors in Algiers numbered only fifty or sixty "at the utmost"; *Last Winter in Algeria*, 335.

4. From the outset, doctors and the management of sickness were an essential element of the French civilizing mission in Algeria; see Turin, *Affrontements culturels*, and more recently, Gallois, *The Administration of Sickness*.

5. See the following biographies: Burton, *Barbara Bodichon*; Herstein, *A Mid-Victorian Feminist*; and Hirsch, *Barbara Leigh Smith Bodichon*. On the Langham Place group, see Rendall, "Langham Place Group."

6. For another reading of Eugénie Luce and her encounter with British feminists, see Cherry, "Shuttling and Soul-Making" and *Beyond the Frame*.

7. Bodichon, *Guide Book*, 92, 72. Like other Europeans, Bodichon reacted strongly to the seclusion of Muslim women, interpreting it as a form of imprisonment.

8. Ibid., 71–73, 92.

9. B.R.P., "Madame Luce, of Algiers"; Bodichon, *Memoir of Madame Luce*.

10. Parkes was similarly interested in education and published *Remarks on the Education of Girls* in 1854. See Lowndes, *Turning Victorian Ladies into Women*.

11. Parkes, "Mme Luce's school in Algiers."

12. Girton College Archives, Cambridge, GCPP Parkes 5/87, Bessie Rayner Parkes to Barbara Bodichon, 30 January 1859.

13. B.R.P., "Madame Luce, of Algiers" (July 1861): 308.

14. Girton College Archives, Cambridge, GCPP Parkes 6/73, Bessie Rayner Parkes to Mary Merryweather, 1857.

15. B.R.P., "Madame Luce, of Algiers" (May 1861): 163–64. (This notion of "approaching the condition" seems to confirm the operative power of Homi Bhabha's concept of "almost the same but not quite" in "Of Mimicry and Man.")

16. Ibid. (June 1861): 227.

17. Davies, *Collected Letters*, 11.

18. Parkes, *Vignettes*, 250–51, 255.

19. Bodichon, *Women and Work*, 47–48, 51. Bodichon relied in her descriptions on other British sources, notably Morell, *Algeria*.

20. Bodichon, *Women and Work*, 51–52.

21. Parkes, *Vignettes*, 253.

22. See Benchérif, *The Image of Algeria*.

23. B.R.P., "Madame Luce, of Algiers" (June 1861): 229.

24. The authors with the dates of publication are as follows: Ellen Rogers (1865), Mabel Crawford (1863), Matilda Betham Edwards (1867), Mrs. Lloyd Evans (1868), Mary Elizabeth Herbert (1872), and Lisbeth Gooch Séguin Strahan (1878).

25. The classic description is Said, *Orientalism*. For a feminist rereading of Said, see Lewis, *Gendering Orientalism* and *Rethinking Orientalism*. For a discussion of how the press contributed to imperial imaginings, see Codell, ed., *Imperial Co-Histories*.

26. *Leaves from a Lady's Diary*, 1:1.

27. F.C., "Winter in Algiers," 655.

28. "Education at Algiers. Madame Luce's school."

29. Crawford, *Through Algeria*, 43. She titles one of her chapters "The Moresque at Home—Her Hopeless Degradation." Her feminist perspective is evident in such articles as "Maltreatment of Wives," *Westminster Review* (March 1893). Inderpal Grewal notes the same response to Indian women's opacity in her English sources; *Home and Harem*, 49–53.

30. Evans, *Last Winter in Algeria*, 9.

31. Bodichon quoted in Benchérif, *Image of Algeria*, 129; Madame Prus, *Residence in Algeria*, 242.

32. Rogers, *A Winter in Algeria*, 58.

33. Scholarship on the social history of indigenous women's lives remains very sparse. See, for example, Clancy-Smith, "A Woman without Her Distaff." For a sociological viewpoint that relies on printed sources and interviews for the most part, see Lazreg, *The Eloquence of Silence*.

34. Rogers, *A Winter in Algeria*, 199.

35. Edwards, *A Winter with the Swallows*, 16.

36. Ibid., 17.

37. See Melman, *Women's Orients*, and Roberts, *Intimate Outsiders*.

38. Edwards, *A Winter with the Swallows*, 49.

39. The British attended their own churches, opened their own library, read their own papers, and interacted mostly among themselves on the slopes of Mustapha Superior; see Benchérif, *The Image of Algeria*, 121–23.

40. "Algiers in 1865," *Cornhill Magazine*, 427.

41. Edwards, *In French-Africa*, 9.

42. Edwards, *Anglo-French Reminiscences*, 157.

43. Edwards, *In French-Africa*, 34.

44. "Review of Current Literature," *Christian Examiner* 65 (July–November 1858): 457.

45. Davies, *Algiers in 1857*, 76.

46. Ibid., 102.

47. *Dublin Review* (February 1860): 297.

48. *Christian Examiner* 65 (July–November 1858): 458.

49. "Education at Algiers. Madame Luce's school."

50. Whatley was the daughter of the archbishop of Dublin, and her portrayal of missionary life in *A Ragged Life in Egypt* (1858) was enormously influential.

51. Rogers, *Winter in Algeria*, 58.

52. Ibid., 198–99.

53. For a discussion of Luce, see *The Monthly Packet of evening readings for members of the English Church* 2 (1866): 402–3; quotation at 403.

54. *Eclectic Review* (1866): 255.

55. Stowell, "Red Algiers," 54–55, quotation at 55.

56. See B.R.P., "Madame Luce, of Algiers" (July 1861): 307.

57. Stowell, "Red Algiers," 56.

58. "Education in Algiers," 102–3.

59. Stowell, "Red Algiers," 57.

60. Herbert, *A Search after Sunshine*, 76–77. For a discussion of Herbert's earlier travel writing, see Melman, *Women's Orients*, 28, 222–23.

61. Herbert, *A Search after Sunshine*, 89.

62. Edwards, *A Winter with the Swallows*, 207.

63. Pope, *The Corsair and His Conqueror*, 84.

64. B.R.P., "Madame Luce and the Great Exhibition," 355.

65. See Gouvernement général de l'Algérie, *L'Algérie à l'exposition universelle de Londres*, 2:204–5, for the list of objects; and 2:241–42, for the prizes received.

66. Parkes, *Vignettes*, 254–56.

67. Rogers, *Winter in Algiers*, 192–93.

68. Evans, *Last Winter in Algeria*, 166, 333.

69. Herbert, *A Search after Sunshine*, 76–77.

70. Bennet, *Winter and Spring*, 508. He, like Henry E. Pope, noted the presence of Jewish girls in the workshop.

71. Cox, *Search for Winter Sunbeams*, 123. Alexander Knox similarly directed his readers to the "strange old house" where Madame Luce conducted her "experiment . . . to provide honest work for young Moorish girls"; *The New Playground*, 183.

72. Murray, *A Handbook for Travelers in Algeria* (1873), 30; Murray, *A Handbook for Travelers* (1874), 71.

73. Strahan, *Walks in Algiers*, 44.

74. *Algerian Advertiser*, advertisements on 3 and 10 March 1889.

75. Playfair, *Handbook for Travelers*, 103.

76. Nugent, *A Land of Mosques and Marabouts*, 38.

77. Hyam, *The Illustrated guide to Algiers*, 51.

78. See Oulebsir, *Les usages politiques du patrimoine*.

79. Crouse, *Algiers*, 153–54.

80. Gautier, *Voyage pittoresque en Algérie*, 54.

81. Tailliart argues that most descriptive texts about Algeria focused on the indigenous population and repeated generalities although descriptions of the Kabyle were more detailed; *L'Algérie dans la littérature française*, 323–438. Monicat notes only scattered references to the legitimacy of French colonization in the texts of the period under consideration; *Itinéraire de l'écriture au féminin*.

82. Sessions, *By Sword and Plow*, 218–20.

83. *Petite bibliotheque*, 20–23.

84. On these guidebooks, see Nordman, "Les *Guides-Joanne*."

85. Piesse, *Itinéraire historique et descriptif de l'Algérie*, xcvix, 63.

86. Fillias, *Nouveau guide général*, 72, 98.

87. Seven Frenchwomen's travel narratives were published between 1851 and Luce's death in 1882, compared with nine written by British women (six of whom mention Madame Luce). The French authors who mention her are Vallory (1866), Dutertre (1866), and Regis (1880). For an analysis of Frenchwomen's travel narratives of Algeria, see Monicat, "L'Algérie des voyageuses."

88. Dutertre, *Voyage de Vermont-sur-Orne*, 539, 543, 557.

89. Ibid., 557.

90. Ibid., 558–59.

91. Vallory, *À l'aventure en Algérie*, 25, 42–43.

92. Ibid., 31, 33.

93. Michèle Salinas argues that the myth of "necessary colonization" developed only

gradually in French travel literature. It needed first to "deorientalize" its vision in order to see an Algeria behind the picturesque; *Voyages et voyageurs*, 371.

94. Régis, *Constantine. Voyage et séjours*, 46–47, 301.

95. Dall, *The College, the Market, and the Court*, 41.

CHAPTER 7

1. Crouzet-Benaben, *Souvenirs*, 73.

2. Ibid., 38.

3. Ibid.

4. For the importance of music in French republicanism, see Pasler, *Composing the Citizen*.

5. Crouzet-Benaben, *Souvenirs*, 40.

6. Ibid., 47.

7. Ibid.

8. Ibid., 73.

9. See Gerson, *The Pride of Place*.

10. AN, F^{17} 22960.

11. CAOM, registres d'état civil, jugement de divorce, 2 June 1886. The Naquet Law in 1884 legalized divorce in France.

12. AD Loir-et-Cher, 6M 525, recensement de 1876. At this point the population of Montrichard was 3,020.

13. Crouzet-Benaben, *Souvenirs*, 68–69.

14. Ibid., 61. Two recent books explore the effect of de Ségur's popular fiction: Sophie Heywood, *Catholicism and Children's Literature in France: The Comtesse de Ségur (1799–1875)* (Manchester: Manchester University Press, 2011); and Maialen Berastegui, *La comtesse de Ségur. De l'art discret de la subversion* (Rennes: Presses Universitaires des Rennes, 2011).

15. See Regourd, "Allons à l'école," 91.

16. Klary published *La photographie d'art à l'exposition universelle de 1900*, edited the journal *Le photogramme. Revue mensuelle illustrée de la photographie* (1897–1906), and wrote frequently about appropriate photographic methods in portraiture. His book *L'éclairage des portraits photographiques* was frequently reprinted in the final decades of the century.

17. Crouzet-Benaben, *Souvenirs*, 130–31.

18. Information about this business is indicated in her will as well as in Gouillon, *Annuaire général de l'Algérie*, 40.

19. In the archives, his name is also spelled Paute-Lafaurie, with or without a hyphen. His administrative dossier lists him as Laforie.

20. AN, F^{17} 21050. He was also the author of *Mémoire d'un Régent de Quatrième sur la réforme des collèges communaux (juin 1849)*, which was published with an introduction by H. Monin in 1913 that offers biographical material about his radical youth (text available at the BHVP).

21. Crouzet-Benaben, *Souvenirs*, 35. The archives indicate that he was in residential arrest with the "assistant of Bouzaréah" as of 5 September 1852. AN, BB^{22} 154/2, grâces du mariage. For information on the radical left and Algeria, see Darriulat, "La gauche républicaine." For internment camps, see Thénault, *Violence ordinaire dans l'Algérie*, esp. 209–13.

22. Crouzet-Benaben, *Souvenirs*, 131.

23. For information about the reinstatement of divorce and its consequences for women, see Pedersen, *Legislating the French Family.*

24. Crouzet-Benaben, *Souvenirs,* 435.

25. Sorbonne Library, MS 1936, correspondance Eugène Manuel E. Paute Laforie, folio 175, letter from Paute Laforie to Eugène Manuel, Paris, 28 April 1893.

26. Crouzet-Benaben, *Souvenirs,* 128.

27. Notarial archives of Maître Billette (Montrichard), dépôt des testaments olographes de Madame Veuve Luce, 6 June 1882.

28. Crouzet-Benaben, *Souvenirs,* 129.

29. Notarial archives of Maître Billette (Montrichard), vente mobilière après le décès de Madame Veuve Luce Berlau, Bureau d'enregistrement de Montrichard, 11 August 1882.

30. Coadaccioni, "Les fortunes à Lille," 358.

31. Crouzet-Benaben, *Souvenirs,* 132.

32. Ibid., 130.

33. For an analysis of Henriette Belly's life in fin-de-siècle Algeria, see Rogers, "Relations entre femmes."

34. CAOM, GGA, 14 H 32 (24), letter from Henriette Benaben to the Governor General, 13 January 1911.

35. Interview with Claude Crouzet, the widow of Henriette Benaben's grandson, 6 November 2006.

36. Eberhardt, *Oeuvres complètes,* quotation at 444.

37. These images are available in the iconothèque of the Quai Branly. See also the album of photos *Vues d'Alger* in the Getty Collection, where his name is spelled Le Roux. The Getty also has 158 plates of images from *L'Algérie Illustrée* between 1888 and 1892.

38. My thanks to Michel Megnin for this information; see Megnin, "Paul et Arnold Vollenweider: L'autre famille de photographes suisses à Alger . . . 1887–1937: de la photocarte à la carte postale," at http://michel.megnin.free.fr/CDV%20Vollenweider.html. See also the postcard of the Benaben workshop by Geiser in Humbert, *Jean Geiser,* 84–85.

39. Jordi, "Le temps des hiverneurs," esp. 33. See also Sebbar, Taraud, and Belorgey, *Femmes d'Afrique du Nord.* Sebbar describes in her essay how Benaben's workshop is the site for the romantic rendezvous of a photographer and a young Muslim woman.

40. Paul Eudel's account of his visit in February and March 1896 captures this interest in domestic spaces, girls' work, and Arabic embroideries nicely; see *Hivernage en Algérie,* 195, 216.

41. See the analysis of Çelik, "Framing the Colony" and "A Lingering Obsession."

42. Klein, *L'enseignement à Alger,* 50, 52. For information about the secularization of madrasas in 1905 and their use as public monuments, see Oulebsir, *Les usages du patrimoine,* 247–54. An image of the Médersa d'Alger is on p. 254.

43. See especially Oulebsir, *Les usages du patrimoine,* 233–60, and Benjamin, *Orientalist Aesthetics.*

44. *Algerian Advertiser,* 3 and 10 March 1889. For her location in Algiers, see *Annuaire commercial, industriel, administratif, agricole et vinicole de l'Algérie et de la Tunisie.* The name of this trade book frequently changed. It is more accurate than the guidebooks.

45. Hyam, *The Illustrated guide to Algiers,* 50–51.

46. Crouzet, "L'art de la broderie Arabe." The article is reproduced in Berque, *L'art antique*, 122–25, and Berque, *L'Algérie, terre d'art et d'histoire*, 289–91.

47. For a similar analysis that addresses only boys' schooling, see Colonna, *Instituteurs algériens*.

48. Coignet, "À propos de l'instruction des indigènes," quotation at 338.

49. AN, F^{17}12333. See also Combes, *Rapport fait au nom de la commission*.

50. Jeanmaire, "Sur l'instruction des indigènes en Algérie"; this is a condensed version of his report in the *Bulletin universitaire de l'Académie d'Alger*. See Bayet, "L'art arabe à Alger."

51. Poulard, *L'enseignement pour les indigènes*; Illio, *L'enseignement des métiers féminin*.

52. See Benaben's undated report "Instruction professionnelle des indigènes" at CAOM. My heartfelt thanks to Leïla Sebbar for sharing this document with me.

53. Brihmat, "École professionnelle," *Bulletin Municipal Official de la Ville d'Alger* (2 May 1899): 783.

54. Gouvernement général de l'Algérie, *Compte des recettes*, 61.

55. Charles-Roux, *Nomade j'étais*, 423.

56. Victor Barrucand, "Figure disparue," *L'Akhbar*, 14 March 1915, 2–3.

57. This museum's name varied over the first decades of its existence and is now known as the National Museum of Antiquities. For its history, see Benjamin, *Orientalist Aesthetics*, and Oulebsir, *Les usages du patrimoine*.

58. Oulebsir, *Les usages du patrimoine*; see also Orif, "De l'art indigène."

59. Marye, "L'éducation artistique."

60. Bel, "La protection de la vie locale en Algérie," 15. See Clancy-Smith, "A Woman without Her Distaff," for a discussion of Bel and female handicraft in colonial North Africa.

61. Illio, *L'enseignement des métiers féminins*, 75. Articles about these developments abound in the *Bulletin de l'Éducation des Indigènes de l'Académie d'Alger*; see in particular "L'enseignement professionnel dans les écoles de filles indigenes," 115 (November 1902): 161–72.

62. Vachon, *Les industries d'art indigène en Algérie*, 79.

63. Violard, *Des industries d'art indigènes*, 29–32.

64. Violard, *De la rénovation*.

65. Alexandre, "Réflexions sur les arts et les industries d'art en Algérie."

66. See *Un grand universitaire*.

67. Hémon, "Les écoles d'art indigène." The surname Benaben is spelled in multiple ways within the sources, in part because many contemporaries mistook the name for being Arabic.

68. For more on Ricard, see Mokhiber, "'Le protectorat dans la peau.'"

69. Ricard, *Pour comprendre l'art musulman*; Golvin, *Les arts populaires en Algérie*.

70. See the description of embroideries in the annual exhibition of objects from indigenous schools and workshops at the Médersa (the madrasa) in Artenac, "Enseignement professionnel," 138, 142.

71. Ricard, *Dentelles algériennes et marocaines*.

72. Greenhalgh, *Ephemeral Vistas*, 52–81.

73. *Algérie: catalogue spécial*, 39, 42.

74. Brihmat, "L'école professionnelle de broderies arabes," 7.

75. Elliott, *Art and Handicraft in the Woman's Building*, 5, 234; Monteils, *Algérie à l'Exposition*, 5–36. Benaben's involvement in placing her exhibit in the Woman's Building is recounted in Weimann, *The Fair Woman*, 272. For a general discussion of the significance of indigenous peoples on display in these exhibitions, see Bancel, Blanchard, Gilles Boëtsch et al., *Zoos humains*.

76. *Exposition franco-britannique*, 37.

77. Hale, *Races on Display*, 118–40.

78. Bayet, "L'art arabe à Alger," 22–23.

79. Marçais, *L'exposition d'art musulman d'Alger*, 159.

80. Georges Doublet and René-Marie La Blanchère, eds., *Musées et collections archéologiques de l'Algérie et de la Tunisie*, vol. 1, Georges Doublet, *Musée d'Alger* (Paris: E. Leroux, 1890).

81. Marçais, "L'art musulman en Algérie."

82. Bel, *Les arts indigènes en Algérie.*

83. Quoted in Carlier, "Medina and Modernity," 65.

84. *Le musée Stéphane Gsell.*

85. *Bulletin municipal official de la ville d'Alger*, 19 May 1922 and 29 August 1934.

86. Turin, *Affrontements culturels*, 52–56.

CONCLUSION

1. Bodichon, *Guide Book*, 92; Berque, *L'art antique et l'art musulman en Algérie*, 122.

2. See Chapter 7 and the obituary, *Le Républicain de Loir-et-Cher*, 11 June 1882.

3. Crouzet-Benaben, *Souvenirs*, 73.

4. See Anderson, *Joyous Greetings*. For the effects of the Second Empire repression on Saint-Simonian women, see Riot-Sarcey, *La démocratie à l'épreuve des femmes*, 263–82.

5. Deroin, *Almanach des femmes.*

6. References to these two letters can be found in Sand, *Correspondance*, 417, 681.

7. Perrot, *Les femmes ou les silences de l'histoire*, 313–57, esp. 340.

8. Auclert, *Les femmes arabes*. See Wiart, "Hubertine Auclert."

9. AN, F[17]12333, undated petition from Hubertine Auclert, Algiers, to M. Bourgeois, Minister of Public Instruction, c. January–April 1892.

10. BHVP, Fonds Bouglé, sous-fonds Hubertine Auclert, boîte 2 correspondance, folio 35–36, Algiers, letter of 8 March 1895 from Jeanmaire to Auclert responding to her letter of 1 March concerning Arab schools for girls.

11. Auclert, *Les femmes arabes*, 76. For an analysis of Auclert's feminist imperialism, see Eichner, "*La Citoyenne* in the World."

12. Offen, "The Second Sex."

13. See *Un grand universitaire*, 19–50.

14. For an analysis of her writings, see Perin, "Le Bulletin de l'enseignement."

15. Turin, *Affrontements culturels*, 52–56.

16. Knibiehler and Goutalier, *La femme au temps des colonies*, 232–33.

17. Brahimi, *Femmes arabes et soeurs musulmanes.*

18. For a recent overview of scholarship on nineteenth-century Algeria, see Blais, Fredj, and Saada, "Un long moment colonial."

19. Cherry, "Shuttling and Soul-Making," 158.

20. Benjamin, *Orientalist Aesthetics,* 191–220, quotations at 197 and 198.

21. Robert-Guiard, *Des Européennes,* 212–14, 227.

22. Morsly, "La classe de Madame Allix-Luce," quotation at 140. She is also the author of "Madame Allix-Luce," in *Féminin/masculin: Portraits de femmes* (Université de Cergy-Pontoise, France: CRTH, 2002), 177–95.

23. Abi-Mershed, *Apostles of Modernity,* 138–43.

24. See in particular the work of Julia Clancy-Smith in English and Christelle Taraud in French. They have both written useful historiographic essays: Clancy-Smith, "Changing Perspectives," and Taraud, "Les femmes, le genre et les sexualités."

25. Blais, Fredj, and Saada devote only one paragraph specifically to gender; "Un long moment colonial," 14–15. For the question of cultural contact, see Blanchard and Thénault, "Quel 'monde du contact'?" For the notion of cultural colonization, see Dulucq and Zytnicki, eds., "La colonisation culturelle."

26. See in particular Cooper and Stoler, eds., *Tensions of Empire.*

27. See Robert-Guiard, *Des Européennes,* 147–241.

28. See Stoler, "Carnal Knowledge and Imperial Power." This classic article has generated a huge scholarship since its publication, but not particularly with respect to Algeria. Clancy-Smith's scholarship constitutes an important exception, especially "Islam, Gender, and Identities."

29. Scholarly interest in the interactions between Europeans and the local population has focused notably on Jews in Algeria. For a succinct presentation of these approaches, see Blais, Fredj, and Saada, "Un long moment colonial," 13–14, and Schreier, *Arabs of the Jewish Faith.* Women are rarely the focus of these studies.

30. See Trumbull, *An Empire of Facts,* 181–209.

31. Taraud, *La prostitution coloniale.*

32. Clancy-Smith, "A Woman without Her Distaff."

33. Berque, *L'art antique,* 122.

34. Champault, "La donation Jean-Philippe Crouzet."

35. Archives of the Musée du quai Branly, DAOO 5023, bill of sale dated 22 October 1946. The different items were sold for 39,150 francs.

36. Archives of the Musée du quai Branly, DAOO 2048, letter of Crouzet to the Director of the Museum, 28 April 1961.

37. Desvages, "L'enseignement des musulmans," 134.

38. Trumbull, *An Empire of Facts,* 181–82.

39. Auclert, *Les femmes arabes,* 68–69. See Surkis, *Sexing the Citizen,* 58–68, who argues that republican educational reformers produced a civilized sexual morality as a universal norm, while postponing the efforts to educate girls, which would have allowed the creation of companionate marriages.

40. Eudel, *Hivernage en Algérie.* See his entries in February and March 1896 describing his visit to the Benaben workshop and then to the White Fathers in Kabylia, esp. 195–96.

41. For the emergence and effects of the religious mission in Algeria, see Direche-Slimani, *Chrétiens de Kabylie*; Abrous, *La société des missionnaires*; and Ghabrial, "Colonial Sisterhood."

42. See the stimulating essay by Burton, "Archive Stories," as well as Chaudhuri, Katz, and Perry, *Contesting Archives.*

43. Tellingly, the volume in the *Cahiers du centenaire* devoted to the creation of Arab-French schools does not mention Eugénie Luce, although she is described in the volumes devoted to art. See Mirante, *La France et les oeuvres indigènes*, 52–54.

44. See the article in Arabic about the museum's embroideries, Sâjiyya, 'Achûrî, "Dirâsa Namâdij min al-mutarrazât al-jazâ'iriyya al-mahfûza bi l-mathaf al-watani li l-athâr," *Annales du Musée National des Antiquités* (1419/1998), 61–83.

45. See Sebbar's description of Benaben's workshop in the short story "L'ouvroir. Esmée, Isabelle," in *Isabelle l'Algérien*, as well as passages in *Voyage en Algérie*, 26 and 191, and in Sebbar, Taraud, and Belorgey, *Femmes d'Afrique du Nord*, 16–17.

BIBLIOGRAPHY

PRIMARY SOURCES

Archives

Centre des Archives d'Outre-Mer (CAOM, Aix-en-Provence)
Series F[80]: Fonds Ministériels
    508, 515, 516, 521: Bureaux Arabes: Rapports, 1852–1856
    1566: Instruction publique; Écoles Oran, 1846–1858
    1572–1573: Écoles arabes françaises et écoles musulmanes
    1732: Instruction publique. Littérature et enseignement musulmans
    "Note explicative sur l'institution de Madame Allix. 5 March 1846.
    Algiers: Imprimerie Besanceney
Gouvernement Général d'Algérie
    Series E: Politique
        Liasse 228 (1) Abd el-Kader au Château d'Amboise, 1849–1852
        Liasse 230 (1) Abd el-Kader au Château d'Amboise, 1850–1851
    Series H: Affaires indigènes. Affaires sociales et économiques
        14 H 1: Bureau de bienfaisance musulmane
        14 H 32 (24): Main d'oeuvre féminine indigene. Enquête générale 1929
    Series S: Instruction Publique et Beaux-Arts
        22 S/2–3: Écoles arabes-françaises, 1850–1876

Bibliothèque des Archives d'Outre-Mer
Belly, Alexis. "Au maréchal Bugeaud," 1844.
École professionnelle des jeunes filles musulmanes. Règlement. Algiers: Gavault, 1879.

Archives nationales (AN)
BB[22] 154/2 Grâces du marriage
F[15] 4044 Loir-et-Cher, Pensions obtenues et réversions de pensions
F[17] *2632 Registre (Loir-et-Cher)
F[17] 10181 Écoles primaires, académie d'Orléans
F[17] 12333 Enseignement primaire en Algérie et aux colonies (1844–1898)
F[17] 21050 Dossiers personnels: Paute Laforie
F[17] 22960 Dossiers personnels: Sténio Leroy
F[18] 267 Contrôle de la presse, de la librairie et du colportage sous le Second Empire, 1852–1870, dossier de Félix Belly

Service Historique de l'Armée de Terre (Vincennes)
34 YC 1186. Registre du 26ᵉ régiment de ligne

Archives départementales (AD), Loir-et-Cher
In addition to consulting civil registers (series E) and series concerning population surveys (L and M), I have consulted the following documents:

Annuaire du département de Loir-et-Cher (1806–1850)

1 M 79: Rapports de police (1832)

3 M 240: Élections Mairie d'Angé

3 P/3/152/1: Cadastre Napoléon, état de sections, Montrichard

300 Q 11: Enregistrements successions: Montrichard

73 Q 20: Saint-Aignan

Series T concerning education but not catalogued

Liasse 380: 1735/2//1002, Instruction primaire, 1812–1828

Liasse TV 375: Instruction primaire. État des écoles primaires et des institutions autorisées dans le département, 1832–1843

Liasse TV 165: Instruction primaire, 1830–1840

Notarial archives of Maître Billette (Loir-et-Cher)

Dépôt des testaments olographes de Madame Veuve Luce, 6 June 1882

Vente mobilière après le décès de Madame Veuve Luce Berlau, Bureau d'enregistrement de Montrichard, 11 August 1882

Archives départementales (AD), Indre-et-Loire

Annuaires du département de l'Indre-et-Loire, 1828–1835

1 T 401: Instruction primaire

1 T 756: Comités cantonaux de surveillance de l'instruction primaire. Rapport, demandes de secours d'instituteurs, États des situations des écoles primaires, 1830–1834

T 432*: Registre des instituteurs, 1831–1832

Archives départementales (AD), Oise

2E 60/253: Testament de Jacques Alexandre Allix

Recensement de la population de Compiègne (1841)

Archives départementales (AD), Paris

Acte de marriage entre Eugénie veuve Allix et Napoléon Louis Luce (19 May 1846)

Archives of the Soeurs de la Doctrine Chrétienne (Nancy)

Annales religieuses des Soeurs de la Doctrine Chrétienne, 1852–1867

Archives of the Musée du quai Branly

"Catalogue des objets": 234 items donated by "Crouzet"

DAOO 5023, bill of sale dated 22 October 1946

DAOO 2048, letter of Crouzet to the Director of the Museum, 28 April 1961

Arsenal (Bibliothèque nationale de France)

Fonds Enfantin, 7679, folios 121–125, correspondence, E. Allix to Enfantin

Girton College Archives, Cambridge, England

Series: Girton College Private Papers (GCPP)

Parkes: 6/71, 6/72, 6/73, Bessie Rayner Parkes to Mary Merryweather

Parkes: 5/87, 5/96, 5/110, 5/113, Bessie Rayner Parkes to Barbara Bodichon

Sorbonne Library
Manuscripts, MS 1936, correspondance Eugène Manuel E. Paute Laforie, folio 175

Bibliothèque historique de la ville de Paris (BHVP)
Fonds Bouglé, sous-fonds Hubertine Auclert, boîte 2 correspondance
Paute-Lafaurie, Nicolas-Eugène. *Mémoire d'un Régent de Quatrième sur la réforme collèges communaux (juin 1849).* Lyon: Imprimeries Réunies, 1913.

Newspapers (full runs of the colonial newspapers are available at the Bibliothèque Frantz Fanon in Algiers)

L'Akhbar, Journal de l'Algérie (consulted from 1839 to 1915)
Algerian Advertiser
L'Algérie. Courrier d'Afrique, d'Orient et de la Méditerranée (1843–1846)
L'Algérie Française. Journal de la Démocratie Algérienne
Bulletin de l'Éducation des Indigènes de l'Académie d'Alger
Bulletin Municipal de la Ville d'Alger (1897–1944)
Journal d'Éducation Populaire. Bulletin de la Société pour l'Instruction Élémentaire
L'Illustration. Journal Universel
Moniteur de la Colonisation
Le Républicain de Loir-et-Cher

Books and Articles

'Achûrî, Sâjiyya. "Dirâsa Namâdij min al-mutarrazât al-jazâ'iriyya al-mahfûza bi l-mathaf al-watani li l-athâr." *Annales du Musée National des Antiquités* (1419/1998), 61–83.
Aire, Marie d'. *Abd-el-Kader. Quelques documents nouveaux, lus et approuvés par l'officier en mission auprès de l'émir.* Amiens: Imprimerie Yvert et Tellier, 1900.
Alexandre, Arsène. "Réflexions sur les arts et les industries d'art en Algérie, 1905." *L'Akhbar* (25 November and 2 December 1906).
Algérie: catalogue spécial, contenant des renseignements statistiques et des notices sur les principaux produits . . . Exposition de 1878. Paris: Imprimerie Nationale, 1878.
"Algiers in 1865." *Cornhill Magazine* 11 (11 April 1865): 426–33.
Allix, Veuve [Widow]. *Requête de Mme Vve Allix au ministre de l'instruction publique en vue d'obtenir une subvention pour la fondation d'une école de jeunes filles indigènes à Alger.* Paris: Imprimerie de Varré et Fils, 1846.
Almanach de l'Algérie. Le guide du colon (publié d'après les documents fournis par le Ministère de la Guerre). Paris: P. Martinon, 1853.
Annuaire commercial, industriel, administratif, agricole et vinicole de l'Algérie et de la Tunisie. Paris: Paul Langard, 1884–1902.
Annuaire de l'État d'Alger. Marseille: Peissat Ainé; Paris: Firmin Didot, 1832.
———. Paris: Carillian-Goeury, 1833.
Artenac, R. d'. "Enseignement professionnel." *Bulletin de l'Éducation des Indigènes de l'Académie d'Alger* 193 (November–December 1909): 132–50.
Auclert, Hubertine. *Les femmes arabes en Algérie.* 1900. Reprint, Paris: L'Harmattan, 2009.
Bayet, Charles. "L'art arabe à Alger." *Revue de l'Art Ancien et Moderne* 18 (July–December 1905): 17–26.

Bel, Marguerite. *Les arts indigènes en Algérie*. Alger: Gouvernement Général de l'Algérie, 1939.

———. "La protection de la vie locale en Algérie." *Congrès international et intercolonial de la société indigène, 5 au 10 octobre, Exposition coloniale internationale de Paris, 1931.* Cahors: Imprimerie Coueslant, 1931.

Belly, Felix. *Les amazones de la Seine et la police*. Paris, 1870.

Bennet, James Henry. *Winter and Spring on the Shores of the Mediterranean: Or, The Riviera*. 5th ed. London: Churchill, 1875.

Bergevin, Louis, and Alexandre Dupré. *Histoire de Blois*. Vol. 2. Blois: E. Dézairs, 1846–1847.

Berque, Augustin. *L'Algérie, terre d'art et d'histoire*. Algiers: Imprimerie de V. Heintz, 1937.

———. *L'art antique et l'art musulman en Algérie*. Vol. 6, *Cahiers du centenaire*. Paris: Publications du Comité National Métropolitain du Centenaire de l'Algérie, 1930.

Bodichon, Barbara Leigh Smith. *Guide Book: Algeria Considered as a Winter Residence for the English*. London: Englishwoman's Journal Office, 1858.

———. *Memoir of Madame Luce, of Algiers; Reprinted from the English Woman's Journal with Alterations and Additions*. London: Emily Faithfull and Co., Victoria Press for the Employment of Women, 1862.

———. *Women and Work*. 1857. Reprinted in *Barbara Leigh Smith Bodichon and the Langham Place Group*, ed. Candida Ann Lacey, 36–73. New York: Routledge and Kegan Paul, 1987.

Brihmat, Ahmed. "L'école professionnelle de broderies arabes, demande de subvention annuelle de 2400¤." *Revue de l'Islam* 38 (January 1899): 5–9.

B.R.P. [Bessie Rayner Parkes]. "Madame Luce and the Great Exhibition." *English Woman's Journal* (July 1862): 355.

———. "Madame Luce, of Algiers." *English Woman's Journal* (May 1861): 157–68; (June 1861): 224–36; (July 1861): 296–308.

———. "Mustapha's House." *English Woman's Journal* (October 1861): 173–79.

Buisson, Ferdinand. *Nouveau dictionnaire de pédagogie et d'instruction primaire*. Paris: Librairie Hachette, 1911, and online at http://www.inrp.fr/edition-electronique/lodel /dictionnaire-ferdinand-buisson.

Cahiers du centenaire. 12 vols. Paris: Publications du Comité National Métropolitain du Centenaire de l'Algérie, 1930.

Catalogue explicatif et raisonné de l'exposition permanente des produits de l'exposition permanente des produits de l'Algérie (rue de Grenelle, Saint Germain, 107), suivi du *Catalogue méthodique des produits algériens à l'exposition universelle de Paris en 1855*. Paris: Imprimerie F. Didot, 1855.

Cherbonneau, Auguste. "Notice sur les écoles arabes-françaises de filles." *Revue Pédagogique* 3 (March 1882): 311–17.

Christianowitsch, Alexandre. *Esquisse historique de la musique arabe aux temps anciens avec dessins d'instruments et quarante mélodies notées et harmonisées*. Cologne: Dumont-Schauberg, 1863.

Coignet, Clarisse. "À propos de l'instruction des indigènes en Algérie." *Revue Pédagogique* 18, no. 4 (April 1891): 336–45.

Combes, Émile. *Rapport fait au nom de la commission chargée d'examiner les modifications à introduire dans la législation et dans l'organisation des divers services de l'Algérie. L'instruction primaire des indigènes*. Paris: P. Mouillot, 1892.

Conseil général. *Procès-verbal des séances du Conseil général.* Algiers: Typographie Duclaux, 1858–1880.

Cox, Samuel Sullivan. *Search for Winter Sunbeams in the Riviera, Corsica, Algiers and Spain.* New York: D. Appleton, 1870.

Crawford, Mabel Sharman. *Through Algeria.* 1863. Reprint, London: Darf, 1984.

Crouse, Mary Elizabeth. *Algiers.* London: Gay and Bird, 1906.

Crouzet, Paul. "L'art de la broderie Arabe." *Le Monde Moderne et la Femme d'Aujourd'hui* 14 (1901): 306–12.

Crouzet-Benaben, Jeanne Paul. *Souvenirs d'une jeune fille bête. Souvenirs autobiographiques d'une des premières agrégées de France.* Paris: Debresse, 1971.

Dall, Caroline Wells Healey. *The College, the Market, and the Court: or, Woman's Relation to Education, Labor and Law.* Boston: Lee and Shepard, 1867.

Davies, E. W. L. *Algiers in 1857. Its accessibility, climate, and resources described with especial reference to English Invalids. Also details of recreation obtainable in its neighbourhood added for the use of travelers in general.* London: Longman, 1858.

Davies, Emily. *Collected Letters: 1861–1875,* ed. Ann B. Murphy and Deidre Raftery. Charlottesville: University of Virginia Press, 2004.

Depeille, Auguste. *Méthode de lecture et de prononciation arabes.* Algiers: F. Bernard, 1850.

Deroin, Jeanne. *Almanach des femmes* (1854–1856). Paris: Chez l'Éditeur, Chez les Marchands de Nouveautés, 1852–1854.

Desprès, Charles. *Les ouvroirs musulmans.* Algiers: Publié par le Courrier de l'Algérie, 1863.

Duchesne, Édouard-Adolphe. *De la prostitution dans la ville d'Alger depuis la conquête.* Paris: J.-B. Baillière, 1853.

Dupré, Alexandre. *Notice historique sur Montrichard.* Blois: E. Dézairs, 1850.

Dutertre, Anaïs. *Voyage de Vermont-sur-Orne à Constantine-sur-l'Oued, Rummel, Sétif, Bougie et Alger par une femme.* Caen: Imprimerie de C. Hommais, 1866.

Eberhardt, Isabelle. *Oeuvres complètes, I. Écrits sur le sable (récits, notes et journaliers).* Ed. Marie-Odile Delacour and Jean-René Heleu. Paris: Grasset, 1988.

"Education in Algiers." *Journal of Education for Upper Canada* 5 (July 1860): 102–3.

"Education at Algiers. Madame Luce's school." *Penny Illustrated Paper* (19 March 1870): 180.

Edwards, Matilda Betham. *Anglo-French Reminiscences, 1871–1899, New and Revised Reminiscences.* London: Chapman and Hall, 1903.

———. *In French-Africa: Scenes and Memories.* London: Chapman and Hall, 1912.

———. *A Winter with the Swallows.* London: Hurst and Blackett, 1867.

Elliott, Maud Howe. *Art and Handicraft in the Woman's Building of the World's Columbian Exposition, Chicago, 1893.* Paris: Boussod, Valadon, 1893.

Enfantin, Barthélémy-Prosper. *Colonisation de l'Algérie.* Paris: P. Bertrand, 1843.

Eudel, Paul. *Hivernage en Algérie.* Paris: Imprimerie de C. Hérissey et Fils, 1909.

Evans, Mrs. Lloyd. *Last Winter in Algeria.* London: Chapman and Hall, 1868.

Exposition franco-britannique, Londres, 1908, Les colonies françaises. Paris: Comité National des Expositions Coloniales, 1909.

Exposition universelle de 1855. Rapports du jury mixte international, publiés sous la direction de S.A.I. le prince Napoléon. Paris: Imprimerie Impériale, 1856.

F. C., "Winter in Algiers." *Once a Week, an Illustrated Miscellany of Literature, Art, Science, and Popular Information* 12 (1865): 653–55.

Fillias, Achille. *Nouveau guide général du voyageur en Algérie.* Paris: Garnier Frères, 1865.

La France algérienne. Revue de l'Afrique. Militaire, agricole, industrielle, commerciale, littéraire, artistique, administrative, biographique, religieuse et judiciaire. 17 January 1846.

Gautier, Théophile. *Voyage pittoresque en Algérie.* 1845. Reprint, Paris: Librairie Droz, 1973.

Golvin, Lucien. *Les arts populaires en Algérie.* Vol. 1, *Les techniques de Tissage.* Algiers: Gouvernement Général d'Algérie, 1950.

Gouillon, Charles. *Annuaire général de l'Algérie.* Algiers: Imprimerie V. Pézé, 1880.

Gouvernement général de l'Algérie. *L'Algérie à l'exposition universelle de Londres, 1862.* 2 vols. Algiers: Librairie Challamel Aîné, 1863.

———. *Compte des recettes et des dépenses départementales: exercice 1900.* Algiers: Imprimerie de P. Fontana, 1901.

Hémon, Félix. "Les écoles d'art indigène en Algérie." *Revue Pédagogique* 50 (January–June 1907): 305–19.

Herbert, Mary Elizabeth. *A Search after Sunshine; or, Algeria in 1871.* London: Richard Bentley and Son, 1872.

Hugonnet, F[erdinand]. "Écoles de garçons et écoles de filles." *L'Illustration,* no. 1 (18 May 1858): 297–98.

Hyam, Joseph C. *The Illustrated guide to Algiers, a practical handbook for travelers.* Algiers: Anglo-French Press Association, 1899.

Illio, Sylviane. *L'enseignement des métiers féminins en Algérie.* Paris: Imprimerie Marchand, 1937.

Jeanmaire, Charles. "Algérie." In Ferdinand Buisson, *Nouveau dictionnaire de pédagogie et d'instruction primaire.* Paris: Librairie Hachette, 1911, and online at http://www.inrp.fr/edition-electronique/lodel/dictionnaire-ferdinand-buisson.

———. "Sur l'instruction des indigènes en Algérie." *Revue Pédagogique* 19, no. 7 (15 July 1891): 9–36.

Klein, Henri. *L'enseignement à Alger depuis la conquête. Souvenirs divers.* Feuillets d'El-Djezaïr, Algiers: Imprimerie de Fontana Frères, 1920.

Knox, Alexander. *The New Playground; or, Wanderings in Algeria.* London: Kegan Paul, 1881.

Lacroix, Frédéric. "Algérie, ses produits à l'exposition universelle." *L'Illustration,* no. 2, (1855): 55–58.

Leaves from a Lady's Diary of Her Travels in Barbary. 2 vols. London: Henry Colburn, 1850.

Levasseur, Émile. *L'enseignement primaire dans les pays civilisés.* Vol. 1. Paris: Berger-Levrault, 1897.

Luce, Louis. *Abrégé théorique et pratique de musique, divisé en deux parties, pour servir d'introduction à l'étude du solfège et des instruments.* Algiers: Lithographie et Autographie Bastide, 1856.

Marçais, Georges. "L'art musulman en Algérie." In *Histoire et historiens de l'Algérie (1830–1840),* ed. J. Alazard, E. Albertini, and A. Bel, 207–30. Paris: Félix Alcan, 1931.

———. *L'exposition d'art musulman d'Alger.* Algiers: Imprimerie Algérienne, 1906.

Marmier, Xavier. *Lettres sur l'Algérie.* Paris: A. Bertrand, 1847.

Martin, A. E. Victor, and L.-E. Foley. *Histoire statistique de la colonisation algérienne du point de vue du peuplement et de l'hygiène.* Paris: Germer-Baillière, 1851.

Marye, Georges. "L'éducation artistique des indigènes en Algérie." *Nouvelle Revue* 83 (June–July 1893): 123–30.

Mirante, Jean. *La France et les oeuvres indigènes en Algérie.* Vol. 11, *Cahiers du centenaire.* Paris: Publications du Comité National Métropolitain du Centenaire de l'Algérie, 1930.

Monteils, E. *Algérie à l'Exposition de Chicago.* Algiers: Imprimerie de P. Fontana, 1894.

Morell, John Reynell. *Algeria: The Topography and History, Political, Social, and Natural of French North Africa.* London: Cooke, 1854.

Murray, John. *A Handbook for Travelers in Algeria. With travelling maps and plan of Algiers.* London: John Murray, 1873.

———. *A Handbook for Travelers in Algeria with map and plan.* London: John Murray, 1874.

Le musée Stéphane Gsell. Musée des antiquités et d'art musulman d'Alger. Algiers: Presses de l'Imprimerie Officielle, 1950.

Nugent, Ermengarda Greville. *A Land of Mosques and Marabouts.* London: Chapman and Hall, 1894.

Parkes, Bessie Rayner. "Mme Luce's school in Algiers." *Waverly Journal* (1 November 1856): 104–5.

———. *Remarks on the Education of Girls with Reference to the Social, Legal, and Industrial Position of Women in the Present Day.* London, 1854.

———. *Vignettes: Twelve Biographical Sketches.* London: Alexander Strahan, 1866.

Peigné, Michel-Auguste. *Méthode de lecture, ouvrage adapté par la Société pour l'instruction élémentaire.* Paris: Armand-Aubré, 1831.

Perrot, A. M. *Alger. Esquisse topographique et historique du royaume et de la ville accompagnée d'une carte générale du royaume et d'un plan du port et de ses environs.* 2nd ed. Paris: Librairie Ladvocat, 1830.

Petite bibliothèque du voyageur en Algérie. Guide à Alger, Alger et ses environs en 1863, vademecum indicateur. Algiers: Tissier, 1863.

Piesse, Louis. *Itinéraire historique et descriptif de l'Algérie, comprenant le Tell et le Sahara.* Paris: Hachette, 1862.

Playfair, Sir R. Lambert. *Handbook for Travelers in Algeria and Tunis.* 4th ed. London: John Murray, 1891.

Pope, Henry E. *The Corsair and His Conqueror: A Winter in Algiers.* London: Richard Bentley, 1860.

Poulard, Maurice. *L'enseignement pour les indigènes.* Algiers: Gojossi, 1910.

Prus, Madame. *Residence in Algeria.* London: W. Pickering, 1852.

Rapport sur l'exposition universelle de 1855, présenté à l'Empereur par S.A.I. le Prince Napoléon. Paris: Imprimerie Impériale, 1857.

Régis, Louis. *Constantine. Voyage et séjours.* Paris: Calmann Lévy, 1880.

Ricard, Prosper. *Dentelles algériennes et marocaines.* Paris: Larose, 1928.

———. *Pour comprendre l'art musulman, dans l'Afrique du nord et en Espagne.* Paris: Hachette, 1921.

Rogers, Mrs. G. Albert [Ellen M.]. *A Winter in Algeria, 1863–64.* London: Sampson Low, Son and Marston, 1865.

Sand, George. *Correspondance.* Vol. 18, *Août 1863–décembre 1864.* Paris: Classiques Garnier, 1964.

Session législative de 1870. Cahiers Algériens. Algiers: Imprimerie Duclaux, 1870.

Stowell, William Hendry. "Red Algiers." *Eclectic Review* 3 (January–June 1860): 45–58.

Strahan, Lisbeth Gooch Séguin. *Walks in Algiers and Its Surrounding.* London: Daldy, Isbister, 1878.

Tableau de la situation des établissements français dans l'Algérie. Paris: Imprimerie Royale, 1838–1867.

Urbain, Ismaÿl. *Algérie. Du gouvernement des tribus. Chrétiens et musulmans, Français et Algériens* (extracts from *Revue de l'Orient et de l'Algérie,* October–November 1847). Paris: J. Rouvier, 1848.

Vachon, Marius. *Les industries d'art indigène en Algérie, mission de conférence et enquête avril–mai 1901.* Algiers: Adolphe Journad, 1902.

Vallory, Louise [Louise Mesnier]. *À l'aventure en Algérie.* Paris: Hetzel, 1863.

Violard, Émile. *De la rénovation des industries d'art indigène en Algérie.* Algiers: F. Montégut, 1922.

———. *Des industries d'art indigènes en Algérie.* Algiers: Imprimerie de Baldachino-Laronde-Viguier, 1902.

Voilquin, Suzanne. *Souvenirs d'une fille du peuple ou la Saint-Simonienne en Egypte.* Paris: François Maspero, 1978 (initially published as *Souvenirs d'une fille du people, ou la Saint-Simonienne en Egypte.* Paris: E. Sauzet, 1866).

Warnier, Auguste. "École de jeunes filles musulmanes." *Atlas. Journal Démocratique de l'Algérie* (26 October 1851).

SECONDARY SOURCES

Abi-Mershed, Osama. *Apostles of Modernity: Saint-Simonians and the Civilizing Mission in Algeria.* Stanford, CA: Stanford University Press, 2010.

Abrous, Dahbia. *La société des missionnaires d'Afrique à l'épreuve du mythe berbère.* Paris: Éditions Peeters, 2007.

Ageron, Charles Robert. *Les Algériens musulmans et la France, 1871–1891.* 2nd ed. 2 vols. Paris: Éditions Bouchène, 2005.

Aldrich, Richard, and Peter Gordon. *Biographical Dictionary of North American and European Educationists.* London: Woburn Press, 1997.

Allen, Cyril. "Felix Belly: Nicaraguan Canal Promoter." *Hispanic American Historical Review* 37, no. 1 (1957): 46–59.

Anderson, Bonnie S. *Joyous Greetings: The First International Women's Movement, 1830–1860.* Oxford: Oxford University Press, 2000.

Arnaudiès, Fernand. *Histoire de l'Opéra d'Alger. Episodes de la vie théâtrale algéroise, 1830–1840.* Algiers: Imprimerie de V. Heintz, 1941.

Association les femmes et la ville. *Germaine Poinso-Chapuis. Femme d'état (1901–1981).* Aix-en-Provence: Edisud, 1998.

———. *Marseillaises, vingt-six siècles d'histoire.* Aix-en-Provence: Edisud, 1999.

Bancel, Nicolas, Pascal Blanchard, Gilles Boëtsch et al. *Zoos humains et exhibitions coloniales: 150 ans d'inventions de l'autre.* Paris: La Découverte, 2011.

Barthélémy, Pascale. *Africaines et diplômées à l'époque coloniale (1918–1957).* Rennes: Presses Universitaires de Rennes, 2010.

Benchérif, Osman. *The Image of Algeria in Anglo-American Writings, 1785–1962.* Lanham, MD: University Press of America, 1997.

Benjamin, Roger. *Orientalist Aesthetics: Art, Colonialism, and French North Africa, 1880–1930.* Berkeley: University of California Press, 2003.

Berenson, Edward. *Heroes of Empire: Five Charismatic Men and the Conquest of Africa.* Berkeley: University of California Press, 2010.

Bhabha, Homi. "Of Mimicry and Man: The Ambivalence of Colonial Discourse." *October* 28 (1984): 125–33.

Blais, Hélène, Claire Fredj, and Emmanuelle Saada. "Un long moment colonial: pour une histoire de l'Algérie au XIXe siècle." *Revue d'Histoire du XIXe Siècle* 41 (2010): 7–35.

Blanchard, Emmanuel, and Sylvie Thénault. "Quel 'monde du contact'? Pour une histoire sociale de l'Algérie pendant la période coloniale." *Le Mouvement Social* 236, no. 3 (2011): 3–7.

Bourguet, Marie-Noëlle, Bernard Lepetit, Daniel Nordman, and Maroula-Sinarellis, eds. *L'invention scientifique de la Méditerranée. Egypte. Morée, Algérie.* Paris: Éditions de l'EHESS, 1998.

Boyer, Pierre. *L'évolution de l'Algérie médiane (ancien département d'Alger de 1830 à 1956).* Paris: Adrien-Maisonneuve, 1960.

———. *La vie politique et les élections à Alger. La révolution française de 1848 en Algérie.* Paris, 1949.

Brahimi, Denise. *Femmes arabes et soeurs musulmanes.* Paris: Éditions Tierce, 1984.

Brouwer, Benjamin Claude. *A Desert Named Peace: The Violence of France's Empire in the Algerian Sahara, 1844–1902.* New York: Columbia University Press, 2009.

Burton, Antoinette. "Archive Stories: Gender in the Making of Imperial and Colonial Histories." In *Empire in Question: Reading, Writing and Teaching British Imperialism,* 94–105. Durham, NC: Duke University Press, 2011.

Burton, Hester. *Barbara Bodichon, 1827–1891.* London: John Murray, 1949.

Caine, Barbara. *Biography and History. Theory and History.* New York: Palgrave Macmillan, 2010.

Cardoza, Thomas. *Intrepid Women: Cantinières and Vivandières of the French Army.* Bloomington: Indiana University Press, 2010.

Carlier, Omar. "Medina and Modernity: The Emergence of Muslim Civil Society in Algiers between the Two World Wars." In *Walls of Algiers: Narratives of the City through Text and Image,* ed. Z. Çelik, J. Clancy-Smith, and F. Terpak, 62–84. Los Angeles: Getty Research Institute in Association with the University of Washington Press, 2009.

Caron, Jean-Claude. *À l'école de la violence. Châtiments et sévices dans l'institution scolaire au XIXe siècle.* Paris: Aubier, 1999.

Çelik, Zeynip. "Framing the Colony: Houses of Algeria Photographed." *Art History* 27, no. 4 (2004): 616–26.

———. "A Lingering Obsession: The Houses of Algiers in French Colonial Discourse." In *Walls of Algiers: Narratives of the City through Text and Image,* ed. Z. Çelik, J. Clancy-Smith, and F. Terpak, 134–60. Los Angeles: Getty Research Institute in Association with the University of Washington Press, 2009.

———. *Urban Forms and Colonial Confrontations: Algiers under French Rule.* Berkeley: University of California Press, 1997.

Chalopin, Michel. *L'enseignement mutuel en Bretagne. Quand les écoliers faisaient la classe.* Rennes: Presses Universitaires de Rennes, 2011.

Champault, Dominique. "La donation Jean-Philippe Crouzet au Département d'Afrique Blanche." *Objets et Mondes: La Revue du Musée de l'Homme* 1–2 (1961): 33–38.

Champion, Renée. "Représentations des femmes dans les récits de voyageuses d'expression française en Orient au XIXe siècle (1848–1911)." Thèse de Doctorat, Université de Paris VII, 2002.

Chapoulie, Jean-Michel. "L'organisation de l'enseignement primaire de la Troisième République: Ses origines provinciales et parisiennes." *Histoire de l'Éducation* 105 (January 2005): 3–44.

Charles-Roux, Edmonde. *Nomade j'étais. Les années africaines d'Isabelle Eberhardt, 1899– 1904*. Paris: Grasset, 1995.

Chaudhuri, Nupur, Sherry J. Katz, and Mary Elizabeth Perry. *Contesting Archives: Finding Women in the Sources*. Urbana: University of Illinois Press, 2011.

Cherry, Deborah. *Beyond the Frame: Feminism and Visual Culture, 1850–1900*. London: Routledge, 2000.

———. "Shuttling and Soul-Making: Tracing the Links between Algeria and Egalitarian Feminism in the 1850s." In *The Victorians and Race*, ed. S. West, 156–70. Aldershot: Scolar Press, 1996.

Christelow, Allan. *Muslim Law Courts and the French Colonial State in Algeria*. Princeton, NJ: Princeton University Press, 1985.

Clancy-Smith, Julia A. "Changing Perspectives on the Historiography of Imperialism: Women, Gender, Empire." In *Middle East Historiographies: Narrating the Twentieth Century*, ed. Israel Gershoni, Amy Singer, and Y. Hakan Erdem, 70–100. Seattle: University of Washington Press, 2006.

———. "Éducation des jeunes filles musulmanes en Tunisie: Missionnaires religieux et laïques." In *Le pouvoir du genre: Laïcités et religions 1905–2005*, ed. Florence Rochefort, 127–43. Toulouse: Presses Universitaires du Mirail, 2007.

———. "Envisioning Knowledge: Educating the Muslim Woman in Colonial North Africa, 1850–1918." In *Iran and Beyond: Essays in Middle Eastern History in Honor of Nikki Keddie*, ed. Beth Baron and Rudi Matthee, 99–118. Los Angeles: Mazda Press, 2000.

———. "Exoticism, Erasures, and Absence. The Peopling of Algiers, 1830–1900." In *Walls of Algiers, Narratives of the City through Text and Image*, ed. Zeynep Çelik, Julia Clancy-Smith, and Frances Terpak, 19–61. Los Angeles: Getty Research Institute in Association with the University of Washington Press, 2009.

———. "Islam, Gender, and Identities in the Making of French Algeria, 1830–1962." In *Domesticating the Empire: Race, Gender, and Family Life in French and Dutch Colonialism*, ed. Julia Clancy-Smith and Frances Gouda, 154–74. Charlottesville: University Press of Virginia, 1998.

———. *Rebel and Saint: Muslim Notables, Populist Protest, Colonial Encounters (Algeria and Tunisia, 1800–1904)*. Berkeley: University of California Press, 1994.

———. "A Woman without Her Distaff: Gender, Work, and Handicraft Production in Colonial North Africa." In *Social History of Women and Gender in the Modern Middle East*, ed. Margaret L. Meriwether and Judith E. Tucker, 25–62. Boulder, CO: Westview Press, 1999.

Coadaccioni, Félix-Paul. "Les fortunes à Lille (1821–1908)." In *Les fortunes françaises au XIXe siècle, Enquête sur la répartition et la composition des capitaux privés à Paris,*

Lyon, Lille, Bordeaux et Toulouse, d'après l'enregistrement des déclarations de succession. Paris: Mouthon, 1963.

Codell, Julie F., ed. *Imperial Co-Histories: National Identities and the British and Colonial Press.* Madison, NJ: Farleigh Dickinson University Press, 2003.

Colonna, Fanny. *Instituteurs algériens, 1883–1939.* Paris: Presses de la Fondation Nationale des Sciences Politiques, 1975.

Cooper, Frederick, and Ann Laura Stoler, eds. *Tensions of Empire: Colonial Cultures in a Bourgeois World.* Berkeley: University of California Press, 1997.

Cova, Anne, and Bruno Dumons, eds. *Destins de femmes. Religion, culture et société (France XIXe–XXe siècles).* Paris: Letouzey et Ané, 2010.

Curtis, Sarah A. *Civilizing Habits: Women and the Revival of French Empire.* Oxford: Oxford University Press, 2010.

———. *Educating the Faithful: Religion, Schooling, and Society in Nineteenth-Century France.* Dekalb: Northern Illinois University Press, 2000.

———. "Emilie de Vialar and the Religious Reconquest of Algeria." *French Historical Studies* 29 (2006): 261–92.

Darriulat, Philippe. "La gauche républicaine et la conquête de l'Algérie, de la prise d'Alger à la reddition d'Abd el-Kader (1830–1847)." *Revue Française d'Histoire d'Outre-mer* 82, no. 307 (1995): 129–47.

Deleigne, Marie-Christine. "Entre la plume et l'*angady* (la bêche): les jardins scolaires des écoles du premier degré à Madagascar (1916–1951)." *Histoire de l'Éducation* 128 (2010): 103–27.

Desvages, Hubert. "L'enseignement des musulmans en Algérie sous le rectorat de Jeanmaire." *Le Mouvement Social* 70 (1970): 109–37.

Diebolt, Évelyne, ed. *Dictionnaire biographique. Militer au XXe siècle. Femmes, feminismes, églises et société.* Paris: Michel Houdiard Editeur, 2009.

Direche-Slimani, Karima. *Chrétiens de Kabylie 1873–1954. Une action missionnaire dans l'Algérie coloniale.* Paris: Éditions Bouchène, 2004.

Dosse, François. *Le pari biographique. Écrire une vie.* Paris: La Découverte, 2005.

Dulucq, Sophie, and Colette Zytnicki, eds. "La colonisation culturelle dans l'empire français: entre visées éducatives et projets muséographiques (XIXe–XXe siècles)." *Outremers. Revue d'Histoire* (December 2007): 356–57.

Dupâquier, Jacques. *Histoire de la population française.* Vol. 3, *De 1789 à 1914.* Paris: Presses Universitaires de France, 1995.

Dupeux, Georges. *Aspects de l'histoire sociale et politique du Loir-et-Cher, 1848–1914.* Paris: Mouthon et Cie, 1962.

Eichner, Carolyn. "*La Citoyenne* in the World: Hubertine Auclert and Feminist Imperialism." *French Historical Studies* 32, no. 1 (2009): 63–84.

Eisenmann, Linda. *Historical Dictionary of Women's Education in the United States.* Westport, CT: Greenwood, 1998.

Emerit, Marcel. *Les Saint-Simoniens en Algérie.* Paris: Les Belles Lettres, 1941.

Ernot, Isabelle. "L'histoire des femmes et ses premières historiennes (XIXe–début XXe siècle)." *Revue d'Histoire des Sciences Humaines* 16, no. 1 (2007): 165–94.

Fakkar, Rouchsi. "Le Saint-Simonisme en Afrique du Nord." *Économies et Sociétés* 17 (January 1973): 149–69.

Farge, Arlette. *Le goût de l'archive.* Paris: Seuil, 1989.

Fortescue, William. "Divorce Debated and Deferred: The French Debate on Divorce and the Failure of the Crémieux Divorce Bill in 1848." *French History* 7 (1993): 137–62.

Fraisse, Geneviève. *Clémence Royer. Philosophe et femme de sciences.* 2nd ed. Paris: La Découverte, 2002.

Frémeaux, Jacques. *Les bureaux arabes dans l'Algérie de la conquête.* Paris: Denoël, 1993.

Furet, François, and Mona Ozouf. *Lire et écrire, l'alphabétisation des français de Calvin à Ferry.* Paris: Éditions des MSH, 1977.

Gallois, William. *The Administration of Sickness: Medicine and Ethics in Nineteenth-Century Algeria.* Basingstoke: Palgrave Macmillan, 2008.

Gerson, Stéphane. *The Pride of Place: Local Memories and Political Culture in Nineteenth-Century France.* Ithaca, NY: Cornell University Press, 2003.

Ghabrial, Sarah. "Colonial Sisterhood: The Missionnaires d'Afrique and 'The Regeneration of the Muslim Woman' in Algeria (1890–1912)." *Genre et Colonisation.* Forthcoming.

Un grand universitaire, Paul Crouzet, 1873–1952. Toulouse: Privat-Didier, 1956.

Greenhalgh, Paul. *Ephemeral Vistas: The Expositions Universelles, Great Exhibitions and World's Fairs, 1851–1939.* Manchester: Manchester University Press, 1988.

Grew, Raymond, and Patrick J. Harrigan. *Schools, State, and Society: The Growth of Elementary Schooling in Nineteenth-Century France, A Quantitative Analysis.* Ann Arbor: University of Michigan Press, 1991.

Grewal, Inderpal. *Home and Harem: Nation, Gender, Empire, and the Cultures of Travel.* Durham, NC: Duke University Press, 1996.

Hale, Dana S. *Races on Display: French Representations of Colonized Peoples, 1886–1940.* Bloomington: Indiana University Press, 2008.

Herstein, Sheila R. *A Mid-Victorian Feminist: Barbara Leigh Smith Bodichon.* New Haven, CT: Yale University Press, 1985.

Hirsch, Pam. *Barbara Leigh Smith Bodichon: Feminist, Artist, and Rebel.* London: Chatto and Windus, 1998.

Houbre, Gabrielle. *Grandeur et décadence de Marie Isabelle, modiste, dresseuse de chevaux, femme d'affaires, etc.* Paris: Perrin, 2003.

Huguet, Françoise. *Les livres pour l'enfance et la jeunesse de Gutenberg à Guizot.* Paris: INRP/Éditions Klincksieck, 1997.

Humbert, Jean-Charles. *Jean Geiser: Photographe, éditeur d'art, Alger 1848–1923.* Paris: Ibis Presse, 2008.

Ihaddeden, Zahir. *Histoire de la presse indigène en Algérie, des origines jusqu'en 1930.* Algiers: ENAL, 1983.

Jordi, Jean-Jacques. "Le temps des hiverneurs: les Anglais en Algérie (1880–1914)." In *Le tourisme dans l'empire français: politiques, pratiques et imaginaires (XIXe–XXe siècle). Un outil de la domination coloniale?*, ed. Colette Zytnicki and Habib Kazdaghli, 29–36. Paris: Publications de la Société Française d'Histoire d'Outre-mer, 2009.

Julien, Charles-André. *Histoire de l'Algérie contemporaine.* Vol. 1, *Conquête et colonisation, 1827–1870.* Paris: Presses Universitaires de France, 1964.

Kateb, Kamel. *Européens, "indigènes" et juifs en Algérie (1830–1962). Représentations et réalités des population.* Paris: Éditions de l'INED, 2001.

Knibiehler, Yvonne, and Régine Goutalier. *La femme au temps des colonies.* Paris: Stock, 1985.

Lançon, Daniel. "Le destin du lettré Nicolas Perron, passeur des cultures arabes." In *L'orientalisme des Saint-Simoniens*, ed. Michel Levallois and Sarga Moussa, 197–219. Paris: Maisonneuve et Larose, 2006.

Laurent, Franck. *Le voyage en Algérie. Anthologie des voyageurs français dans l'Algérie coloniale, 1830–1930.* Paris: Robert Laffont, 2008.

Lazreg, Marnia. *The Eloquence of Silence: Algerian, Woman in Question.* New York: Routledge, 1994.

Léon, Antoine. *Colonisation, enseignement et éducation.* Paris: L'Harmattan, 1991.

Levallois, Michel. *Ismaÿl Urbain, 1812–84. Une autre conquête de l'Algérie.* Paris: Maisonneuve et Larose, 2001.

Levallois, Michel, and Sarga Moussa, eds. *L'orientalisme des Saint-Simoniens.* Paris: Maisonneuve et Larose, 2006.

Lewis, Reina. *Gendering Orientalism: Race, Femininity and Representation.* London: Routledge, 1996.

———. *Rethinking Orientalism: Women, Travel, and the Ottoman Harem.* London: J. B. Tauris, 2004.

Lorcin, Patricia. *Imperial Identities: Stereotyping, Prejudice and Race in Colonial Algeria.* London: St. Martin's, 1995.

Lowndes, Emma. *Turning Victorian Ladies into Women: The Life of Bessie Rayner Parkes, 1829–1925.* Palo Alto, CA: Academia Press, 2011.

Luc, Jean-Noël. *L'invention du jeune enfant au XIXe siècle. De la salle d'asile à l'école maternelle.* Paris: Belin, 1997.

Lyons, Martin. "Les nouveaux lecteurs au XIXe siècle: femmes, enfants, ouvriers." In *Histoire de la lecture dans le monde occidental*, ed. Guglielmo Cavallo and Roger Chartier, 365–400. Paris: Seuil, 1997.

———. *Readers and Society in Nineteenth-Century France.* Basingstoke: Palgrave, 2001.

Mainardi, Patricia. *Husbands, Wives, and Lovers: Marriage and Its Discontents in Nineteenth-Century France.* New Haven, CT: Yale University Press, 2003.

Margadant, Jo Burr. *The New Biography: Performing Femininity in Nineteenth-Century France.* Berkeley: University of California Press, 2000.

Mayeur, Françoise. *Histoire de l'enseignement et de l'éducation en France.* Vol. 3, *De la révolution à l'école républicaine*, ed. L.-H. Parias. Paris: Nouvelle Librairie de France, 1981.

McBride, Theresa. "Public Authority and Private Lives: Divorce after the French Revolution." *French Historical Studies* 17 (Spring 1992): 747–68.

Melman, Billie. *Women's Orients: English Women and the Middle East, 1718–1918. Sexuality, Religion and Work.* 2nd ed. London: Macmillan, 1995.

Merle, Isabelle. "De la 'légalisation' de la violence en contexte colonial. Le régime de l'indigénat en question." *Politix* 17, no. 66 (2004): 137–62.

Messaoudi, Alain. "Savants, conseillers, médiateurs: les arabisants et la France coloniale (vers 1830–vers 1930)." 3 vols. Thèse de Doctorat, Université Paris I–Panthéon-Sorbonne, 2008.

Mokhiber, James. "'Le Protectorat dans la peau': Prosper Ricard and the 'native arts' in French Colonial North Africa 1899–1952." In *Revisiting the Colonial Past in Morocco*, ed. Driss Maghraoui. New York: Routledge, forthcoming 2013.

Mondenard, Anne de. "L'Algérie, terre oubliée des photographes en Orient." In *De Delacroix à Renoir: l'Algérie des peintres*, ed. Institut du Monde Arabe, 108–14. Paris: Hazan, 2003.

Monicat, Bénédicte. "L'Algérie des voyageuses." In *Stendhal, l'Italie, le voyage: mélanges offerts à V. Del Litto*, ed. Emanuelle Kanceff, 377–88. Moncalieri: CIRVI, 2003.

———. *Itinéraire de l'écriture au féminin. Voyageuses du 19e siècle.* Amsterdam: Rodolphi, 1996.

Morsly, Dalila. "La classe de Madame Allix-Luce. Quand des 'jeunes filles musulmanes' apprenaient le français (Alger 1846–1861)." In *L'enseignement du français en colonies. Expériences inaugurales dans l'enseignement primaire*, ed. D. Morsly, 139–56. Paris: L'Harmattan, 2010.

Moses, Claire. *French Feminism in the 19th Century*. Albany, NY: SUNY Press, 1984.

Nordman, Daniel. "Les *Guides-Joanne*: ancêtres des Guides Bleus." In *Lieux de memoire*. Vol. 2, *La Nation*, book 1, ed. Pierre Nora, 529–68. Paris: Gallimard, 1986.

Offen, Karen. "The Second Sex and the Baccalauréat in Republican France, 1880–1924." *French Historical Studies* 3, no. 2 (Autumn 1983): 252–86.

———. "Women's Memory, Women's History, Women's Political Action: The French Revolution in Retrospect, 1789–1889–1989." *Journal of Women's History* 1, no. 3 (Winter 1990): 211–30.

Orif, Mustapha. "De l'art indigène à l'art algérien." *Actes de la Recherche en Sciences Sociales* 33 (November 1988): 35–49.

Oulebsir, Nabila. *Les usages du patrimoine. Monuments, musées et histoire en Algérie (1830–1930)*. Paris: Éditions de la MSH, 2004.

Parayre, Séverine. *L'hygiène à l'école, histoire des pratiques de santé XVIIIe–XIXe siècles*. Saint-Étienne: Presses Universitaires de Saint-Étienne, 2011.

Pasler, Jann. *Composing the Citizen: Music as Public Utility in Third Republic France*. Berkeley: University of California Press, 2009.

Pedersen, Jean. *Legislating the French Family: Feminism, Theater, and Republican Politics, 1870–1920*. New Brunswick, NJ: Rutgers University Press, 2003.

Perin, Estelle. "Le Bulletin de l'enseignement secondaire des jeunes filles: la formation intellectuelle des femmes dans la France de l'entre-deux-guerres vue par Jeanne P. Crouzet Ben Aben." Master's thesis. Université Marc Bloch, 2007.

Perrot, Michelle. *Les femmes ou les silences de l'histoire*. Paris: Flammarion, 1998.

Picon, Antoine. *Les Saint-Simoniens. Raison, imaginaire et utopie*. Paris: Belin, 2002.

Pouillon, Francis. "Simplification ethnique en Afrique du Nord: Maures, Berbères et Arabes (18e–20e siècles)." *Cahiers d'Études Africaines* 129 (1993): 37–49.

Prochaska, David. *Making Algeria French: Colonialism in Bône, 1870–1920*. Cambridge: Cambridge University Press, 1990.

Redouane, Joëlle. "Les Anglais et l'Algérie." Thèse de Doctorat, Université de Rennes, 1988.

———. "La présence anglaise en Algérie de 1830 à 1930." *Revue de l'Occident Musulman et de la Mediterranée* 38 (1984): 15–35.

Régnier, Philippe. *Les Saint-Simoniens en Egypte, 1833–1851*. Cairo: Banque de l'union européenne, 1989.

Regourd, Jacqueline. "Allons à l'école. Histoire de l'évolution de l'école à Montrichard." *Les Cahiers des Amis du Vieux Montrichard* (1993): 1–100.

Rendall, Jane. "Langham Place Group (*act.* 1857–1866)." In *Oxford Dictionary of National Biography*. Oxford: Oxford University Press, 2005.

Renson, Marie-Edmonde. "Les soeurs de la doctrine chrétienne en Algérie. Fondation et expansion." In *Histoire des soeurs de la doctrine chrétienne en Algérie*. Vol. 4, *L'expansion au Luxembourg et en Algérie*, ed. Jacques Bombardier and Anne-Marie Lepage. Nancy: Doctrine Chrétienne, 1999.

Rey-Goldzeiguer, Annie. *Le Royaume Arabe: la politique algérienne de Napoléon III, 1861–1870*. Algiers: Société Nationale d'Édition et de Diffusion, 1977.

Riot-Sarcey, Michèle. *La démocratie à l'épreuve des femmes. Trois figures critiques du pouvoir, 1830–48*. Paris: Albin Michel, 1994.

———, ed. *De la liberté des femmes: lettres de dames au "Globe," 1831–1832*. Paris: Côté-femmes, 1992.

Robert-Guiard, Claudine. *Des Européennes en situation coloniale, Algérie, 1830–1939*. Aix-en-Provence: Publications de l'Université de Provence, 2009.

Roberts, Mary. *Intimate Outsiders: The Harem in Ottoman and Orientalist Art and Travel Literature*. Durham, NC: Duke University Press, 2007.

Rogers, Rebecca. "L'éducation des filles: un siècle et demi d'historiographie." *Histoire de l'Éducation* 115–16 (2007): 37–79.

———. *From the Salon to the Schoolroom: Educating Bourgeois Girls in Nineteenth-Century France*. University Park: Pennsylvania State University Press, 2005.

———. "Language Learning versus Vocational Training: French, Arab and British Voices Speak about Indigenous Girls' Education in 19th-Century Colonial Algeria." *Paedagogica Historica* (2012): 1–11.

———. "Relations entre femmes dans l'Alger colonial: Henriette Benaben (1847–1915) et son école de broderie 'indigène.'" *Genre et Colonisation*. Forthcoming.

———. "Retrograde or Modern?: Unveiling the Teaching Nun in Nineteenth-Century France." *Social History* 23 (May 1998): 146–64.

———. "Teaching Morality and Religion in Nineteenth-Century Colonial Algeria: Gender and the Civilizing Mission." *History of Education* 40, no. 6 (2011): 741–59.

———. "Telling Stories about the Colonies: British and French Women in Algeria in the Nineteenth Century." *Gender and History* 21 (April 2009): 39–59.

Ronsin, Francis. *Les divorciaires. Affrontements politiques et conceptions du mariage dans la France du XIXe siècle*. Paris: Aubier, 1992.

"Roundtable: Historians and Biography." *American Historical Review* 114, no. 3 (June 2009): 573–661.

Said, Edward W. *Orientalism*. New York: Pantheon, 1978.

Salinas, Claire. "Colonies without Colonists: Colonial Emigration, Algeria and Liberal Politics in France, 1848–1870." PhD diss., Stanford University, 2005.

Salinas, Michèle. *Voyages et voyageurs en Algérie, 1830–1930*. Toulouse: Privat, 1989.

Schlick, Yaël Rachel. "Travel as Praxis: Suzanne Voilquin and the Saint-Simonian 'Call to the Women.'" *European Romantic Review* 21, no. 6 (2010): 693–710.

Schreier, Joshua. *Arabs of the Jewish Faith: The Civilizing Mission in Colonial Algeria*. New Brunswick, NJ: Rutgers University Press, 2010.

Sebbar, Leïla. *Isabelle l'Algérien. Un portrait d'Isabelle Eberhardt*. Neuilly: Al Mannar, 2005.

———. *Voyage en Algérie autour de ma chambre. Abécédaire*. Paris: Bleu Autour, 2008.

Sebbar, Leïla, Christelle Taraud, and Jean-Michel Belorgey. *Femmes d'Afrique du Nord. Cartes postales (1885–1930)*. 2nd ed. Paris: Bleu Autour, 2006.

Sessions, Jennifer E. *By Sword and Plow: France and the Conquest of Algeria.* Ithaca, NY: Cornell University Press, 2011.

Sklar, Kathryn Kish. *Catherine Beecher: A Study in American Domesticity.* New York: Norton, 1973.

Smith, Bonnie. *The Gender of History: Men, Women, and Historical Practice.* Cambridge, MA: Harvard University Press, 1998.

Stoler, Ann. "Carnal Knowledge and Imperial Power: Gender, Race, and Morality in Colonial Asia." In *Feminism and History,* ed. Joan Wallach Scott, 209–66. Oxford: Oxford University Press, 1996.

Surkis, Judith. "Propriété, polygamie et statut personnel en Algérie coloniale, 1830–1873." *Revue d'Histoire du XIXe Siècle* 41, no. 2 (2010): 27–48.

———. *Sexing the Citizen: Morality and Masculinity in France, 1870–1920.* Ithaca, NY: Cornell University Press, 2006.

Tailliart, Charles. *L'Algérie dans la littérature française.* Paris: Champion, 1925.

Taithe, Bernard. "Algerian Orphans and Colonial Christianity in Algeria, 1866–1939." *French History* 20, no. 4 (2006): 240–59.

Taraud, Christelle. "Les femmes, le genre et les sexualités dans le Maghreb colonial (1830–1962)." *Clio, Histoire, Femmes et Sociétés* 33 (2011): 157–91.

———. *La prostitution coloniale. Algérie, Tunisie, Maroc (1830–1962).* Paris: Payot, 2003.

———. "La virilité en situation coloniale." In *Histoire de la virilité.* Vol. 2, *Le triomphe de la virilité. Le XIXe siècle,* ed. Alain Corbin, 331–47. Paris: Seuil, 2011.

Thébaud, Françoise. *Écrire l'histoire des femmes et du genre.* 2nd ed. Lyon: ENS Éditions, 2007.

Thénault, Sylvie. *Violence ordinaire dans l'Algérie coloniale. Camps, internements, assignations à residence.* Paris: Odile Jacob, 2012.

Trumbull, George R., IV. *An Empire of Facts: Colonial Power, Cultural Knowledge, and Islam in Algeria, 1870–1914.* Cambridge: Cambridge University Press, 2009.

Turin, Yvonne. *Affrontements culturels dans l'Algérie coloniale. Écoles, médecines, religion, 1830–1880.* Paris: François Maspero, 1971.

———. "Une page de publicité scolaire: la distribution de prix des écoles arabes-françaises à Alger, en 1852." *Revue d'Histoire Maghrebine* 21–22 (April 1981): 71–86.

Veauvy, Christiane, and Laura Pisano. *Paroles oubliées. Les femmes et la construction de l'état-nation en France et en Italie, 1789–1860.* Paris: Armand Colin, 1997.

Vidalenc, Jean. "Les techniques de la propagande Saint-Simonienne à la fin de 1831." *Archives de Sociologie des Religions* 10 (July–December 1960): 3–20.

Walton, Whitney. *Eve's Proud Descendants: Four Women Writers and Republican Politics in Nineteenth-Century France.* Stanford, CA: Stanford University Press, 2000.

Weimann, Jeanne Madeline. *The Fair Women.* Chicago: Academy Chicago, 1981.

White, Owen, and J. P. Daughton, eds. *In God's Empire: French Missionaries in the Modern World.* Oxford: Oxford University Press, 2012.

Wiart, Carole. "Hubertine Auclert, une féministe en Algérie (1888–1892)." Master's thesis. Université de Paris 8, 1997.

INDEX

Italic page numbers indicate illustrations.